# Pilot Error

Also by Phaedra Hise

*Entrepreneur America*
*Growing Your Business Online*
*301 Great Ideas for Managing Technology*

# Pilot Error

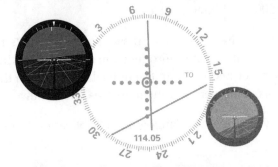

# THE ANATOMY OF A PLANE CRASH

# Phaedra Hise

Brassey's, Inc.

WASHINGTON, D.C.

Library of Congress Cataloging-in-Publication Data

Hise, Phaedra.
 Pilot error : the anatomy of a plane crash / Phaedra Hise.–1st ed.
     p.cm.
Includes index.
 ISBN 1-57488-325-9 (cloth : alk. paper)
1.   Aircraft accidents–Human factors. 2.  Aircraft
accidents–Investigation. 3. Private flying–Accidents. I. Title.
  TL553.6 .H57 2002
  363.12'414--dc21

                                2002001307

Printed in the United States of America on acid-free paper that meets the American National Standards Institute Z39-48 Standard.

Brassey's, Inc.
22841 Quicksilver Drive
Dulles, Virginia 20166

Cover design by Kathleen Dyson
Text design by PEN & PALETTE Unlimited
Maps by Jay Karamales

First Edition

10 9 8 7 6 5 4 3 2 1

# Contents

But who am I to judge his crisis-action while I lie snugly here in bed? Fonck had to decide in seconds what his critics have had days to talk about. And what pilot is immune to errors? We all commit them, as every honest man will say. Usually our errors don't end in a crash. But when a man is unlucky, does that make him more to blame?

— Charles Lindbergh, *The Spirit of St. Louis*

# Acknowledgments

It was Miriam Goderich who, in a coffee shop in Charlottesville, Virginia, first said, "I like this idea a lot." She and Jane Dystel at Jane Dystel Literary Management patiently waited a year for the proposal, made insightful edits, and then tirelessly shopped it until it found a home. Jane's expert guidance got me a book that I loved writing.

The editors at Brassey's generously involved me in the publishing process, something I hadn't been privy to with my other books. Don Jacobs was great to work with, carefully reading all the copy and marking it up with thoughtful comments.

I couldn't have finished this book without the help of the writers and editors whose opinion I respect most: David H. Freedman, who apparently is never too busy to offer advice and do some hangar flying; Leslie Brokaw, one of the few I believe when she says it's good; and Caroline Kettlewell, who kept me on a tight schedule by reading each chapter as it came, making insightful suggestions, and asking for more. I'm also very thankful that Tom Turner and Ken Ibold, experienced pilots and aviation writers, read the whole draft carefully and caught my technical errors.

Many other people and organizations helped create the time, space and perspective needed to write the book, including my husband; my mother, Barbara Lemont; my grandparents, Eugene and Lillian Hise; Patricia and William Hargis, Sr.; Jack and Sydney Waring; the Key West Literary Seminar; the Virginia Center for the Creative Arts; and Amtrak's delightfully quiet and comfortable Acela train between Washington and Boston.

I was prepared to write this book without Marsha Sinzheimer's cooperation, but in retrospect I see that would have been almost impossible, particularly given the loyalty of Ron and Marsha's family and many friends. Marsha answered all of my questions, in detail and without flinching. Without Marsha, this would merely have been a book about a flight. Because of her, it also became a book about people.

Some of those people were very nervous. Aviation has seen more than its share of lawsuits and bungled media coverage, so it's not surprising that mechanics, pilots and government officials deeply distrust notebook-toting journalists asking questions about a fatal accident. I am indebted to those who spent many hours with me digging through their memories, or patiently explaining some obscure technical detail.

I'm particularly grateful to Bob Hancock at the National Transportation Safety Board. Not only did he write the thorough and interesting report that leaped out at me from among the many I read, but he also answered my endless niggling questions years after the event. His help, and that of Terry Williams in Washington, was invaluable.

I owe a huge debt to the personnel of the United States Coast Guard, who were polite, patient and thorough. Likewise the volunteers of the Civil Air Patrol, who shared their documentation and memories. The men and women at Cape TRACON let me look over their shoulders, and I'm particularly grateful to David Loring for generously recounting his experience and thoughts.

Dave Meier was kind enough to teach me about Grummans by letting me crawl all over his plane, taking me up for touch and goes, and copying information from the maintenance manual. Ron Levy, the Safety Director for the American Yankee Association, provided a wealth of information about Grummans and their history. Oscar Rolan gave us permission to use (and modify) photographs of his handsome Grumman Traveler, which had a similar registration number and the same paint scheme as Ron Sinzheimer's. The guys on my Beechcraft Bonanza mailing list pointed me toward several sources and responded to my informal surveys about different aspects of flying. Many thanks to the Aircraft Owners and Pilots Association for mining their databases, research and statistics on general aviation.

Material from the National Park Service, the Massachusetts Division of Marine Fisheries, and web sites for the newspapers *Provincetown Banner* and *Cape Cod Times* served to outline the social, economic and geological history of Provincetown and Cape Cod. The online newspaper archives proved useful in establishing details and firm dates for events about which the participants themselves were fuzzy. The National Oceanic and Atmospheric Administration's historical weather images and charts were invaluable sources to which I returned again and again.

All of the scenes and dialog in the book came from the personal recollections of the people involved. Dialog in quotes is from Air

Traffic Control transcripts and Coast Guard logs, personal interviews or standard aviation phraseology that is used in given situations.

In some cases the people I interviewed did not remember the minute details of an event—where someone stood, or what their exact words were. I have in those cases filled in the probable particulars based on observations and information gathered in interviews and on visits. This dialog is not in quotes.

Although this book is about an accident, it is also intended to celebrate the skill, risks and joy that go into flying. My biggest thanks go to all who work and play in the aviation industry—both my fellow pilots and those who keep us in the air.

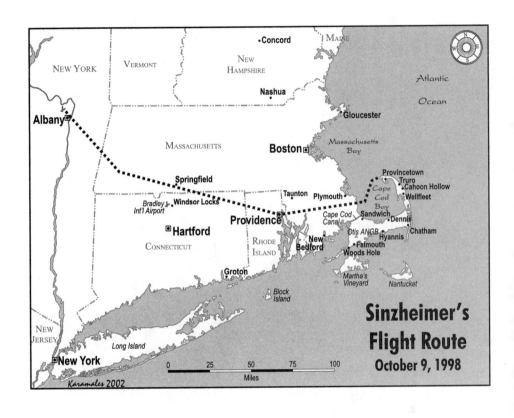

Sinzheimer's
**Flight Route**
October 9, 1998

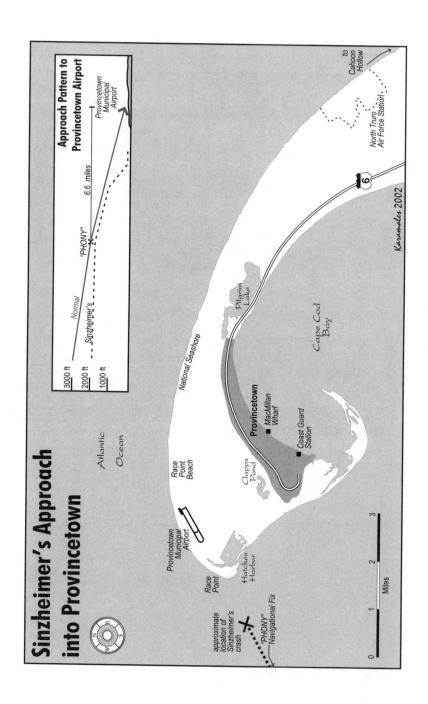

# Sinzheimer's Approach into Provincetown

Atlantic Ocean

Approach Pattern to Provincetown Airport

Normal

"PHONY"

Sinzheimer's

6.6 miles

Provincetown Municipal Airport

3000 ft

2000 ft

1000 ft

National Seashore

Race Point Beach

Provincetown Municipal Airport

Race Point

Hatches Harbor

Clapps Pond

Pilgrim Lake

Provincetown

MacMillan Wharf

Coast Guard Station

Cape Cod Bay

North Truro Air Force Station

to Cahoon Hollow

6

Kessmeier 2002

approximate location of Sinzheimer's crash

"PHONY" Navigational Fix

Miles

0    1    2    3

# Chapter 1

# The Accident

SIXTEEN YEARS OF TELLING PILOTS where to go and air traffic controller David Loring had never lost an airplane. Until tonight, apparently. Where the hell was Grumman 7100L?

Loring stood outside the break room door, a thin figure crouching near the side of the air traffic control building to stay out of the night rain. His baseball hat was pulled low over his wavy graying hair. With jittery fingers he sucked on a cigarette and recapped the evening's events.

At 2:00 P.M. his shift had begun. On his way in to the radar room he had stepped outside the break room door for a smoke. The seagulls were walking, he remembered. Gusting winds, mist and low clouds kept them on the ground. Not surprisingly, things were busy in the radar room that night. Cape TRACON was the radar facility that worked Cape Cod's approach and departure flights. The controllers were based at Otis Air National Guard Base on Cape Cod.

"Cape Approach, Seven One Zero Zero Lima is with you five with a request," the voice came over the tiny speaker in Loring's earpiece at 7:20 P.M. He knew the plane was coming. In the darkened radar room he had been watching the blip cruise along at 5,000 feet for a few miles before it started flashing on his screen. The flash was Loring's signal to accept the handoff from Providence Approach. Loring had a "strip" on the blip, a narrow piece of paper with the flight plan information. It listed the destination as Provincetown.

Provincetown is the fist of Cape Cod's bent arm. Chatham is the elbow, Hyannis the bicep. Falmouth, home of the base and Cape TRACON, is at the Cape's shoulder. Boston lies about 40 miles across Cape Cod Bay to the northwest. The Grumman was inbound from Providence, Rhode Island, which is 45 miles to the west of Falmouth.

"Ah, Zero Zero Lima, Cape Approach, standby with your request." At the moment the single-engine Grumman Traveler was the only customer for the small airport at Provincetown. Loring had several other planes headed for Hyannis and he had to line them up before he could talk to the Grumman. It took a couple of minutes.

He called the Provincetown pilot back. "Zero Zero Lima, go ahead with your request, make it simple."

"The weather at P-town is showing below minimums, sir. Do you have any other suggestions for an alternate on the Cape?"

The pilot was talking about the visibility at Provincetown and the ceiling, or the cloud cover hanging over the airport. As Loring glanced at the weather reports on the screen above his radarscope, he noticed that the visibility was three-quarters of a mile. That was the minimum required to land at the airport. The weather was right at minimums; it was on the edge, but not below. The pilot misunderstood the conditions. It was perfectly legal to shoot the approach.

Not that Loring would have recommended it. In addition to the low scud layer over the airport, the winds at Provincetown were even gustier than usual. At the moment, Loring knew, Hyannis weather was slightly better. Nobody was having trouble landing there.

"Ah, yes sir," Loring said. "The Hyannis airport is available. Advise with weather for that, please."

The answer was quick. The pilot had already listened to the pre-recorded weather broadcast. "I do have weather for Hyannis. Let me try the approach into P-town and then Hyannis if I can't make it, sir."

"Roger," Loring answered.

The Grumman worried him a little. Loring prided himself on his sixth sense, his ability to tell if something were a little off, about to go wrong. He felt it about the Grumman but he couldn't explain why. The pilot's voice was calm and he worked the radios well. The plane steadily held its course.

In bad weather pilots frequently tried approaches when the ceilings were at minimums. Often they made it, scooting in just under the cloud layer. But clouds were fickle things, and sometimes they would drop below minimums just as the pilot reached the decision point. When the clouds stayed shut the pilot climbed back up on the go-around and headed for an alternate landing site.

Loring didn't worry when pilots tried an approach to minimum altitude. Well, maybe if a guy sounded nervous, asked a lot of questions. Then Loring might encourage trying Hyannis right off the bat. He was no stranger to the occasional save, talking non-instrument-rated pilots out of the clouds, or vectoring a disoriented pilot back from heading out to sea. He saved the heroics for the neophytes who sounded scared or wandered off course. The rest of them took care of themselves. They followed their flight plans and generally did what they were supposed to.

The Hyannis-bound planes coming in from the north needed sharp turns to line them up for the runway, and that turn was getting tricky in the bad weather. The Grumman's flight plan was simpler, clearing it to make a slight turn left once it passed Gails, a navigational fix floating in the air a few miles off the Massachusetts coastline. As Loring watched, the little green blip crossed Gails and then made the turn north on the radar screen. Good, he thought. This guy is making my job easier.

"Grumman Zero Zero Lima, fly present heading join the ILS Seven final approach course, proceed inbound."

He didn't feel right about the plane, but there wasn't anything to do. The pilot decided where to go, the controller just told him the path to take. And those planes at Hyannis needed a lot of attention.

With nothing else landing at Provincetown, the Grumman was cleared to continue until it intercepted the track from the Instrument Landing System. From there, its navigational instruments would track the the descent to the airport. The runway was about 15 nautical miles away.

"Zero Zero Lima, descend and maintain three thousand," Loring called out, authorizing the descent.

"Down to three, Zero Zero Lima," the pilot acknowledged.

Dan Duda had landed at Provincetown earlier. He dumped his load of weekenders and was sitting in the cockpit alone, ready to fly his empty twin Cessna back to Boston for the next load. As usual, it was a busy Friday night for Cape Air, the regional airline that serviced Boston, the Cape and Islands. Alan Davis was inbound with a load of passengers from Boston, just crossing Cape Cod Bay. Pete Kacergis was on the ground at Provincetown, in the cockpit of another Cessna 402, ready to start up and take off behind Duda.

The cloud cover was at minimums—hairy even for Kacergis, who had logged over 7,000 hours of Cape Cod flight time, much of it spent flying approaches to the minimum decision height. The low ceiling, intermittent rain and turbulence put him on full alert. After four years of flying for Cape Air he knew Provincetown's approach by heart but tonight he got out the charts and approach plates to double-check frequencies and altitudes. No slacking, no complacency. Do it all by the book.

A noncommercial pilot can easily go months, years, without flying a single instrument approach to its minimum altitude of a few hundred feet above the ground. Kacergis had workdays where he flew a dozen. Each one to 200 feet, then spot the lights at the threshold and descend another white-knuckling hundred to finally see the runway. That's what the Cape's changeable weather demanded. Kacergis was a little concerned for some of Cape Air's newer hires who were flying in and out of Boston, Hyannis, and Provincetown that night.

He knew that a hundred feet above the ground was a dangerous place to be. Towers, buildings, telephone and power lines needled up into the clouds, closing the actual terrain clearance to 50 or 30 feet. A slight error in the altimeter could knock off another 20 to 50 feet. Pretty soon the plane's belly was scraping along on the tiniest of air cushions. A sneeze, a blink, a downdraft, any error could wham it down in half a second.

At 7:30 P.M. the Grumman was 15 nautical miles (17 statute miles) west of Provincetown and fast approaching Phony, the final navigational fix for the landing approach. A minute after clearing the plane for a descent to 3,000 feet, David Loring called back with the clearance. His voice was deep, with the even cadence and crisp syllables of a professional radio announcer.

"Grumman Zero Zero Lima is eleven miles from Phony, cleared for the ILS Runway Seven approach."

"Zero Zero Lima is cleared for the approach," the pilot acknowledged briefly.

After the clearance, the airspace around Provincetown belonged to the Grumman. Loring held Cape Air pilot Alan Davis west of the field, where he swung his twin Cessna around in a holding pattern, waiting for 7100L to land. On the ground, Dan Duda and Pete Kacergis sat in their respective cockpits, waiting to depart. Nobody could move at Provincetown until the Grumman touched down and its pilot radioed to say he had arrived safely.

The Grumman descended to 2,000 feet. In a minute or two, it would cross Phony, the navigational fix six miles west of the airport. From there it would begin to fly the constant rate of descent on the ILS.

By 7:37, the Grumman was close enough to Provincetown that David Loring's work was done. He radioed the Grumman one last time, jamming the words all together in one rapid sentence.

"Grumman Zero Zero Lima is four miles from Phony, frequency change is approved, report cancellation as soon as possible on the ground on one two zero point six five, have departure traffic waiting."

The Grumman was to switch from Cape Approach to the Provincetown radio frequency and announce the landing. The other pilots waiting on the ground would listen, mentally tracking the inbound airplane and preparing to takeoff as soon as it landed.

The pilot confirmed the call, light static crackling over the frequency as he radioed back, "Zero Zero Lima."

On the ground, Pete Kacergis started taxiing toward the end of the runway. He keyed his radio microphone, hitting the "talk" button five times to turn on the runway lights. Kacergis guessed the ceiling was about 100 feet. Even with the lights he didn't think the Grumman pilot would see the runway until he was right on top of it.

Kacergis parked the Cessna, stopping well short of the runway to give the approaching airplane some space. It was a bad night, he figured, and the plane might break out of the clouds right or left of the runway. Kacergis didn't want to crowd the touchdown zone. He shut down the engines and climbed out onto the wing of his plane, scanning the sky. The rain had stopped but he couldn't see the beacon of the lighthouse, a mile away on the shore.

In the sky, Davis continued flying a holding pattern as the Grumman headed toward the airport. On the radar screen the little green blip descended, down to 500 feet. It was three miles from the runway, still over the ocean, when it dipped from 400 to 100 feet. On the next radar sweep it was still at 100 feet. Twelve seconds later, two miles from the runway at 7:43 P.M., the Grumman vanished.

# Chapter 2

# The Last Warm Weekend

OUTSIDE THE WINDOW of Ron Sinzheimer's office in downtown Albany, New York, the sky was quiet. An overcast layer of ragged-bottom clouds drifted in the warm fall afternoon. It was well past 2:00 P.M., and Sinzheimer hoped to leave the office by 4:00.

He worked at his desk at the back of the first floor, in what had once been the tall row house's dining room. Marie Newman, his bookkeeper, filed paperwork upstairs in her office. Two secretaries shuffled law briefs in the front room, they were wrapping it up for the weekend. It was Friday, October 9, 1998, and still warm enough to be considered late summer.

Sinzheimer's weekend plans were the same as they had been all summer long, and the summers before that for the past 12 years: Head for the house on Cape Cod. This weekend would stretch the Cape season into October for one last lobster boil, one more tennis match, one final pass at fixing a few house details before closing it for the winter. Marsha had stayed out there most of the summer instead of driving back every week. It was easy for Ron to make the commute—he had the plane.

He planned to take off from Albany International airport by 4:30 P.M. The weather was not cooperating.

Sinzheimer's office at the back of 23 Elk Street faced north, away from the state capitol and shade trees of Academy Park, where Albany's law offices were clustered. Usually the sunlight from the office's large bay window lit up the back rooms. But today was gray and cruddy, punctuated by intermittent rain. The air in Albany was balmy but the sky cover was solid, no blue patches in sight. No clues about what was up there on the other side of the cloud layer. Rain? Turbulence? The Weather Channel painted green and angry yellow Doppler returns showing rain covering Maine and threatening the New York coastline. The air churned and rushed from low pressure to high. Clear flight corridors opened, then slammed shut, then opened again as rainstorms popped up and burned out all over New England.

The air in New England bristled, but at 3:30 P.M. Sinzheimer's narrow flight path from Albany to Cape Cod looked quiet. He picked up the telephone on his desk and punched in 1-800-WX-BRIEF. An aviation weather briefer answered the call.

"Burlington Flight Service," he said.

Sinzheimer rattled off a string of coded information—numbers and letters that marked him as a pilot and identified his airplane. "I'll be leaving Albany around 4:30 to go to Provincetown, Massachusetts, could I have a weather briefing, please?"

Sinzheimer waited while the briefer entered the aircraft number into the computer.

"Route of flight, time en route?" the briefer asked.

"Uh, I'll take Victor one forty six to Providence and Victor one fifty one over to Gails intersection then to Provincetown, about two hours," Sinzheimer said, listing the aerial highways that he planned to follow for the 220-mile trip. "So Providence, Boston, uh, Hyannis would be the closest airports."

Like most of the country's small airports, Provincetown is too understaffed to plot weather forecasts. Instead, briefers check the forecasts for larger airports nearby. The briefer typed the three-letter airport abbreviations into the computer—PVD, BOS, HYA—and started reading the forecasts.

Two offshore stationary fronts were heading toward the Atlantic coastline, pushing rain and low clouds over Cape Hatteras up to Nova Scotia. The unstable low-pressure system off the New Jersey coastline was predicted to drift north, due to center on Cape Cod by 7:00 P.M. That front carried ice, rain and low ceilings, with clouds stacked in the sky from 1,000 to 20,000 feet above the ground. At the moment, it was parked off the New England coast, boiling up a mass of quickly-changing weather that nobody could accurately predict.

The briefer droned on, reading the conditions at airports in Connecticut and Massachusetts, along Sinzheimer's route of flight.

"Bradley, overcast clouds between one thousand through two thousand eight hundred feet... Westover through Taunton, light rain showers and mist with broken to overcast clouds... New Bedford broken to overcast clouds at one hundred feet." The ceilings were pretty decent through New York and Connecticut, but deteriorated rapidly at the Massachusetts coastline.

When the forecasts are good, most experienced pilots just nod while they listen to the briefers. Student pilots, novices, are the ones who bother to take notes about cloud layers, temperatures and wind speeds along the route. But when weather forecasts start sounding bad, worse than the previous evening's Weather Channel predictions, all pilots drop the blasé act and grab a nearby empty envelope or notepad, jotting down the locations of frontal boundaries and precipitation levels. As they write, they build pictures in their minds—little weather maps for the flight.

From Albany to Providence, Sinzheimer's trip would be cloudy, but nothing difficult for an instrument-rated pilot who had logged over a thousand flight hours. He would be flying among cloud layers that the briefer said were stacked in the sky, rising from a few hundred feet above the ground's surface to over 20,000 feet into the sky. A soup of gray and white clouds would surround the cockpit windows. The view would be dreary but the air would probably be smooth and quiet, with light rain and mist. A typical instrument flight.

After Providence, Rhode Island, however, things sounded a bit more hairy.

"Rain... moderate to occasionally isolated strong showers," the briefer said. "Forecast Boston through six P.M. ceiling three hundred feet overcast, temporarily one mile visibility in light rain and mist. Provincetown currently at one and a quarter miles visibility, two hundred foot scattered ceiling."

After flying over Providence and turning north for the Cape, Sinzheimer might be flying through strong rain showers that would drum on the airplane canopy. The winds would increase, bumping the airplane around a bit. There was a chance that the scattered clouds at

Provincetown Municipal Airport might tighten into a solid layer, hanging too low for Sinzheimer to fly out of the bottoms and land. There was a chance that the clouds all along the shoreline would be too low to land anywhere.

Sinzheimer listened as the briefer ran through a list of New England airport forecasts for his time of arrival. Taunton, bad. Bradley, New Bedford, both bad. Sinzheimer needed a forecast of clouds at least a thousand feet above the ground and one and a half miles of visibility to file the airport as his legal alternate landing spot.

"Could you give me forecast for Hyannis and a suggestion for an alternate?" he asked, explaining about the thousand-foot limit.

The briefer paused, scrolling through computer screens, "Hyannis is not gonna meet that. Nantucket, not gonna meet it, Portland's not gonna meet it. Augusta's out." Coastal ceilings were two hundred to five hundred feet from Rhode Island to Maine.

Sinzheimer interrupted, "How about Providence?"

"Manchester's out," the briefer continued. "Providence is out. Uh, Concord forecast is showing winds gusting from twelve knots to twenty, three miles in light rain and mist, ceiling two thousand overcast."

Concord, New Hampshire. The closest forecast for "good" weather—rain, low visibilities and strong wind gusts—was in another state, almost 90 miles northwest of Sinzheimer's destination. A three- or four-hour drive to the Cape. He'd take it.

He read his flight plan to the weather briefer: Takeoff at 4:30, fly at 5,000 feet above sea level from Albany to the Providence, Rhode Island airport, then on to Provincetown. He predicted that the trip would take just under two hours. If Provincetown's weather proved too bad to land, he would turn for his alternate, Concord.

At the end of every flight plan, the pilot lists "number of souls aboard."

"One person," Sinzheimer said.

The briefer misunderstood, reading back, "That's two on board."

"One person," Sinzheimer repeated. He didn't mention that there would, in fact, be two aboard the airplane. The passenger would be his dog, Theo, a nine-month-old Chow.

The call took eight minutes. It was 2:30 P.M. when Sinzheimer hung up and turned back to his paperwork.

Did it occur to him not to go? He could have taken one of the cars or even the motorcycle. He had made the six-hour drive alone on the Harley most weekends over the past three summers. But Sinzheimer drove only as a last resort. To drive was to be stuck on the ground with the yahoos, glancing up wistfully at the sky and cursing the traffic. To drive was to waste the years of training, the thousands of dollars spent on airplane equipment.

Why bother to keep a plane if you don't use it? Ever since buying the Grumman in late May, Sinzheimer had been flying it out to the Cape. It had been a sunny summer. About the only bad weather had been in June, the weekend of Ron and Marsha's 21st wedding anniversary. Torrential rain then, but he had made it there and home again. No big deal. Why should this flight be any different?

When Marsha had asked if she should close the house up, Ron had said no. Give it one more weekend. Labor Day marked the official end of Cape Cod's high season. Some tourists tried to stretch vacations into late September, enjoying the warmish days and crisp nights. Good sleeping weather. October pushed it because the weather was unpredictable. Some weekends were glorious, golden and warm enough for shorts and a light sweater. But it was just as likely to rain for days at a stretch. Few tourists making pricey hotel reservations months in advance were willing to take the chance. Cape Cod's October visitors usually owned summer houses and were squeezing in one last beach visit before shutting down for the season.

In Truro, Marsha Sinzheimer sat on a barstool at the kitchen counter and gazed through the wide bank of windows with the view across Cape Cod Bay. She stared at the dark clouds with mixed feelings. Ron shouldn't fly through crap like that, she thought. But at the same time she wanted nothing more than to meet him at the Provincetown airport—her tall, dark and handsome husband, lugging the two or three books he planned to read over the weekend.

He was over six feet tall and had only gained a pound or two over the years. He was 49 and fit enough to keep winning tennis tournaments. The dark hair had started thinning, but thank goodness he didn't do that hopeless comb-over thing.

They would play doubles at the club and then he would cook lobster. Marsha thought it would be lovely to have one more weekend with Ron on the Cape.

Well, it wasn't her choice whether or not he came anyway. Ron never listened to her about the airplane.

She opened the slim paper bag and pulled out the nightgown she had bought that morning. Ron rode her about her weight, and she had to admit that she had put on a few pounds. But this was nice, it flattered her tall figure. She reached for an elastic band and gathered up her shoulder-length, reddish brown hair. It was on the frizzy side, a little wild.

Marsha was a woman who had always gotten out a lot. Even before Ron, when she was cutting hair in Cleveland, she tended to look at dates, trips and concerts and ask herself, "why not?" The south of France, Cape Cod, and even Woodstock in 1969. Marsha had driven her new Volkswagon Beetle from Cleveland, struggling with the funky "automatic shift" transmission that shifted like a stick, but had no clutch. Her bosses at the beauty shop had said to call if she got arrested, they'd bail her out. The traffic in Saugerties had been so bad that Marsha and her friend parked the bug and caught a ride on the hood of a Chevy. The event itself was somewhat of a letdown. She couldn't hear much of the music; people were too busy jabbering.

She had met Ron in 1972, through mutual friends on a day ski trip on slopes outside Cleveland. She was 30, he was 23 and talked and joked with her all day. He impressed her so much that she handed over her phone number. They dated for two years and after Ron graduated from Case Western law school in 1974, he asked her to move to Albany with him.

Different as they were, the relationship had worked out. Ron was the only child of conservative German and Austrian parents, putting himself through law school. He was a detail-oriented guy. He didn't just buy a dog, he researched breeds and bloodlines, visited breeders and trainers. But he wasn't all business, thank goodness. Marsha liked his crazy side. Ron was quick to wisecrack or flick someone with a rolled-up dishtowel. There was also a wild streak. He liked to drive fast and had started taking glider lessons.

They married in 1977 and launched into a life of skiing and vacation houses, gourmet food and Caribbean beaches, purebred dogs and expensive cars. Ron made the decisions. Marsha always felt as if he were just a couple of steps ahead of everyone else in life's game. He always seemed to know where to buy property, when to change jobs, what investment to choose. Marsha enjoyed most of Ron's adventures, but never developed a taste for speed. She clung, scared, to the back of his motorcycle and never rode very far.

The airplane terrified her.

At first she had tried to go along with it all. She used to go watch him fly the gliders at the airport. Gliding, Ron explained, was so dramatic and quiet that he would never take powered flight lessons.

Well, that didn't last. He earned his pilot's license in 1980, tried hang-gliding, even parachuted out of an airplane once but that scared even him. He bought a nice airplane, then a series of larger and faster airplanes, and she had to admit it was convenient to hop in and a few hours later land in Vermont or Provincetown. She had fought her fear, gritted her teeth and climbed into the cockpit for 14 years.

Then there was that flight over Pennsylvania. The engine had started coughing, sputtering as the plane flew over the ridges and valleys below. Carburetor picked up a little ice, Ron explained, pointing the nose down in a gradual descent, looking for warmer air. The engine revived, but Marsha wanted to land anyway. Ron laughed. The engine was fine now, he said. But Marsha insisted, and he had finally landed at Allentown. They rented a car and drove home to Albany. He drove back later to pick up the plane, and Marsha had never gotten in it again.

In the kitchen at the Cape Cod house, Marsha's phone rang. Ron's mother calling from Manhattan. The weather was bad, she pointed out, maybe Ron wouldn't be able to come. Would Marsha like some company over the weekend?

No, Marsha would not. Ron's mother made her feel self-conscious, as if she didn't quite fit into their careful Manhattan lifestyle. Well, Ron didn't fit either, she reminded herself. She was older than he was and a hairdresser to boot, and yet he had married her. He loved her sense of humor, her honesty, loved that she wasn't uptight. Even loved that she was Jewish, which Ron's parents had been running from ever since the Holocaust.

After Sulamith hung up, Marsha dialed Ron's office.

Your mother just called me, she told him. You bum, did you tell her to call? She thought you might not be able to come and that she would come instead.

They laughed.

Well, maybe she's right, Marsha suggested. Was the weather too bad to come?

No, it's no problem, he reassured her. He would fly on instruments.

She pushed him: It's pretty bad here in Truro. Maybe you shouldn't come.

Ah, it'll be fine, he shrugged her off. Don't worry so much. I'm running a little late, probably be there around 7:00 and you can take me to dinner. Take me somewhere nice.

She laughed and chatted about her day. After I talked to you this morning I went shopping, she told him. I got a new nightgown from that little shop in Provincetown.

A few minutes later they hung up. Twenty-one years of marriage and a grown child, Marsha giggled, and we're still getting excited about lingerie.

In Albany, Ron was running late. It was after 4:00 P.M. and the two secretaries had gone for the day. Marie Newman came downstairs from her second-floor office at the back of the brownstone and sat working at one of the desks in the front room. She was finishing typing a brief for Sinzheimer to review, and waited to catch him at the door.

If he were quick about picking up the dog and his flight bag at the house, he could possibly take off by 5:30 and make it to Provincetown by 7:30. Would Andrew ride along? He had been invited, but an 18-year-old boy with a girlfriend probably had better ways to spend a weekend. Sinzheimer would double-check with his son when he stopped at the house.

What time did the briefer say the front would settle along the coast? Seven? Maybe it would be delayed. Maybe he'd get in right at the leading edge.

Anyway, how bad could it be? The freezing level was far above where Sinzheimer would be flying, so he wouldn't pick up any ice like that time over Pennsylvania. That was in his previous plane, the Mooney, and worse than the carburetor ice he had experienced when Marsha insisted they land. Marie Newman and her husband Bill had dozed off for most of the ride, but Bill perked up when the wings started frosting over. Sinzheimer chattered on the radio as he flew lower and lower, looking for warmer air. His passengers blanched as the Mooney bumped along low over the Pennsylvania ridgelines. Fuel was running low and Sinzheimer made an unscheduled landing at a small airport.

On the ground he had really let Flight Service have it, yelling over the phone about the unforecast ice. The group took off again within the hour and Ron flew far west of their Louisville, Kentucky, destination, steering clear of the storm.

It was too warm for ice on this flight. More likely it would be like the one a few years ago out to the Cape. He had flown Bill Newman out to Provincetown in the Mooney. Marsha, Marie and the kids had driven out earlier. Over Cape Cod Bay the only sign of Boston was a glow of lights through the fog bank. Ron had descended down into the fog, flying on instruments, and asked Bill to keep an eye on the altimeter. Call out the altitudes as we pass through them, he said.

Newman had nervously called out each tick mark: Six hundred, five hundred, Ron, we're four hundred feet off the water.

Couldn't blame the guy for worrying. He didn't know that they could go as low as 200 feet above the ground before they had to see the airport. Sinzheimer told Newman to expect the clouds to be pretty low, maybe a hundred feet.

Down they had flown through the fog, Ron at the controls and Bill eyeing the altimeter as it fell to 208. Ron keyed the "talk" button for his microphone to turn on the pilot-controlled runway lights. Then he dropped even lower, below the decision height. At 150 feet Newman finally saw the runway ahead.

Ron had admitted that he was happy to be on the ground. On the way to the bar Bill complimented him on his nerves, how smooth the approach was. Ron had over 1,000 hours logged at that point, but it had been hairy even for him. That fog was pretty low, he told Bill.

He always got in. Ice, low fog, rain, turbulence, that's what the instrument license was for—to help a pilot navigate through bad weather.

He could have waited until the morning, as Marsha suggested, but there was no indication that Saturday's weather would be any better. By Sunday, he might as well not bother since he had to be back in Albany on Monday morning. Waiting meant that he wouldn't get to see the remodeled bathroom in the Cape house, or install the faucet he was bringing. Also the bedroom blinds, which were in his car—Marsha had towels over the windows. He hadn't seen Marsha for a week and it was one of the last warm weekends before the New England snow started to fly.

Sinzheimer was ready to go by 4:30, but had one last call to make before leaving the office. He picked up the phone and called the airport.

Signature Flight Service, the desk clerk answered.

Ron Sinzheimer in Grumman Seven One Zero Zero Lima, he said. I need a fuel top-off, both tanks please, as soon as possible.

No problem, Mr. Sinzheimer, we'll send the fuel truck out to the plane right away.

The plane would be fueled up and ready to go. No waiting at the airport. Sinzheimer hung up and gathered his things. He walked through the bottom floor rooms of the restored Victorian townhouse, through the second parlor and its massive gilt-framed mirrors, salvaged when it was converted to a library and spare office. Marie sat at one of the desks in the former front parlor.

I have to stop by the house, he told her. Have to change and pick up the dog before I go.

She asked if he had time to scan the brief. She had been working all afternoon, trying to finish it before he left. Maybe he wanted to take it with him?

Monday, he said, smiling. Gotta go, goodbye.

Home was twenty minutes away, the massive stone landmark at 2 Manning Boulevard. It was quite a step up from the seedy student apartments where he had lived in Cleveland, or the fixer-upper townhouse in downtown Albany, where Andrew was born. Two Manning Boulevard dominated the street corner and announced Sinzheimer's success to anyone driving by.

It was fortunate that the law firm did well because Ron liked to play with expensive toys—the houses, the antique Jaguar and red Ferrari, the motorcycles and airplanes. Albany's legal and political powers all knew the rising star who had set a few precedents in environmental law. He protected his corporate clients from land cleanup responsibilities, but stuck it to them when his client was the little guy. What impressed both clients and opponents was Sinzheimer's creativity. When negotiations got tense, Ron would come up with an ingenious solution that would somehow manage to answer everyone's needs. He pulled stuff like that out of thin air. Clients loved it.

He and Marsha had bought the big house in 1987 and Ron spent ten years adding fun little touches. The pool table and Jacuzzi each dominated its own front parlor. The gourmet kitchen was Ron's domain, where he cooked for dinner parties and canned dilly beans. He built the upstairs bookshelves for his collection of science fiction paperbacks, and added one set of shelves that pulled open to reveal a hidden passage to a secret room.

When the roof leaked, Ron researched historic slate colors and coppersmithing techniques, coming up with an intricate herringbone pattern that the roofer would curse. He gave Marsha the choice between an outdoor pool or tennis court. The pool was more social, Marsha decided. They installed it behind the garage, which housed Sinzheimer's revolving collection of sports cars and motorcycles—the BMW, the antique Jaguar, the Alfa Romeo that was always in the shop, the red Ferrari and Mercedes convertible.

In a typical day Ron would settle a complicated case at the office in the morning, win a tennis match at lunch, land a hot client in the afternoon, drive his Jaguar home to cook lamb chops for dinner, then read the latest novel from cover to cover before bedtime. His intensity and intelligence tended to intimidate people. Except Marsha. He could always count on her to cut right to the point and give him an honest opinion. Also, she made him laugh. He was looking forward to seeing her this weekend.

Sinzheimer parked out front and walked up the brick herringbone sidewalk. The Chow met him at the door. Good boy, Theo.

Andrew? He called upstairs but no answer. Sinzheimer climbed the stairs and knocked on his son's door.

Andrew had been taking a nap and looked up, groggy, from the bed.

You going with me? Sinzheimer already knew the answer. Over the years he and Andrew had made many "boys' weekend" flights together, holing up in nice hotels in Orlando and Key West, sampling fine restaurants. But Andrew had a girlfriend now, and spent less time with his family.

Nah, Dad. I'll stay here this weekend, you and Mom have fun.

Okay, I'm going. See you Monday.

Okay Dad, bye. Andrew rolled back into the pillow.

Sinzheimer didn't bother to grab a bag; he had extra clothes, a toothbrush and everything else he needed at the Cape house. He changed into jeans and a short-sleeved knit shirt, rounded up Theo and headed for the car.

At 5:15, Sinzheimer parked in the far corner of the general aviation lot at Albany International airport and shooed the big Chow out of the back seat. They walked through Signature's wide lobby, with its two-story glass front wall and sweeping 180-degree view from west to east.

In the pilot briefing room the computer weather screen showed that the coastal rain had moved offshore. At the moment, Sinzheimer had a clear shot between Albany and Provincetown. The weather didn't look like much of a factor for an instrument-rated pilot familiar with the route. But the problem with an unstable front is that it's fast and unpredictable.

Sinzheimer headed past the desk clerk, through the sliding glass doors leading to the ramp. The sun was setting but the air was still warm, in the sixties. Sinzheimer didn't need a jacket as he and Theo walked the hundred or so yards, past a few of the 30 other small airplanes on the ramp, each tied down by the wings and tail in its parking place. Sinzheimer's plane was in the third row. Single engine, low wings. It was a Grumman AA-5 Traveler, white with wide brown stripes along the sides and marked on the tail with the five-inch-high registration number, "N7100L."

The cockpits of most single-engine airplanes are narrower than the average economy car. Pilot and copilot sit shoulder-to-shoulder, the tops of their headsets clearing the ceiling by an inch or two. The headroom is so low that in turbulence pilots tighten their seatbelts, lest they bonk their heads during a downdraft.

To cut down on structural weight, most airplanes have a single door on the passenger side. The Grumman is famous for being set up a little differently. It has a bubble-shaped sliding canopy, similar to a World War II Mustang fighter plane. The canopy creates a visual illusion of extra space for those riding inside, plus it offers better views out the top and sides. The Plexiglas curves down far enough on the sides so that when it slides back the pilot and passengers can step out over the low metal sides, onto the wings. It's an important safety feature during an emergency exit—the pilot doesn't have to climb across the cockpit to get out of a passenger-side door.

The Grumman Traveler was created by Jim Bede. He was the finest aircraft designer who ever lived, Grumman owners will argue, but not a money man. He ran out of capital in the 1960s while developing a foldable-wing airplane. Investors bailed him out and renamed Bede's Cleveland-based company American Aviation. It built the first Grumman Yankee in the early 1970s. Later came the more popular model, the Traveler.

American was eventually acquired by Grumman Aerospace, the company that built the Hellcat and Wildcat for World War II pilots. Grumman also built a series of beautiful twin-engine amphibians in the 1930s—the Goose, Widgeon and Albatross (Jimmy Buffet flies one). In 1973, Grumman's manufacturing moved to Savannah, Georgia, where famous speed-king designer Roy LoPresti souped up the Traveler, adding a larger engine and reworking the nose and tail to reduce drag and add speed. It was called the Tiger, and later, the Cheetah, and produced until 1979. These popular airplanes are common at small airports.

All small Grummans are instantly recognizable by that rounded canopy and the castering nosewheel, which sits at the end of a curved strut and rotates through 180 degrees left and right for tight taxi turns. They're faster than the popular high-wing Cessnas in use at so many of the country's flight schools. They're snazzier looking than Piper's chunky Cherokees. Grummans are like Volkswagons—entry-level, affordable planes with extra cachet.

Sinzheimer's Traveler was the last model year before LoPresti got hold of it. It was a basic "platform," in pilot lingo. A four-seater with a 150-horsepower engine and simple systems. The propeller was fixed, meaning that it stayed at the same setting all the time so that the pilot didn't have to adjust the pitch in climb, cruise and landing. The landing gear was also fixed, so that the pilot didn't have to retract it on takeoff, then remember to put it down again just before landing.

All in all, the Traveler was a simple machine. Keep the airspeed in the green, jockey the throttle and mixture around a little bit, and it will keep flying. It was exactly what Sinzheimer wanted for getting back and forth to the Cape. A bit more pedestrian than his Mooney, which had been a fast, high-performance airplane with sophisticated instrumentation. The Grumman was simpler, but it got him back in the air again after three years of driving. He had seen the ad for it in *Trade-A-Plane* and bought it without telling Marsha until after the deed was done.

He knew that the Grumman would be easy to maintain and operate. He wouldn't have to remember the landing gear, or monitor the engine temperature and pressure of the turbocharger like he had in the

Mooney. When it came time for the annual inspection—the yearly tear-down, examination and repair event that every airplane goes through—there would be fewer systems to check, which meant fewer things to go wrong.

The Grumman had a standard instrument package, nothing fancy but enough to shoot an approach and fly through clouds. The Century autopilot was very basic, one that generally kept the wings level but didn't turn automatically to headings or hold an altitude like the Mooney's had. It had been a long time since Sinzheimer had flown anything this basic, but he welcomed the change.

Sinzheimer walked out to the plane and slid the canopy open. He flipped on the master switch and the lights to check that they were working. As Theo walked around the plane with him, he started the preflight check.

Before every flight is the preflight. Most planes require the same basic routine—the pilot checks the airplane, touching, smelling, listening for potential problems. Wiggle the ailerons and elevator, the moveable control surfaces on the back of each wing and the tail—they're free and clear with no grinding noises. Run a hand over the fronts of the wings and propeller—slick and smooth and ready to generate lift.

Flick the tiny stall-warning vane, listening for the corresponding warning horn from the cockpit. Check the engine's oil level. Open the fuel tank lids and sniff for 100 low-lead's sharp gasoline smell. Jet fuel, which sometimes finds its way into prop planes by mistake, smells like kerosene and will destroy a piston engine. Drain a few tablespoons of the blue fuel, verify that there's no pink jet fuel or water rolling around in the bottom of the strainer. At the end of a thorough preflight, pilots have oily, gasoline-scented hands.

The Grumman would fly for about four and a half hours with its full tanks. Plenty of time to get to Provincetown and then turn north and make Concord if necessary.

Sinzheimer shooed Theo into the back seat. Some pilots stuffed their dogs into travel crates, or strapped them to the seatbelts with little harnesses. Sinzheimer didn't bother. If the plane crashed, he told friends, Theo ought to be able to wiggle free and climb out.

He did not carry life vests or a raft in the Grumman. He would not be flying further than 50 nautical miles from shore, so according to the FAA regulations he was not required to carry any flotation devices.

Few pilots of small airplanes do, preferring to trust their luck rather than cram one more thing into a cockpit crowded with passengers, luggage and tools. The chances are slim, they argue, that they'd be able to rustle around the back for the life vest and then get it on while also struggling to fly the plane through an emergency procedure.

A friend once asked Ron why he didn't carry a life raft for the frequent flights over Cape Cod Bay. Because of the added weight, Ron answered. Life rafts, provisioned with signaling equipment, water and rations, are heavy and a pilot must cut back on baggage. Sinzheimer didn't think it would help much anyway. If anything happened, he had always explained to Marsha, he'd just set the plane down in Cape Cod Bay and wait for rescue crews to come get him. How long could it take when there were Coast Guard stations scattered all along Cape Cod?

Sinzheimer wedged his six-foot, two-inch frame into the Grumman's small cockpit, running his hands and eyes over the instruments. In the center of the panel were the dials and gauges. Over to the right of the panel was the stack of navigational and communications radios. Next to that a stack of engine gauges—fuel and oil pressure, oil temperature. Along the bottom of the panel were the circuit breakers and a row of rocker switches—fuel pump, radio master switch, panel lights. Below that were the knobs for the throttle, carburetor heat and mixture control. Unlike cars, airplane engines must operate at drastically different air pressures. The pilot has to adjust the air/fuel mixture to keep the pistons firing.

Below the throttle quadrant were the fuel gauges and the switch for the fuel tanks. Sinzheimer had flown enough hours in this cockpit to scan it all with a practiced eye, running through the simple start-up checklist: seat belts on, brakes on, fuel on, flip a few switches, check a gauge or two.

"Clear," he yelled out of the open canopy. It means, "I'm about to swing this big blade in front of my plane, get out of the way."

Sinzheimer pressed the starter button. The engine coughed, the two-bladed propeller spun. It was 5:36 P.M.

# Chapter 3

# Cleared for Takeoff

ON THE RAMP AT ALBANY, the small plane's engine sparked and caught. Sinzheimer busied himself flipping communication radio switches, checking the oil pressure gauge and turning on the cabin instrument lights. He turned the radio dials, tuning in the frequency to pick up his departure clearance. He had filed for a 4:30 P.M. departure and it was now past 5:30, but Air Traffic Control holds instrument flight plans for two hours. His was still in the system.

"Clearance delivery, Grumman Seven One Zero Zero Lima is IFR to Provincetown," he announced.

The controller called back, but didn't say the magic words every pilot wants to hear, "cleared as filed." Instead he said, "revised routing, advise when ready to copy." That meant that Sinzheimer's requested route had been changed. It was to be expected on such a busy day for ATC. With bad weather creeping up the coast, small planes were lining up for their instrument-flight clearances through the clouds. ATC had to clear each one through the complicated network of aerial highways and assigned altitudes, keeping five miles of air between them. Sinzheimer's requested course conflicted with someone else's, someone who had taken off earlier.

"Zero Zero Lima, cleared to Provincetown via the Albany Three Departure, radar vectors to Victor one thirty to Bradley, Victor four zero five to Providence, Victor one fifty one to Gails intersection, then direct Provincetown. Maintain three thousand feet, expect seven thousand one zero minutes after departure," the controller read the new clearance.

A quick rustle of the charts, the thin tissue paper criss-crossed with black Victor airways and aerial intersections. Sinzheimer studied the dark lines with their tiny labels—Victor 130, 405, 151. The new routing was a minor change, fortunately. The new altitude would be 7,000 feet instead of the 5,000 he had requested. That was fine, still well below the freezing layer at 8,000 feet. The new routing sent him just south of his planned course, he would overfly Windsor Locks, Connecticut. Only about four miles added to the flight. It was a good routing, no reason to dicker with the controller and ask for something better.

Sinzheimer read the instructions back to verify that he had copied them correctly.

"Zero Zero Lima, readback correct. Verify you have information Bravo," the controller said.

"Zero Zero Lima has Bravo," Sinzheimer said. Just after starting the engine he had listened to it, the looped recording of airport weather that was updated every hour and given a new name—Alpha, Bravo, Charlie, etc. Bravo had reported that Albany's ceilings were overcast at 3,000 feet, winds were out of the east at eight knots, temperature 13 Celsius, dew point 11, altimeter setting 30.09, the active was Runway 1.

Switching radio frequencies, Sinzheimer called Ground control and announced that he was ready to taxi toward the takeoff end of Runway 1. The controller cleared him and Sinzheimer pushed the throttle knob forward, eased out of his parking space and turned left onto taxiway Foxtrot, then right onto taxiway Alpha, paralleling Runway 1.

No passengers to chat with on this flight, just a panting Theo in the back seat. On Labor Day weekend a few weeks earlier Ron had taken John Dorfman along for his first ride in the Grumman. A fellow lawyer, Dorfman had a house in Truro near Ron's and had been going along for flights to the Cape since the 1980s. Dorfman was a calm passenger, especially for a self-confessed white-knuckle flier.

The Grumman took almost two hours to reach Provincetown. The dog rested in the back, so calmly that Ron never bothered to strap him in. Dorfman kept an eye on the scattered clouds and waited expectantly for yet another smooth landing from Ron. He got it. Ron touched down at Provincetown and then slid the canopy open to get fresh air in the cockpit. Another non-eventful flight to the Cape.

"I thought Ron was an excellent pilot," Dorfman said later. "He knew that trip like the back of his hand. He'd come in to land to Provincetown and there would always be turbulence and crosswinds but he'd lay that plane down like he was putting down a piece of cotton. I felt very secure with Ron. I was comfortable that I was in good hands. I always told that to my wife. She was nervous about me being up in something so small."

Sinzheimer had plenty of friends eager to ride along. Years before, he had thrilled his bookkeeper Marie Newman with a ride out to Long Island for a deposition. New York had a special sightseeing corridor that kept small aircraft away from the busy air space near LaGuardia and JFK airports. It was the Hudson River. Heading south, pilots turned left at Sing Sing prison and flew along the right side of the river past the hovering traffic and tourist helicopters, past Yankee Stadium and Central Park, toward Lady Liberty and the Verrazano bridge.

Marie was so impressed that she later brought her Girl Scout troop out to the airport. They sat in the Mooney and Ron explained what all the technical gadgets were. She told the girls what a confident and smart pilot Ron was.

Tom Wiltshire was an Albany attorney who had begun flying with Sinzheimer many years earlier, then started taking flying lessons himself. He had even bought from Sinzheimer his first plane, a Piper Cherokee.

"He had the ability to be in control of his aircraft," Wiltshire remembered. "Ron was seamlessly wedded to his machinery, he was smooth. He was probably one of the most intelligent people I've ever met, he could instantly comprehend complex data, then synthesize that data into a course of action. I've seen him do it when faced with complex legal issues: he could immediately see the core issue."

It was a skill that served Sinzheimer well in the airplane, Wiltshire noticed. "He was always thinking three or four steps ahead. I watched him work toward his instrument rating, and really admired his proficiency and confidence. I'd watch him bring that plane down [on instruments] and there was the runway dead ahead, on the glide slope. It was marvelous to watch, he always nailed it."

Lance Moore was an old friend of Sinzhimer's. The two men had started taking flying lessons at the same time, years earlier. Moore felt that his friend's confidence could sometimes run away with him. "Ron was extremely proficient," Moore said. "But proficient and professional people like doctors and lawyers get killed all the time because they're used to being in command of the situation. They don't factor in a lot of things. The biggest problem with noncommercial pilots is they think they can jump in aircraft and go out there. A lot of times they don't keep their hours real current."

On the ramp in Albany the rumbling engine vibrated the Grumman. The radios crackled and buzzed with chatter from the controllers announcing clearances and from airplanes acknowledging as they landed and headed for the ramp and home. The Grumman's instrument panel glowed softly, the dimmed lights designed to keep the pilot's eyes dilated for night vision, ready to glance out at the darkened taxiway.

Outside the cockpit flashed the navigational lights—red on the left wingtip, green on the right, white on the tail—designed to telegraph in which direction the plane was traveling in the air. Sinzheimer steered with his feet, pressing on the pedals, down where the gas and brake are on a car, to keep the nosewheel centered on the taxiway's yellow line.

As he taxied, he double-checked the instruments on which his cloudy night flight would depend: Airspeed indicator fixed on zero as the plane taxied; Current setting of 30.09 into the tiny altimeter window—like the date window on a wristwatch—so that altitude readout was within 75 feet of Albany's airport elevation of 285 feet above sea level; Attitude Indicator showed a little plane planted level on its horizon; Directional Gyroscope on the proper heading from the wet compass, and it turned correspondingly as Sinzheimer taxied left, then right; Turn and Bank gauge turned also; Tachometer at about 1,000 revolutions per minute. Fuel and oil gauges in the green.

In nice weather flights, a pilot can do most of the work just by looking out the window. Keep an eye on the horizon to gauge wings and nose level or turning. Match landmarks below to the chart, or map, to make sure the plane is on course. It's easy to see how far the plane is above the runway.

To fly in the clouds, pilots need to earn an additional rating. The training for an instrument rating is as difficult to master, and can take as long, as that for the pilot's license. It focuses on perfecting the "scan," glancing from instrument to instrument, teasing out the pertinent information and double-checking it against the rest of the panel.

To get a feel for the tense work of instrument flying, imagine driving a car in the rain. The fog is too thick to see anything through the windows, but the car is still speeding ahead. All of the normal road sounds are still there—the rain drumming the windshield, wind whistling over the windows, thuds as the wheels hit bumps, the revving of the accelerating engine. The sounds offer scant few clues as to what is happening. When the wind noise gets louder, the car is probably speeding up. When the car hits a lot of bumps, it has probably drifted over to the shoulder.

Instead of watching the road, you can only tell where the car is headed by staring at the screen full of instruments on the panel behind the steering wheel. The big circular gauge in the center has a miniature car sitting in the middle of a painted black road. If the mini-car starts to head too far right, you must pull the steering wheel left. Ease the wheel to the new heading to avoid over-correcting and running off the left-hand side of the road. Listen to the outside noise as the car turns. Is it bumping along on the shoulder now? Pay attention.

Remember to occasionally check the fuel levels, rate of fuel flow and pressure. And the oil temperature, engine temperature, the rate at which the alternator is charging and the RPM level. While you're scanning these gauges, making small corrections, talking on the radio and juggling navigational frequencies, the speedometer indicates that you're zipping along at 150 miles per hour. At that speed, you don't have a lot of time to recover from mistakes.

Mastering the quick scan is one of the most important lessons of instrument training. Fixating on any one gauge can make a pilot focus on only one aspect of flying the plane—just keeping the wings level and forgetting about heading in the right direction, for example. Or not noticing when fuel levels dip. Or when the nose drops perilously low and the plane runs out of altitude.

It can be overwhelming at first but after a few hours of flying, the dials begin to speak English, and that's the first half of instrument training: learning to scan the gauges. The second half is learning to trust them. That's how to fight off vertigo, the deadly enemy of instrument pilots.

There is an infamous simulator called the Vertigon, created to teach pilots how insidious and overwhelming vertigo is. The machine, set up like a small airplane cockpit, rotates. The pilot inside is instructed to reach forward, as if picking up a dropped pencil. When he sits back up, he's gone. Vertigo makes your head spin, your stomach sick. It feels like the airplane is turning, but in which direction? Your head warns that you're in a climbing right turn, but the instruments say diving left. Which do you believe?

It takes hours and hours of instrument training to learn to trust the gauges. Then, if vertigo attacks, a pilot knows to ignore that churning gut and spinning inner ear. Instrument pilots grit their teeth and obey the gauges.

That's why pilots check them while taxiing out to the runway. Once airborne, the gauges are the only guide to a safe flight and landing.

At the end of the taxiway, Sinzheimer finished his pre-takeoff checklist: Fuel switch set to the fullest tank. Wiggle the control yoke to make sure the airplane's ailerons and elevator, which bank and turn the airplane, respond properly. Set the navigational radios to the beacons at Albany and Windsor Locks. Switch the two communication radios over to the Tower and Departure Control frequencies. He pushed the throttle forward to run the engine up to a higher power setting, checking to make sure everything was firing properly. Six minutes after getting his clearance, Sinzheimer announced to the Tower that he was ready for takeoff.

The Tower called back, "Zero Zero Lima, hold short, landing traffic." Another airplane was in the clouds above the airport, on final approach to landing. The Grumman waited until the approaching airplane landed and taxied off the runway.

At 5:47, the Grumman was cleared into position. Sinzheimer pointed the nose straight down the runway and held his toes on the brakes.

"Zero Zero Lima, cleared for takeoff, fly heading four zero," announced the Tower controller. Sinzheimer released the brakes and pushed the throttle all the way in. The vibration in the cockpit grew as the small plane rumbled down the runway, picking up speed as it bumped and fought to stay pointed down the center yellow line.

Takeoffs and landings are when pilots have the highest workload. That's when there is the most stuff to do, the least time to do it in, and the slimmest margin for error. The key elements are airspeed and altitude, and the more of each the better.

Sinzheimer kept his eye on the Airspeed Indicator, to the left on the instrument panel. He watched to make sure it came alive, showing 20 miles an hour, then 30, 40. He was waiting for it to hit 60 miles an hour, the "rotation" speed for liftoff.

Each plane has its own airspeeds, determined by wind-tunnel testing of the prototype. There are landing-gear-extension airspeeds (too fast and the gear doors might buckle from the wind resistance), flap-extension airspeeds, best speed for different types of climbs and descents, maximum airspeeds in bumpy weather, special speeds for specific rates of fuel burn: Pilots don't have to memorize them all, they're in the flight manual. The important ones are marked on the dial itself with colored arcs. White for landing speed ranges, green for normal cruise, yellow is where the plane is flying fast enough that sudden maneuvers could buckle the airframe, or yank the wings and tail off. Past that is the red line. When pilots hit the red line and live to tell the tale, they consider themselves lucky.

The Grumman's airspeed indicator climbed past 40 miles an hour, then 50. At 60 miles an hour, Sinzheimer pulled back on the yoke.

Liftoff—and the plane felt right. The cockpit got a little quieter as it left the rough asphalt behind. No more stomping on the rudder pedals trying to steer the rushing machine along the narrow runway. Sinzheimer's hands took over, nudging the yoke back to pull the nose up. The Grumman built speed, climbing at about 100 miles an hour, about 500 vertical feet per minute. As it climbed past the end of the runway, the Tower controller called for the handoff.

"Grumman Zero Zero Lima, contact Departure."

Sinzheimer confirmed the call, rolled to his assigned heading of 40 degrees and switched radio frequencies.

Lift is what makes airplanes fly and sailboats race along at top speed. It seems like the plane should just fly along the way a kite does, or your hand when you stick it out of the car window. The strong wind pushes your hand and the kite up until they're "flying." A headwind does help, which is why planes usually take off into the wind. But that's not lift.

What happens in lift is that wind whisks toward the wing. It breaks apart at the blunt leading edge of the wing and passes along the top and the bottom, meeting up again at the sharp trailing edge.

An airfoil, the shape of the wing, is designed so that the top is rounded and the bottom is flat. A cross-section looks sort of like a sideways teardrop, flatter on the bottom. As air rushes along the top, it has farther to travel than the air running along the bottom. This makes it run a little faster to meet up with the air at the trailing edge of the wing.

The faster air moving over the top of the airplane wing has correspondingly lower pressure than the air on the bottom. The lower pressure above the wings creates a vacuum. The wing is, essentially, being sucked up into the sky. That's lift. Boats generate it across the airfoil of the sail, which is why they are sucked along faster by a quartering headwind than by a pushing tailwind.

The whole thing hinges on the Bernoulli Effect, an impressive-sounding scientific name that pilots trot out from time to time when they talk about takeoffs and stall speeds. Bernoulli discovered that pressure is lower in a faster-moving fluid than in a stationary fluid—like the air moving over the top of an airfoil. Lower pressure equals vacuum equals lift.

When pilots talk about an airplane "stall" it's not the engine they mean but the wing. When the plane stalls, the wing quits creating lift. The angle of the wing increases and the airspeed drops until there is not the required smooth air flowing over the wing to keep it flying. The plane falls out of the sky even though the engine is still running. Given enough altitude, the pilot can recover by pointing the nose down to get air flowing over the wings again, then leveling off.

It's all very scientific, but that doesn't explain the sheer joy pilots feel when their planes lift off the runway. A ton of metal and fiberglass, floating through the air! All physics aside, there's simply a moment of magic in that. First-time soloers and jaded airline pilots alike still feel the quick gasp of excitement, still announce, sometimes aloud, "We're flying!" as the plane leaves the ground.

"Albany Departure, Grumman Zero Zero Lima is with you climbing through eight hundred feet," Sinzheimer announced to the air traffic controller.

The controller replied, "Roger, Zero Zero Lima is radar contact. Climb to seven thousand feet and turn right heading zero niner zero."

"Niner zero and out of two for seven," Sinzheimer confirmed. Routine radio chatter.

He expected the turn east. His takeoff heading had been north of his route, to keep the Grumman plane clear of other airplanes taking off from and landing at Albany. He banked the airplane to the right, keeping an eye on his compass heading. Although the turn east helped, Sinzheimer knew that he was still a bit off his planned routing. Because he was flying an instrument plan he would have to wait for the controllers to clear him before he could turn to his on-course heading.

As he turned, he glanced at the most useful flight gauge—placed front and center—the Attitude Indicator (AI) which is also called the Artificial Horizon. Its circle was divided by a horizontal line into a blue half, above, and a brown half, below. A little plane sat in the middle, a tiny picture of the Grumman in flight. As Sinzheimer turned right, the little horizon banked left. As he raised the nose to climb, the little horizon dipped. A glance at the AI gave Sinzheimer instant information about the attitude of the plane in two dimensions—the roll of the wings and the pitch of the nose.

To make a turn, pilots don't just point the nose left or right like in a car. That would swing all the passengers over to one side, like kids smashing into each other in the back seat every time Dad goes around an exit curve on the highway. An airplane does point the nose left but it also rolls the wings. This keeps the turn "coordinated" so that everyone stays centered in the seats. It is what pilots mean when they say, "fly by the seat of your pants."

Famous aerobatic pilot Bob Hoover perfected a stunt in which he rolled his plane while pouring coffee into a cup affixed to the panel. Although the plane rolled upside down and back again, it was so perfectly coordinated that the coffee flowed continuously right into the cup.

To keep his turn coordinated, Sinzheimer also eyed the Turn and Bank indicator which monitored the "yaw" of the plane's nose, or whether it was pointed left or right. The gauge was black with a small white airplane and below it a ball floating in a tiny curved glass tube. As the Grumman turned right, the instrument's little plane dipped the right wing and the ball swung to the right. To keep the nose centered, Sinzheimer "stepped on the ball," pushing right rudder to guide nose to the right.

Below, Sinzheimer could see the lights of the Albany airport as he rolled out of the turn. As he pulled on the yoke to keep the nose climbing, the altimeter marked the plane's passage through 1,500 feet at about a hundred miles an hour. The Vertical Speed Indicator read 500 feet per minute. It would take another 11 minutes to reach 7,000 feet.

The Altimeter was on the right half of the panel. It looked like a clock—the little hand for thousands, the big hand for hundreds. The little hand was on one and the big hand was on eight, passing through 1,800 feet.

Glancing up through the clear canopy of his airplane as it climbed, Sinzheimer eyed gray clouds' jagged bottoms. Another few minutes and he would be in them. Then two long hours in and out of the soup, with an instrument approach to landing. No big deal, he'd done it a hundred times in the Mooney.

"Zero Zero Lima, turn right heading one six zero and intercept your course," the controller instructed.

Sinzheimer rolled the airplane over to the right and pushed the little button on the control yoke that broadcast his voice to the controller, "Turn right one six zero to intercept."

He rolled out of the turn with an eye on the Directional Gyroscope, or DG, which worked like a compass. It had an arrow fixed at the top, with a dial of numbers rotating around it. As the airplane turned, the DG rotated to the new heading of 160 degrees. Sinzheimer stopped the turn in time to line up the arrow with 160 to fly that heading: East was 90 degrees, south 180 degrees, west 270 degrees, north 360 degrees.

He was heading almost due south. From there, he would fly toward a mid-air highway, a line on his map between Albany and a radio beacon almost 40 miles away. That was his airway, Victor 130. He flew toward it at a slight angle, and would turn onto the airway once he got closer.

To intercept, he would use the VOR radio (for "very high-frequency omnidirectional range"). He had already dialed in the frequency for Albany's VOR beacon. The gauge had an outer ring with compass headings and a center needle that pointed to the ground beacon. Sinzheimer turned the outer ring to Victor 130's bearing of 147 degrees. The VOR needle pointed to the right, meaning that his airway was still off to the plane's right.

As the Grumman neared the airway, the VOR needle began to swing from the right to the center of the gauge. As the needle slid toward the instrument's center, Sinzheimer turned the plane slightly left, rolling out on the airway heading of 147 degrees. He would hold that heading and keep that needle centered, following the airway, or radial, just over 30 miles to the next VOR beacon at Bradley International Airport in Windsor Locks, Connecticut.

A lot going on, but it was a mere five minutes after takeoff. Sinzheimer's altimeter read 2,800 feet as the little plane started poking in and out of the wispy cloud vapor, one minute blinding Sinzheimer to the outside, another minute revealing the street and parking lot lights just coming on in the city of Troy, below.

Glancing outside to eye the approaching clouds is easy, almost irresistible. But switching from clouds to instruments and back again can be confusing, often inducing vertigo. To avoid the temptation, pilots switching from visual to instrument flying make it a very distinct transition. As the planes punch through the clouds at over a hundred miles an hour, pilots are trained to tell themselves, sometimes announcing aloud, "I'm on the gauges." From that point on, they fly by scanning the panel full of instruments.

Twelve minutes after taking off and Sinzheimer was flying blind in the clouds. He scanned the gauges as the plane reached 7,000 feet. In one smooth motion, he released the yoke with his left hand, letting the nose of the plane lower a bit to settle level, and with his right hand set the throttle knob to cruise power. He leaned the fuel mixture a bit and glanced again across the gauges. The airplane was established in level flight.

When Sinzheimer carried passengers to Provincetown in the Mooney he would reach cruising altitude, turn on the autopilot, then spend the next hour or so chatting about the towns they flew over, and pointing out airplanes they passed. At the end of the flight he would swoop down across the Bay, circle and float in for a landing. His feel for the plane was so practiced that he always managed a smooth touchdown even in Provincetown's near-constant crosswinds and gusts. He had loved that plane.

He had owned two Mooneys, actually. A 1968 M20C which he flew for three years then sold for a 1978 M20K. It was ten years old then, practically new in the world of aviation, where World War II era Mustangs dominate the national speed races in Reno, Nevada. Sinzheimer's K-model, also called a Mooney 231, was fast. It had a turbo-charged engine and whizzed along at over 200 miles an hour.

Like the later Grummans, the Mooney had been touched by LoPresti, and was a sleek four-seater, as famous for its speed and fuel-efficiency as for its cramped cockpit. The "Ferrari of airplanes," pilots call it, explaining that you don't get in it so much as put it on, like a pair of jeans. Mooneys have a unique tail design for the vertical fin, or stabilizer. Instead of sticking straight up it slants backwards, leaning toward the airplane's nose.

Sinzheimer soon learned that the Mooney was not as stable as some airplanes, which tend to stay on course even if the pilot gets distracted. This plane could dip the nose or a wing, demanding that he pay close attention to all three dimensions while also managing a lot of high-end equipment. Zipping along at 180 miles an hour in instrument flight meant that a moment's distraction could snowball into tragedy.

The Mooney had retractable landing gear, an adjustable prop, and a panel full of fun toys. The King KFC-200 autopilot was one of the best available. It interfaced with the navigational instruments and could fly the plane almost down to the ground on an instrument approach. The radar altimeter—rare in small airplanes—measured the exact distance from the plane to what was directly below it, and could be set to beep at a particular altitude. The plane had a backup vacuum system to power the all-important attitude and heading instruments. It was a "mission capable" aircraft that could punch through weather and get a pilot to almost any destination.

But it had cost a lot to maintain. And once Marsha gave up riding along, Ron hadn't seen much point in keeping the Mooney. After seven blissful years of flying it around the country for work, to the house on Cape Cod and the ski lodge in Vermont, he sold it to a friend in 1995. He spent three long summers riding the booming Harley back and forth every weekend, a seven-hour trip one-way.

The Grumman was certainly better than that. It was a good plane shaking off the rust after years of being on the ground. Sinzheimer was getting back in touch with the instrument skills he had honed in the sensitive Mooney, a speed demon that punched through storms and ice. He trusted his piloting ability. He believed that he could always get to his destination, even in the Grumman. But he missed the Mooney.

The Grumman was flying toward the beacon at Windor Locks' Bradley International Airport. Sinzheimer scanned the gauges, glancing from one needle to the other, verifying the proper settings. Wings level, airspeed in the green, heading 147 degrees, fuel gauges reading full, oil pressure in the green, fuel flow steady, and then back to checking wings level. Over and over, Sinzheimer faced two hours of tedious gauge-scanning.

The little plane droned on, the engine roar muffled by Sinzheimer's headset. How far away was the beacon, anyway? Nothing like a little math calculation to keep a pilot awake. Let's see, a cruise speed of a 150 knots (nautical miles per hour) and Bradley is about 70 nautical miles from Albany. Turn it into a word problem: It takes the plane an hour to fly 150 nautical miles, how long will it take it to fly 70? Okay, 70 is what percentage of 150? A little more than half—this is quick cockpit math, no pencils involved. So a little more than half an hour total time from Albany to Bradley. Add a pinch of time for the minutes spent climbing out at 100 knots instead of 150. So, 35 minutes total.

He had been up for, what, 15 minutes? In another ten it would be a good time to start watching the VOR needle. It would begin its little warning dance, meaning that the beacon was near. Then, suddenly, a little white triangle next to the needle would flip upside down. If Sinzheimer missed the flip he might keep following the blind needle and wander further southeast, toward Norwich.

Most pilots would catch the problem before long, noticing that the triangle was pointing in the wrong direction. If not, no matter. Airplanes on instrument flight plans are almost always on someone's radar. Controllers radio drifting planes, "You're off course, say your intentions." They can offer new headings to help disoriented pilots get back home. Even with that backup coverage, pilots watch their VOR needles for the dance and flip. No pilot likes to be embarrassed by missing the course, drifting off into la-la land while the controllers watch his wandering blip on radar and wonder, "What is that idiot doing now?"

The sun had set before Sinzheimer took off, and twenty minutes into the flight it was dark. Inside the cockpit, instrument lights glowed a gentle red; a color chosen for its ease on the eyes in dim environments. Outside, the little lights on the airplane's wings flashed red and green, lighting the Grumman up for other planes to spot. On a clear night, Sinzheimer could have seen the ground, might have noticed the lights of Springfield, Massachusetts, in the distance. The city lay just north of Bradley airport. Grumman 7100L was about halfway to Providence, Rhode Island.

"Grumman Zero Zero Lima, contact Bradley Approach on one two five point zero," the controller's voice zapped into the quiet, dark cockpit. Bradley airspace, already? That was quick, especially with headwinds from the north.

Sinzheimer confirmed the handoff, "Over to Bradley on twenty five zero, Zero Zero Lima."

# Chapter 4

# Radio Work

FROM THE OUTSIDE Building 130 was modest, as if some minor lieutenant sat inside shuffling base paperwork. The squat cinderblocks were painted an afterthought shade of tan, number 130 on the side in brown. It sat behind a cluster of drab buildings and their parking lots at one end of Otis Air National Guard Base in Falmouth, Massachusetts, on Cape Cod.

The quiet atmosphere inside matched the image, but it did not stem from bored desk workers. The employees were concentrating on a very tense job. Building 130 was the home of Cape Cod's Terminal Radar Approach Facility otherwise known as TRACON. In a darkened room, at the end of the hall behind a security door at the entrance, air traffic controllers focused on a wall of round radarscopes. They tracked every airplane below 10,000 feet that passed over Martha's Vineyard, Nantucket, or Cape Cod—about 50,000 a month during the summer.

On Friday, October 9, 1998, David Loring's shift started at 2:00 P.M. Loring was wiry with a face lined from years of Cape Cod suntans. No sign of the pasty skin and thick belly you might expect from a desk jockey who spent his days in a windowless room. He had the kind of nervous energy that kept him in motion, physically and verbally, trading wisecracks across the radar room. Loring's graying dark hair and sideburns curled out from under a blue Cape Air baseball cap. He wore pretty much whatever he wanted to work, which was usually shorts or jeans.

Just before it was time for him to hop on position on a radarscope that Friday afternoon, Loring headed down the hall to the small break room to start his evening off on the right note.

Hey you bum, he said to one of the controllers sitting on the couch. What are you doing in here being lazy? All the planes are gonna fall out of the sky.

Oh no, Dave is here! The controller waved his arms over his head. Mr. Former Supervisor's gonna make us fill out some paperwork!

Yeah, bite me, Loring said, laughing. What's it like tonight?

Not bad, a little gusty. They're having a little trouble holding the ILS, but nothing major.

Loring cracked the back door and glanced outside. Raining, but if he stood close enough to the open door he could have a smoke and not get too wet. The clouds were low, he figured, a couple hundred feet with visibility of a few miles. He couldn't make out the giant Coast Guard hangar on the other side of the runway and the seagulls were walking. He could tell that he was going to have a scope full of instrument traffic, none of the pilots able to see anything. They were gonna be going missed on the approaches, he'd have to turn them back around to try again. They would ask for alternates, weather updates, new routings, new altitudes where things weren't so bumpy. He was going to be hopping.

One last deep drag then Loring stubbed out the butt, shut the door and walked down the short hallway to the radar room.

The room was dark, so dark that for a moment it seemed as if Loring had walked right into a coat closet. He could hear the familiar buzz of controllers muttering into their headsets, "Cape Air Fifty Five, turn left heading three four zero," "Cessna One Eight Hotel, descend and maintain four thousand."

He didn't stand at the doorway to let his eyes adjust, but plunged right into the dim room, knowing the layout by heart. The first thing he could see were the low spotlights aimed at the paperwork on the supervisor's large desk at the back of the room. Then the monitor with the weather radar, painting a lot of blue and green tonight for rain, a few patches of yellow and red off the coast of Rhode Island where it got heavier. Then he could make out the sweeping arms and blips of the six radarscopes, four on the long wall facing the door, two along the short wall to the right. At the far end, along the short wall opposite the door, was the desk for the Flight Data controller.

There were two controllers on the scopes that afternoon. One worked the two sectors that handled Nantucket. In summers, Nantucket became the second-busiest airport in all of New England, surpassed only by Boston's Logan. By early October traffic had slowed a bit, but it was still too busy to fold Nantucket into another sector. The other controller worked everything else.

The supervisor pointed toward that radarscope. Start off on High sector, Dave, he said. Go relieve him.

Loring stood next to the controller who was working approaches and departures for the four sectors covering Plymouth, the grass strip at Cape Cod airport, Otis National Guard Base, Falmouth, Hyannis, the two airports on Martha's Vineyard, Chatham, and Provincetown. He hooked the black earpiece over his right ear, inserting the small pink earplug. He pivoted the tiny boom microphone, no bigger around than a toothpick, into position next to his mouth and slid the jack into the plug just under the counter top as the controller started rattling off an update for the sector.

Okay, mostly Cape Air between the Vineyard and Hyannis tonight, the controller pointed at the screen. Hyannis is running the ILS one five. These guys are lined up for the approach. This one already has clearance. This guy just took off over here. His radar tag will start flashing for the handoff to you in a minute.

The other controller stood up and headed for the break room as Loring sat down and rolled the chair into position. He jiggled his leg and absently tapped his pen on the metal countertop that served as a narrow desk in front of the scopes. When he spoke to his planes he pushed the white button attached to the headset cable.

Loring's voice was deep and scratched by years of Marlboro Lights. His cadence was rhythmic, with the occasional accent on an unexpected word to keep listeners interested. It was a voice of a professional, one that could have preached sermons, called games at Fenway Park, or hawked rip-off carney games on a boardwalk, which in fact Loring had done in high school. It was a voice that his pilots trusted, knew to be willing to share a joke or a local weather update.

Pilots rely on the static-tinged voices that come into the cockpit. Those voices on the radio describe what's going on in the rest of the sky. And when a pilot has a problem, that voice is the only link to the rest of the world that lies below.

A typical example of the emotional dependence on controllers is the story of a doomed pilot who got lost over the Bahamas. She circled the islands, low on fuel. An anxious controller tried, and failed, to pinpoint the airplane's position. As the sun began to set, the pilot still had not found a place to land. The controller offered headings for the pilot to fly, trying to steer her toward the mainland. She ignored the directions, saying that she was more comforted by the sound of his voice, "Just keep talking to me, I need it."

Even in calmer times, pilots will sometimes chat with controllers, asking for ballgame scores or for information that could be looked up on a chart. The voice helps keep them from getting bored on long, lonely flights.

One of Loring's radar screen blips had an aircraft identifier number that he knew.

Good evening, Captain, he said. Climb to niner thousand and left turn on course.

Niner thousand and on course, Dave! How are you today? Loring could hear the smile come through the earpiece. One of his regulars.

Excellent, Captain, nice to see you again but now I've got to let you go. Talk to Cape on one twenty four point seven.

Loring handed the flight to the next controller's sector, waving his hand across the screen as if to scoot the plane through the air.

As Loring slid into his chair in the radar room on one side of the runway at Otis, a fresh Coast Guard Search and Rescue team reported for duty on the other side.

Lieutenant Commander Scott Womack was a tall, pale Georgia boy from Cobb County, in his early forties and looking trim in his royal blue flight suit. As he walked across the parking lot to the building that housed the flight operations center, Womack glanced up at the low cloud cover. It looks like Alaska, he thought.

He jogged the stairs to the flight planning room to collect his pager and ran into Robin Starrett.

Hey there Scottie, Starrett said.

Womack smiled at his old friend. Looking nasty out there tonight, he said.

The two had flown together only a few times since Starrett transferred from Kodiak two months earlier, following Womack to Cape Cod. On the Cape they had been spending most of their air time on fisheries patrol. That consisted of flying a grid pattern off Stellwagen and George's Bank to make sure the fleet stayed off whichever nearly-depleted fishing grounds were currently forbidden. Law enforcement duty was not glamorous, even when they had flown in Alaska. Womack never liked being pitted against the mariners. He'd rather run Search and Rescue—skimming the Jayhawk helicopter over the water to winch some injured fisherman out of a capsizing boat. Today's hero, flying toward disaster and saving a life.

Womack and Starrett would be on call for the next 24 hours, along with a rescue swimmer and flight mechanic. The crew covered the Coast Guard District One territory that ran from the Canadian border down through New Jersey. Their machine was the Sikorsky HH60 "Jayhawk" helicopter.

The Jayhawk is an orange and white monster 17 feet tall and 65 feet long. Its most distinctive feature is the bulbous black nose that houses its radar antenna. The helicopter's two turbo shaft engines can carry a maximum gross weight of around 22,000 lbs. It's a massive, complicated machine that makes a pilot's heart leap with lust, with the desire to climb into the cockpit, power the beast up into the air, flip its switches, dive it, bank it, climb it, yank it around until it screams and then glide it down again smoothly. Hot toys like the Jayhawk are what make enlistees sign up.

At the air station, the four Jayhawks sat in different stages of readiness. "Alfa" helicopters were out on actual missions. "Bravo" aircraft sat in the hangar or out on the ramp, ready to go. "Charlie" status meant the helicopter was down for maintenance. Jayhawk number 6021 was on Bravo status, parked on the spotless hangar's white-painted floor. It had received its one thorough preflight for the day, a four-hour operation performed by maintenance specialists that crawled over every inch of the machine, poking and prodding. The cabin, aft of the pilots' cockpit, held the standard equipment: the wire rescue basket, the emergency water pump and a basic first-aid kit.

Womack and Starrett left the flight planning room and headed downstairs and across the parking lot, over to the barracks to find a television or something to read. The pagers were all very well, but on a night like this they planned on staying close, within range of the air station's emergency sirens.

The controller working the Flight Data desk walked over with a fresh load of strips for Loring's rack. The narrow pieces of paper held flight-plan information for all planes traveling through Cape TRACON's airspace that evening. Strips gave controllers advance notice of which planes would show up when and where. The controller pulled Loring's old strips out of their narrow plastic holders and replaced them with the new ones.

Fresh load for you Dave, you think you can handle it?

Ah, piss off, Loring smiled. Go rip your strips, you're not good enough to work a scope tonight.

The controller laughed and took some strips over to the Nantucket controller.

Dave's hot tonight, he joked. Maybe you should just give him your sector too and go home.

Yeah, yeah, Loring said. Run around the room a little more, maybe you'll lose some weight. He grabbed the strip for the next takeoff from Hyannis and tapped it on the metal counter top as he turned back to the scope.

The scope was full of blips, but not all of them were his. Some belonged to Boston Center, cruising along above 10,000 feet and headed over the pond for Europe. Others belonged to Boston Approach, which worked lower-level flights around Logan's airspace. Some belonged to the Cape controller who sat a few scopes away, working the two Nantucket sectors. On a bad-weather night like this, every plane in the air was talking to a controller—at an airport tower, a TRACON, or a Center. Nobody moved without a controller's radar clearance for the flight plan.

Most of the blips on Loring's scope were tagged with two lines of coded text, listing the airplane's "call sign," or registration number, its altitude, type of aircraft, destination and airspeed. Loring's planes were marked with an "I," an abbreviation for the "High" sector he was working that evening.

Most controllers got distracted by the other blips and tags and adjusted their scopes to filter out all traffic except their own. But Loring preferred the big picture, liked to see what everyone was doing and where they were headed. He fiddled with the knobs along the top and right side of the scope, leaving all the blips in but blocking out the map of the coastline. He wanted to see the airspace the way the pilots saw it that afternoon—a gray soup of clouds with no shoreline, no cities below. Instead, the sky was full of aerial fixes and navigational beacon signals.

On Loring's screen only the airplanes had tags. None of the fixes or beacons themselves were marked by any identifying text. Each was represented by a faint mark, as if a child had hesitantly pressed a green marker on the living room wall. After 16 years Loring recognized them all at a glance, and had no use for the overlay that tagged them with their identifier codes. He turned on the scope's range rings, the concentric circles five miles apart. They made it easy to tell how far an airplane was from an airport or a fix. When a pilot took off and climbed to altitude in the soup, unable to see the ground or any landmarks, Loring could say "Radar contact five miles from Phony," and the distance wasn't just a guess.

Cape Approach, Cessna Six Two Uniform with a pirep.

A pilot was calling Loring with a pilot report on what the weather was like up there. Loring didn't key his talk button. He glanced at the controller in the next chair: A pirep?

As if on cue they chanted, laughing: Pirep? We don't need no stinking pirep!

But on the frequency, Loring listened as the pilot told him he was between cloud layers, occasional rain. Loring was polite and thanked him but didn't write the information down. That was a Flight Service job. The pilot should switch over to frequency 122.2 and call it in himself. Loring had bigger fish to fry, had to keep these planes from getting tangled up in the messy weather.

The scope painted the standard assortment of Cape Air flights, running between Boston, Hyannis, Provincetown, and Nantucket. Most of his action was in Hyannis, smack in the middle of Cape Cod's bicep, where the landing planes were using the ILS approach for Runway 15. The winds were shifting, now headed out of the south, which gave planes inbound from Nantucket, to the south, a tailwind. The tailwind made the tight turn to the southeast-facing runway tricky. It swept planes though a larger turn radius than normal.

Most of Loring's work that afternoon and evening would center around getting planes from Nantucket to Hyannis, keeping them clear of the landing path for Martha's Vineyard to the west, then giving them sharp right turns for the final approach into Hyannis.

Provincetown would be even worse, Loring thought, its near-constant gusty crosswinds exacerbated by the bad weather. Good thing it was just Cape Air in and out of there tonight. Those guys worked Provincetown all the time. They would have no trouble.

In the dance between ATC and their planes, pilots lead. They decide where to go and where to land. Controllers tell them how to get there. Up for negotiation are the routings and altitudes. The pilot makes a request for a certain heading, then the controller decides if there is enough space between other airplanes in the sector to grant it. But the bottom line, which Loring never forgot once he took a few flying lessons, was that the pilot was the one up there in the sky, trying to survive the flight. The controller, in the comfortable chair on the ground, was there to help.

On an instrument flight plan, before a plane even takes off, it gets a clearance. That spells out where the plane will land and what Victor airways it will take to get there. The pilot sometimes marks the path on the tissue-paper chart with a highlighter.

The controllers also know what the plane is going to do. In radar rooms all along the plane's route of flight, computers spit out strips. The strips list the plane's "N" number, type of aircraft, flight path, altitude and destination.

Commercial jets cruise in the airspace above 18,000 feet. From there, they talk to Center controllers, fly pre-approved routes and rarely see a propeller airplane. The props duke it out in the radar sectors below 18,000, a jumble of Centers, TRACONs and airport towers. On a clear day, sometimes a pilot has to talk to a controller and sometimes not, depending on the type of airspace. But when a flight is on instruments, there's no option. Everyone talks to TRACON and Center.

Sometimes the strips for a radar facility conflict and so the pilot's routing must change in flight. Maybe the Victor airway the plane had a bend in it which turned to the west. "West is best," goes the saying, meaning that west-bound planes fly at even altitudes. A controller will call the pilot, saying, "I need you at an even altitude for that direction of flight, you want 6,000 or 8,000?" The pilot chooses 8,000. Or maybe asks for 10,000. When the controller hands the pilot to the next sector, he says thanks for the help on the altitude change.

Controllers complain about pilots in the same way that a café owner complains about his customers. They are rude, annoying, stupid, and they get in the way. But they are the reason we are here. If a flight develops problems and a pilot asks for help, the controller will rearrange the whole sky to accommodate.

In Building 130, Loring was fresh back on the scope for another two-hour shift after his second cigarette break. He was working Cape Air flights, mostly. They flew to and from their airports every hour, sticking a dozen planes into Cape's airspace at any given moment. On clear days they didn't bother to call in, scooting below the controlled space at 1,000 or 2,000 feet. But today everyone was going IFR, following Victor airway 141 to intersections and fixes with entertaining names like Drunk, Grogg, Wimpy, Celts and Clamy. Somebody in the airspace department at the FAA had a sense of humor.

One of the data tags on a blip started flashing at Loring. The controller at Boston TRACON was signaling to hand the plane off to Cape. Loring used his radarscope's trackball to center the cursor over the tag's "B." He typed "I" for his sector, hit "enter" and the tag stopped flashing as he accepted the handoff. A few minutes later, the pilot radioed in. He used the common identifier for Cape Air flights, "Care."

Cape Approach, Care Six Eight Five at four thousand for Provincetown, he said. In rapid-fire pilot-speak it all ran together with a few shortcuts, sounding more like, "'Proach Care Six Eight Five Four P-town."

Good evening Care Four Eight Five, you guys are working hard tonight, Loring shot back. Provincetown altimeter zero zero zero, present heading to intercept ILS Runway Seven.

In other words, he gave the mandatory current altimeter setting, which the pilot needed in order to set the instrument for his location. Loring also directed the pilot to intercept the final course for the runway, although he wasn't yet cleared for the actual landing. The pilot radioed back.

Four Eight Five, present heading ILS seven. Translation: Okay, we've got 30.00 as the current altimeter setting and we'll stay on our current heading until we intercept the approach path for the instrument landing to Runway Seven at Provincetown.

Rrrrrogah, Loring answered, rolling the first R and dropping the last, New England style.

As Loring worked, his focus tightened. It hadn't been a great week. He and his wife had called it quits a few days before. It was almost a relief to come into work, to get the planes funneled into their airports. Something productive, something complicated that turned out well. The rest of his life might be sagging a little at the moment, but the controller thing was working out.

Care Four Eight Five, descend and maintain two thousand, he radioed the Cape Air pilot bound for Provincetown.

Out of four for two, Care Four Eight Five, the pilot answered.

Hey, how was the company party this year? Loring asked.

Good, the pilot said. I didn't stay too late but I heard people were there past midnight.

Loring watched as the altitude number for the blip changed: 40, 35, 30, 25, 20 as it leveled off at 2,000 feet. It took about five minutes.

Care Two Two Six, turn left heading three three zero, Loring directed another flight.

Two Two Six, left three three zero, the pilot responded.

Alan, right? Loring asked. He could hear the British accent. Are you going south this winter to fly those Caribbean routes?

Nah, not this year, Alan Davis answered. Got a job flying a Citation for a company out of Connecticut. Start in a few months.

Some controllers kept the dialog all business, just jargon about altitudes and fixes. But Loring figured that if he could amuse his customers they'd be a lot more likely to help him out with a sharp turn or quick descent if he needed it. Besides, if you couldn't have fun at your job, what was the point? That's why Loring had chucked the supervisor position two weeks earlier. Twice the responsibility for twenty cents more per hour? Forget about it.

Care Four Eight Five is seven miles from Phony, cleared for ILS seven into P-town, Loring announced in his deep voice, rolling his chair forward and tapping the strip holder on the counter.

Care Four Eight Five, cleared ILS seven, the pilot answered. Loring watched as the blip turned right, toward the east, heading right toward the runway. The guy was picking up the radio signal for the ILS approach. It was time to cut him loose.

Care Four Eight Five, frequency change approved, report cancellation on the ground, he announced.

Care Four Eight Five, advisories.

It meant, we will switch to the Provincetown advisory frequency to announce our landing at the airport.

Loring didn't talk to him after that. For a few minutes he could still see the radar blip on the right side of his screen, crossing Phony and descending at 500 feet per minute.

At 1,600 feet, the blip's tag started flashing, just like with a handoff but the tag identifier had switched to "ZZ" instead of Loring's "I." Cape's radar was losing contact with the plane as it descended behind a small rise in the terrain to the east of Otis. The scope painted the blip for another few sweeps, but the data was pure conjecture, a projection based on the plane's most recent actual position. The plane could have started doing something random and Loring would never have known.

If it were landing at Hyannis, Loring would have handed the blip off to the Hyannis tower. Its radar controllers would then track the plane down to the runway. But Provincetown and Chatham do not have towers. It is up to the pilot to report landing safely.

After half a dozen radar sweeps, the blip disappeared completely. Loring turned a few more airplanes and picked up another departure from the Vineyard. The Provincetown flight was off the screen but not forgotten, its flight plan strip would sit in Cape's radar room until the pilot cancelled. In a few minutes, Loring knew, the pilot would call to verify that he had landed.

Sure enough: Care Four Eight Five on the ground in P-town, canceling IFR. The pilot radioed the Flight Data Controller to cancel his flight plan.

Son of a bitch. The controller next to Loring swore under his breath. Loring's ears perked up but he didn't look over. Let the guy handle it without an audience, whatever it was.

Give me some room, Dave. The controller sounded resigned, a little angry. I got a guy can't do shit because he lost his gyros.

Instrument failure. Either no Attitude Indicator or no Directional Gyro. Those critical instruments told the pilot where the plane was pointed or where it was in relation to the invisible horizon. A terrifying situation in a cloudy sky.

No problem, Loring said without looking over. He gave directions to his planes over the microphone. He tightened his traffic, opening some space near the border of his radar sector. The no-gyro airplane would have to make wider turns than usual, flying by the bouncy wet compass. It might cross over into his airspace.

The joking in the room stopped for a moment. The radar room radio was tuned to a music station, Van Morrison singing "Moondance." The room kept humming with the low murmers of controllers talking and the occasional click of plastic strip holders tapping on the metal counter.

Behind Loring, the supervisor meandered over to the other controller, stood behind him. Loring watched on his own scope as the blip made a wide turn and started to descend to the airport. It was a Cape Air flight. A commercial pilot who knew how to keep the wings and nose in position by watching the backup instruments, the Turn and Bank and Airspeed indicators. If anyone could handle the situation, this pilot could.

Loring talked to his planes, leaning forward and resting his elbows on the counter. Every so often he glanced at the no-gyro blip, which was managing to descend on the glide slope.

Cessna Four Oh Seven, he announced to one of his landing aircraft. Descend and maintain three thousand, advise you have Delta.

Down to three and we'll go get Delta.

Ah, I've got nothing better to do, Loring answered. He read from the weather screen above his radarscope, broadcasting the information to all the planes on his frequency: Hyannis information Delta, winds zero one zero at seven, visibility three and mist, overcast two thousand, expect ILS one five.

Cessna Four Oh Seven copies Delta, thanks.

Yeah, thanks Cape, Citation Five Eight Lima copies also.

Loring looked over at the no-gyro blip again. It had landed. The supervisor had wandered away, unnoticed. Business as usual.

The Flight Data controller walked by with a fresh load of strips. Loring glanced at them and noticed something new. A Grumman for Provincetown, it would be inbound from Providence, Rhode Island at about 7:00 P.M. The Providence VOR beacon was at the far left edge of Loring's scope, a tiny green dash. When the plane crossed that VOR, it would start flashing for the handoff from Providence. An hour yet. Loring put the strip at the bottom of his rack and turned back to his radarscope.

# Chapter 5

# Cape Air

AT 5:45 P.M., as Ron Sinzheimer took off from Albany, Pete Kacergis crawled into the cockpit of the twin-engine Cessna 402 that sat on the ramp in Boston. He settled into the pilot's seat, straightened his dark tie and loosened the seatbelt a bit before clicking it closed. He had been at work since 6:15 A.M. but didn't look tired, a late summer's tan still blooming on his face and arms. Above, the sky was dark but Kacergis didn't even bother to look up. He knew he'd get into Provincetown on instruments, just like he'd been doing for the past six years.

Without his uniform, the striped epaulets on the shoulders of the sharply-ironed white shirt, Kacergis didn't look the part of an airline pilot. He was not tall, maybe five foot seven and barrel-chested with a bit of a gut. He combed his dark wavy hair to one side but it flopped pretty much straight down over his forehead. His shoelaces seemed to keep coming untied.

But in the cockpit, Kacergis was a pure professional. As he flew, Kacergis moved with the deliberateness of airline pilots everywhere. He was quick, but the pace of his hands was even, never too fast, never too slow. Airline pilots are trained not to alarm the passengers by getting excited or flipping switches too quickly. They also pay attention to their flight maneuvers. On the bigs, the major airlines, pilots like to say, "Don't spill the coffee." In other words, no abrupt turns, climbs or descents that might shake the passengers up and dump their snacks in their laps. Cape Air didn't offer cabin service, but if anyone cracked open a can of soda from the airport lobby machine, Kacergis would make sure nobody ended up wearing it.

He handled the Cessna with relaxed confidence. His hands moved through the preflight check, flipping switches and moving levers, verifying the procedures with a glance at the checklists. After a few seconds Cape Air flight 90 was ready for boarding. A full load of passengers—nine people—were leaving Boston for the half-hour flight to Provincetown, Massachusetts.

Kacergis could always tell the first-timers. They walked hesitantly out on the ramp and smiled nervously, saying, "It's so small," as they caught sight of the plane. Some of them didn't like having to put their purses and briefcases in the wing lockers, the small storage compartments outside the cabin, on the inner section of the wings. The ground crew had to explain that this wasn't like a jet flight, there was no overhead storage or space under the seats. It would be noisy, and a little bumpier than a jet.

The regulars were different. Most of them loved the thrill of these small, sporty planes that flew low over the ocean. They lined up early to board, elbowing each other aside for the chance to race out on the ramp and be the first to choose a seat. Each wanted to be the lucky passenger who rode up front, next to the pilot.

Kacergis liked those passengers—they asked good questions. Explaining what he was doing kept Kacergis in the ballgame, kept him paying close attention to each flight instead of taking the day for granted as one long monotonous stream of indistinguishable takeoffs and landings. They kept him from getting complacent—so comfortable that he quit paying attention, losing respect for the risks of his job.

Every year the FAA publishes the updated rulebook for pilots and aircraft mechanics. General aviation pilots, the ones flying around in their own airplanes, operate under one set of rules, called Part 91. Charter operations have stricter rules, called Part 135. Some regional airlines (like Cape Air) also operate under Part 135. The pickiest rules of all are those for air carriers, or the major airlines, under Part 121.

For example, the rules regarding takeoffs in instrument conditions vary. A general aviation pilot can legally depart if the visibility and ceiling at the airport are zero/zero. But an air carrier must wait until the weather is above the landing minimums, in case the plane must circle back and make an emergency landing.

The FAA's reasoning for the different levels of rules is this: Why slap regs all over some little guy in a Piper Cub who just goes up for sightseeing flights on weekends? There's not much incentive to because the pilot is only risking himself (regulations keep him a certain distance from populated areas and other airplanes). If the FAA did hit these general aviation pilots with a bunch of additional rules, it is likely that many would stop flying altogether. The companies that manufacture small airplanes wouldn't like that. It would look like the FAA was failing to uphold part of its mission—promoting aviation.

But a pilot taking up fare-paying passengers, that's another story. The FAA gets very interested in protecting people who pay for rides. The regulations are stricter and better enforced. A general aviation pilot can fly for years without ever meeting an FAA representative. They hang around the air carrier operations, checking up on the pilots and mechanics.

Another example of the difference in regulations involves flotation devices. A general aviation pilot need only carry life vests if the plane will be 50 nautical miles from the nearest shore (50 nautical miles is about the distance from Boston to Martha's Vineyard). If the flight will be 100 nautical miles from shore, it's required to carry a heavily-provisioned life raft.

But if a flight is "for hire" (that is, carrying paying passengers), it must carry life vests if it flies outside the power-off gliding distance from shore. At the low altitudes that Cape Air flies, the airline is required to carry flotation devices for each passenger.

A Grumman, however, is not. If it lost power in the middle of Cape Cod Bay, a Grumman would have to be at 6,000 feet to reach the shore in a perfect power-off glide. If it were making a "for-hire" flight at that altitude or lower, it would be required to carry life vests. But not on a normal pleasure flight.

That's because private pilots don't usually make frequent flights over water, the way that a scheduled commercial carrier does. The chances are very slim that one of the few they do make would end in an emergency landing. And so the FAA doesn't require pilots to carry life vests except when beyond the 50 nautical mile range of shore. Life vests are like smoke hoods—one more gadget to buy and tote along, with million-to-one odds it will ever get used. Mandate enough of those kinds of things and pretty soon there's not enough room in single-engine cockpits for the pilot and an overnight bag.

Understandably, the regulations create the following situation: The commercial operators have stricter rules, get more training, fly better equipment and log more flight time. Part 91 pilots have fewer rules, less stringent training, less sophisticated equipment and fewer flight hours. So what happens? They crash more often.

Pete Kacergis grew up in Halifax, halfway between Boston and the Cape. After his parents moved to Provincetown he spent summers in his dad's welding shop or in the water, wearing scuba gear to scrape barnacles from boat bellies. After a few years of that, Kacergis figured it was time to go up. He majored in flying at Bridgewater State College, near Halifax.

He got a job loading baggage at Cape Air. After a few months of that, they offered him the copilot's seat and $6 for each mail flight he made. Kacergis took the cut in pay and hopped into the cockpit, logging time until he qualified to pilot the passenger flights and make more money.

In 11 years of flying Kacergis had logged 7,000 flight hours, a number that more than qualified him to move to the feeder routes for the "bigs," the major airlines. But why bother? Kacergis had seniority at Cape Air and he didn't want to move off-Cape. He didn't want to take overnight trips, away from his wife and teenaged son who sometimes rode along on his dad's flights. Kacergis preferred an easy pace to his life, liked living near his parents and grandparents and having the time to restore his 1941 Chevy.

At Logan Airport, Kacergis ran through the departure procedure. Logan is one of the nation's busiest airports, but for pilots it operates just like any other airport with a control tower: Nobody moves in or out without talking to a series of air traffic controllers. Kacergis put on his headset and flipped the radios on, monitoring two frequencies at once. On the first, he listened to Clearance Delivery, waiting for a break in the conversation to hop in and get his routing to Boston. On the second radio he monitored the recorded voice of the weather broadcast.

"Boston automated weather Yankee, winds three six zero at niner, few clouds at two hundred, overcast five hundred, visibility niner, temperature twelve, dew point twelve, altimeter three zero zero four..." the broadcast went on to give taxi information for Logan's busy airport.

A low scud of a cloud layer, Kacergis thought. Temperature and dew point the same, which meant fog was likely to pop up. Hyannis, Provincetown and Boston lie within roughly 50 miles of each other along Cape Cod Bay, but often have very different weather. It wasn't unusual for Kacergis to leave Boston in sun and find Provincetown banked under a plop of fog. He didn't put much faith in forecasts. Like Lindbergh, who on mail flights sometimes tossed the printed weather brief out of the cockpit without reading it, Kacergis preferred to arrive and gauge the situation first-hand, then decide whether or not to try a landing.

The weather had been cruddy all day, and the night didn't promise to be any better. This flight would be like the half-dozen others he had made that Friday: in and out of layers of clouds, rainy and probably bumpy. The tourists wouldn't be happy, with no view out the windows.

Cape Air operations wasn't happy on IFR days either because its pilots had to file instrument flight plans, sticking to the Victor airways at assigned altitudes and circling in holding patterns to wait in line for the landing approaches. IFR planes had to line up like proper soldiers with three miles of separation. Any deviation from the flight plan had to be cleared in advance or an anxious controller would call, prompting the pilot to get back in line. Lining up like that wasted time, fuel, and money for the small airline, but rules were rules.

Pete Kacergis was a quiet, relaxed kind of guy. He didn't wave his hands in the air when telling a story. Instead, he stood around with his hands in his pockets. When he walked from the plane to the tarmac, it was with an easy roll, glancing up at the bright sun then out to the picnic table to scope out a shady lunch spot. But in one thing Kacergis had speed, and that was in the cockpit of an airplane. As he flipped switches, his mind was already whizzing ahead to the next procedure. He talked on the radios at an astonishing pace, blurting out mind-numbing streams of jargon. He moved with the rapid confidence of a Japanese steak-house chef flinging knives over the heads of the excited diners.

Kacergis heard a brief silence on Boston's Clearance frequency and broke in: Clearance Delivery, Care Ninety IFR to Provincetown with Yankee.

He made the announcement using Cape Air's call sign of "Care." The response was quick.

Roger Care Ninety, cleared as filed to Provincetown, maintain two thousand expect five thousand one zero minutes after departure, departure frequency is one three three zero, squawk four three zero two.

The controller's instructions cleared Kacergis to fly the IFR route he had filed earlier with Flight Service. The "squawk" code was a number to dial into the transponder radio, which would then broadcast to ATC to distinguish Cape Air 90 from all the other silent green blips on the radarscope. Clearance would pass Cape Air 90's flight strip across the room to the Boston TRACON controller who worked the sector Kacergis would fly through. The controller would match the strip to Kacergis' squawking blip.

He already had the first two digits of the squawk code dialed in, had been anticipating the frequency. Kacergis dialed in the other two digits and read back the clearance, expertly jamming together the instructions so it sounded like, "Care Ninety as filed, maintain two, expect five ten one three three zero four three zero two."

The controller spoke the same language, answering: Readback correct.

Kacergis switched the first radio over to Ground Control, and the second over to Cape Air's private operations frequency.

Cape Air's passengers climbed aboard through the back door, crouching and tugging their way up between the seats, a space too narrow to be properly called an "aisle." Pete got a quiet one in the front seat. She didn't ask any questions but she watched as his hands worked the controls preparing to start the left engine. As the passengers struggled with their seatbelts, Kacergis ran through the safety address, telling them where the fire extinguisher was and that flotation devices were under every seat.

The blonde working ground crew that evening was energetic, swirling her hand around in the circular "startup" pattern and then a thumbs-up after pointing to the left engine. Kacergis pushed the left mixture and propeller levers full forward, then pressed the starter button. The engine cranked. The girl on the ramp pointed to the right engine, swirled and gave thumbs-up. Kacergis cranked the right and passed a thumbs-up back before throttling forward to turn the airplane to point toward the taxiway.

He keyed the mike to ask for taxi clearance, as pilots on the Cape Air frequency chattered in the background. Ground, Care Ninety, taxi with Yankee, he announced in a swift monotone.

Care Ninety, cross Runway One Five Right, taxi to Runway Two Two Right via taxiways Alpha, November, the controller instructed. Logan has five runways, two of which are parallel. That night the parallels were active: 22 Right and 22 Left.

In regular conversation, Kacergis didn't rush his words. He had a habit of stuttering a little, as if to hold his place while he thought about how to finish a sentence. But on the airplane radios he always knew what to say next.

Alpha, November, cross one five for Two Two, he answered while pushing forward on the throttle levers. The plane rolled onto the taxiway and headed for the end of Runway 22 Right.

The Cessna inched forward in the line of jets waiting to take off. Number seven for departure. A few minutes later, number six. The clock ticked as controllers waited for spacing between planes. Number five. The Cessna's cockpit stank of jet exhaust from the 727 immediately ahead in line. Number four. Number three. When the 727 finally took off, Kacergis switched frequencies. The second radio he flipped over to his departure frequency, for the controller he would talk to after takeoff. The first he set for Tower.

Tower, Care Ninety number one for departure.

Roger Care Ninety, Runway Two Two Right, position and hold.

Position and hold. Kacergis taxied the plane onto the end of the runway and put on the brakes.

Care Ninety, cleared for takeoff Two Two Right, fly runway heading.

Rolling Two Two Right, runway heading, Kacergis answered and pushed the two throttle levers forward. He held the brakes and revved the engines to full speed, then released the brakes and started rolling down the runway. At 115 miles an hour he eased back on the yoke and lifted the plane into the air. He flipped a lever and sent the landing gear up into its storage wells.

Care Ninety, contact Departure, the controller announced. Kacergis confirmed and flipped the second radio back to Cape Air's operations frequency. He announced on the first radio, which was on Boston TRACON.

Departure, Care Ninety climbing through four hundred, he announced. He had poked through the first thin layer of cloud cover and now nosed up into the solid ceiling, the cabin windows filmed with solid gray haze.

For the passengers, the trip to Provincetown IFR was just a dull, gray ride with nothing to see. For Kacergis it was a busy mental game of staying ahead of the plane—scanning the gauges and double-checking them against each other, making backup plans in case an instrument should fail or the weather should worsen, setting radios for the next navigational fix, the next controller frequency.

Care Ninety, radar contact, turn heading one eight zero and climb to three thousand, said the Departure controller.

One eight zero and three, Kacergis answered. He flipped the selector switch back to the second radio, set for Cape Air's private Hyannis operations frequency, and announced: Care Ninety is off Boston with eight plus one. Eight fare-paying passengers, one "non-rev" riding along on a free pass from a Cape Air employee.

Roger Pete, report landing.

Kacergis left both radios chattering away—TRACON on one, the Cape Air ops people on the other talking about flights getting into Hyannis, discussing the weather at Nantucket.

A few minutes later he tuned the second radio to the automated weather at Provincetown. Was the visibility staying high enough to shoot the approach? So far, so good. He flipped to the automated weather at Hyannis to verify it was good enough to serve as a backup.

Even with an autopilot and the fancy navigational instruments that the Cessna had, Kacergis was busily scanning, flipping, talking and turning as he flew. His confident radio work was an extra, an aviation nicety that only very experienced pilots master. Low-time pilots are slow on the frequencies, carefully repeating back each instruction, stumbling over names of the waypoints, sometimes telling a controller to "standby" before accepting a new heading or altitude change. That's because flying the airplane is paramount. Neophyte pilots are busy holding the plane steady and studying their navigational position. Once the airplane is under control, then come the radios. "Fly first, talk second," the saying goes.

Cape Air passengers may have joked about how small Pete Kacergis's plane is, but to most general aviation pilots the Cessna 402 is big. There are a couple of guidelines to use when evaluating a propeller airplane and the main thing to bear in mind is this: The more expensive and complicated a plane is, the better.

Most obvious, is it a single or a twin? Flying two engines requires earning a multi-engine rating by flying with an instructor and then taking a check ride with an examiner. Twins are expensive to operate—twice as many engines means twice as much maintenance and fuel cost. But they don't fly twice as fast as singles. The reason pilots fly them isn't for speed, but for safety. If an engine fails on a twin, the remaining engine still makes enough power to reach a nearby runway.

Next, does it have fixed or retractable landing gear? "Retracts" rack up more points than fixed gear because the landing gear system is more complicated. They have higher insurance rates because, as the saying goes, there are two types of retractable-gear pilots: those who have landed gear up, and those who are going to.

Is the engine full of pistons or is it a turboprop? Flying the turboprop, a small jet intake that boosts the propeller power, requires yet more instruction, another check ride, more details to memorize, more problems that can develop. More expensive and complicated to fly—bump it up a notch on the list. (A jet, like a Citation or a Gulfstream, is in a class by itself, far above the noisy, oily world of pistons and propellers.)

Across the country, hangar-flying pilots argue the merits of this plane or that, of Cessna models versus those of Beechcraft, of the efficiency of a single-engine versus the safety of a twin, of cloth-covered, aerobatic taildraggers versus standard tricycle-gear, instrument-equipped planes. Some pilots like to fly low and slow, others prefer whizzing along, playing with the latest instruments. In general, most pilots yearn to "transition up" to more complicated airplanes. Bigger is usually better.

The Cessna 402 is a twin with turbo-charged engines and retractable gear. It is 36 feet long with a 39-foot wingspan. It sounds impressive, but there's another factor on which to evaluate it, and it is the most important of all: Speed.

At 200 miles an hour, the 402 is pokey for a twin. The 12-passenger Beechcraft King Air cruises at 260 miles per hour. Small private twins like the six-seater Beechcraft Baron or Piper Cheyenne cruise at 215–240. The Cessna is slow but reliable, a workhorse of a plane that was designed to make short commute hops and not burn too much expensive fuel. Called the "Businessliner" or "Utiliner" by Cessna, the 402 is not very glamorous. Most Cape Air pilots considered it a pit stop. They buzzed through a year or so at the airline to build time before jumping to a DeHavilland Dash-8 at a major commuter or a corporation's private Cessna Citation.

Kacergis liked to fly the 402. Liked it better than flying "Willie," the cloth-covered antique Stinson that gave sightseeing flights over Provincetown's beaches during summers. Three years of that burned him out. He liked the 402 better than instructing, although his patience and calm in the cockpit translated well to students. He had been willing to let them fly into their mistakes for a long time, knowing they would learn more from discovering the problems themselves than from his instant correction.

There was one particular airplane in the fleet that Kacergis preferred, and he was flying it today. It was the one that nobody else wanted. Cessna 548GA did not have weather radar, no global positioning system, radar altimeter or other fancy navigation toys. Kacergis didn't care. He liked the basics, liked to "hand-fly" without aid from the autopilot, even in instrument conditions on an approach. It kept him from getting bored.

In the air over Marshfield, Massachusetts, Kacergis flew along the coastline on the heading Boston Approach had assigned. He had cleared the path jets were flying through Boston Harbor and then climbed to 5,000 feet as directed by Cape Approach. He tuned his radio to the automated weather broadcast for Provincetown and listened again as the computer-generated voice haltingly listed the conditions. Kacergis waited to hear visibility—which dictated whether or not he could legally attempt the approach—and ceilings, which gave him an idea of whether or not he would be able to get in.

On an instrument approach, ceiling and visibility dictate whether or not it is legal to land. If the visibility at the airport is less than the number published on the approach plate, no landings are allowed. Ceilings are different for general aviation pilots, who can shoot the approach no matter what the ceiling is, but cannot legally dip below the decision height on the approach plate.

Kacergis was in luck. Provincetown's minimum was three-quarters of a mile. For the moment the actual visibility was over that, at a mile, so he could legally land. The ceiling was 300 feet, almost 100 feet above the decision height of 208 on the plate. He would break out of the cloud bottoms 300 feet above the ground. Plenty of altitude to see the runway and land.

Care Ninety, contact Cape Approach one twenty-six point three, the Boston controller gave the handoff.

Over to Cape, good day, Kacergis answered. He flipped the radio selector to the new frequency.

Approach, Care Ninety at five thousand.

Good evening Care Ninety, altimeter zero zero zero, fly heading one two zero, expect radar vectors for ILS seven at Provincetown, David Loring answered. Kacergis recognized the voice. He knew Loring mostly over the frequency but had met him once or twice at Cape Air's annual company party in Hyannis, to which the controllers were invited. Hearing the voice was reassuring, knowing that someone experienced and helpful was on the frequency.

Zero zero zero, flying one two zero for ILS seven, Kacergis shot back.

He pulled his thick binder out of the flight bag at his feet and glanced at the landing plate for Runway 7's ILS, to refresh his memory. Then he put it away. He didn't want any distractions while flying the approach. He knew that moving his head around—glancing down at the plate, up at the instruments, out the window to search for the airport—could induce vertigo. Better to memorize the procedure and then concentrate on flying the airplane.

Boston and Provincetown are two very different airports, and not just in the amount of traffic they handle. In Boston, nobody moves without talking to ATC in the control tower. Provincetown, like most of the country's small airports, has no control tower. After being cleared for the approach by Cape, pilots switch to a common radio frequency for Provincetown. On clear days all area pilots listen to that frequency and keep their eyes open, applying the traditional "see and avoid" method of air traffic control. In IFR conditions, only instrument-rated pilots can fly. They are required to talk to Cape TRACON, which makes them take turns using the runway at Provincetown.

Kacergis dialed in the frequency for the Runway 7 approach. He turned the arrow to the proper setting on the Horizontal Situation Indicator, or HSI. The instrument was a combination of the VOR and Directional Gyro, which showed the plane's current heading and navigational information.

Care Ninety descend and maintain three thousand, Loring announced.

Out of five for three, Kacergis answered and eased the throttles back and the nose down. He was getting close to Phony, the final approach fix in the air 6.6 miles from the airport. The procedure was to cross Phony at 2000 feet. Loring was stepping him down instead of hitting him with a 3,000-foot descent at the last minute. Good work.

The needle on the HSI was fully deflected off to the right of the Cessna's heading of 120 degrees. The instrument was tuned to the ILS beacon, picking up a signal that created an airway lying diagonally across the Cessna's flight path. As the Cessna neared the ILS, the needle would begin to float toward center and Kacergis would turn left to pick up that airway, flying a 75-degree heading. He would cross Phony and then descend on that heading directly toward the runway, and hopefully break out of the clouds before the 208-foot minimum altitude.

If he didn't see the runway at 208 feet above sea level, Kacergis planned to follow the procedure for the missed approach. He had that memorized too: Climb back into the clouds to 2,000 feet, turn left toward a navigational beacon at Provincetown, and hold there, flying a three-mile-long oval in the air, until Cape Approach cleared him to try the whole thing again or divert to another airport with better weather.

Kacergis leveled off at 3,000 and Loring called again.

Care Ninety, descend and maintain two thousand.

Out of three for two, Kacergis said.

A few minutes later he leveled off at 2,000 feet. The HSI needle began to drift toward the center of the dial. Kacergis turned left and centered the airplane on the heading on the instrument.

The controller called again: Care Ninety is twelve miles from Phony, cleared for ILS Runway Seven approach.

Care Ninety cleared ILS Seven P-town, Kacergis answered. Now the airport was his. The Clearance controller wouldn't clear anyone else to land or take off until Cape Air flight 90 taxied off the runway and called to report the safe landing.

Most private pilots go months, years, without flying a single approach to minimums. Many refuse to do it, knowing that they simply are not staying proficient enough to accurately control the airplane at low airspeeds, close to the ground and unable to see anything but the cluttered instrument panel. But Kacergis was an approach machine, a pilot who had flown 200 approaches one particularly overcast summer, 16 of those in a single day. He had flown the same airplane almost daily for six years. He knew his equipment, he knew the airport and he knew the routine. True to commercial airline standards, he never let his confidence tempt him into departing from the procedure.

Loring made his last call to Kacergis: Care Ninety is three miles from Phony, frequency change approved. Report cancellation on the ground on one twenty point six five.

Over to advisories, Kacergis answered. See you on the way back.

He flipped the second radio over to Provincetown's Unicom frequency. Every plane using the field listens to and broadcasts on Unicom, as does the Cape Air ticket clerk working the desk in the small Provincetown terminal. She would know that Kacergis was inbound and ready the fuel truck and baggage handlers.

Provincetown traffic, Care Ninety is at Phony ILS Runway Seven P-town, Kacergis announced. Many airports share the same frequency, so pilots broadcast the name of their particular airport at the beginning and end of each transmission.

After crossing Phony, Kacergis pulled the throttles back and flipped a switch to lower the landing gear. The airplane responded with a 500-foot-per-minute descent, perfect for keeping the plane on the evenly slanted three-degree descent path required for the ILS.

He had procedure memorized: Descend at 500 feet per minute and keep the HSI needle centered. It represented the runway. If the needle drifted to the right it meant the plane was wandering left of the runway. Stay on course and on the gradual descent to 208 feet above sea level.

Down came the Cessna as Kacergis eyed the altimeter, scanning the HSI, the airspeed indicator and the vertical speed indicator. Outside the cockpit windows clouds still hid the ground and sky. Only the instrument's needles told Kacergis where he was. He scanned the cockpit panel continually: wings level, airspeed steady, HSI needle centered, steady rate of descent, confirm gear is down and locked, propellers and throttles set for landing.

The other planes had radar altimeters that could be set to beep at 208 feet, reminding the pilot not to go below unless he saw the runway. Instead, Kacergis watched the altimeter as the plane descended.

The ceiling had lowered, or maybe fog had set in. Kacergis passed through 300 feet, where the automated weather had said the cloud bottoms were. He was still in the soup.

Hand on the throttle, ready for the go-around, Kacergis kept his eyes on the panel. He descended to 210 feet and glanced out the window. Ahead, the glow of fuzzy runway lights shone through the haze, but he didn't have a sharp view of the ground. The bottoms of the clouds may have been at 300 feet, like the weather broadcast said, but haze or mist or something was making everything blurry.

Kacergis knew the rules—his view of the "runway environment" allowed him to descend further. He turned back to the instruments. Down another hundred feet in hopes of seeing the runway itself.

He nosed down for a few seconds to lose the altitude and glanced outside again. There was the runway, coming up to meet the plane. He flared, lifting the nose to bleed off some extra airspeed. The two main landing gear wheels touched first, then the nose wheel. Kacergis rolled the full length of the 3,500-foot runway, letting the plane slow down on its own, saving the tires and brakes.

A pretty standard landing for Kacergis, but he worried that it might not be for some of Cape Air's newer pilots up that night. When he flew with new hires, he trained them not to rubberneck it, looking out the window, back at the altimeter, back out the window while trying to see the runway. That kind of thing could give you vertigo. Better to stay on the instruments and then make that one quick glance at the last minute.

He turned onto the taxiway and flipped the radio to Cape TRACON's Clearance Delivery frequency.

Cape, Care Ninety on the ground at P-town.

Roger Care Ninety, IFR cancelled, have a good one.

The Cessna rolled to a stop in front of the small terminal and the engines stopped. The passengers smiled as they wiggled out of the plane, happy for one more weekend on the Cape, bad weather or not. Kacergis shut off the master power switch, unstrapped his belt and crouched through the plane, climbing down the stairs onto the ramp. He checked the scrap of paper on which he had scribbled his schedule that morning. His next flight would be back to Boston. Nobody goes from the Cape to Boston on Friday night. He would be ferrying an empty plane back to overnight in Boston, then ride jump seat back to Hyannis where his car was parked. Kacergis headed for the cramped break room behind the ticket counter. He would get something to eat before his departure time of 7:30 P.M.

# Chapter 6

# Direct Providence

RON AND HIS FRIEND LANCE MOORE had started taking flying lessons in 1978 at the tiny airport in Freehold, New York. By then Sinzheimer had been soaring around in gliders for years. Moore didn't remember if it was Ron's idea or his own, it was just something that kept coming up while Ron and Marsha hung out at his neighborhood restaurant in downtown Albany. Flying lessons? Yeah, I've been meaning to do that, too. Before long, the two were sharing rides out at Freehold, taking turns in the front seat with the instructor.

Clem Hoovler was old-school, warning the two pals, I'm going to teach you to fly an airplane by the seat of your pants. It's not a car, you can't pull over and park it. If it bites you in the butt it's going to kill you.

He worked them hard, in and out of the short runway for takeoffs, landings, takeoffs, more landings. Hoovler remembered Ron as being supremely confident in the cockpit. "You don't see that in most students. Most are a little scared. To be a pilot it takes a lot of confidence, that's the whole game. You have to feel good about what you're doing. As soon as you lose confidence it all starts to go bad."

At first, before he went into private practice and was still lawyering for the state, Ron was not flush and took lessons when he could afford them. Marsha waited tables for Lance, and he and Ron used to steal her tips on Saturday mornings to go buy bagels. The two friends had a race on to see who got his pilot's license first.

By late summer of 1979, Ron had passed his written exam and was ready for his check ride, the deciding test for a pilot's license. Hoovler remembered. "He would push the envelope, Ronnie would. He would fly a lot and then he'd go away from it. You'd get him ready for the check ride and then he'd get busy. You wouldn't see him a week, three weeks, then he'd walk in and say he was ready for the check ride, sign him off." After several months, Hoovler got his student ready and sent him off to the examiner in August. Like a lot of pilots, Sinzheimer failed his first try, botching touch-and-go landings and stall recovery.

It took Ron a year to return. It was a busy one for both friends— Moore sold the restaurant and went into the construction business while Ron opened his own law firm. He and Marsha finished rehabbing the brownstone they had bought on Jay Street. Marsha became pregnant.

Ron won the race with his friend, passing his check ride in August 1980. Hoovler didn't see much of Ron after he earned his license, then started his instrument training. Ron tended to jump around among instructors, flying with whomever was free at the right time.

Moore's wife later had a baby of their own and Moore gave up on flying altogether. But Ron's legal work started making money and he flew even more. He took the whole baby thing in stride, Hoovler remembered, dropping little Andrew off at the airport office. "At first my wife didn't mind, but after a while she had to tell him she had a business to run and couldn't watch his kid."

After his check ride the law firm business picked up, and Sinzheimer bought a four-seater Piper Cherokee to fly for work. Every so often he flew it in to Freehold for Hoovler to do this or that small repair. He didn't stay to chat, the responsibilities of the job and baby Andrew were keeping him on a tight schedule. He flew into Freehold sporadically over the next 18 years. Hoovler didn't see Ron much, but knew he had sold the Cherokee and bought the first and the second Mooney, then the Grumman.

A week before his last flight to Provincetown, Ron had flown the Grumman out to Freehold for some "hangar flying," talking about flying and showing Hoovler the new plane. Hoovler wasn't around, and Ron looked at an antique Piper J-3 Cub for sale.

By then, he had already decided he was going to sell the Grumman. On a flight up to Syracuse and Buffalo he had gotten into some turbulence and bumped his head on the top of the canopy. The plane was a little small, a bit too Spartan and slow. It had been a good re-entry plane after three years of not flying at all, and a nice change from the complexity of the Mooney. But it was not, Sinzheimer decided, the right plane for getting him out to the Cape and back every weekend.

The little Grumman had been in the air for 23 minutes. At 6:11 P.M. Sinzheimer was 7,000 feet over the small town of Lenox, Massachusetts, home of the Tanglewood Music Center where the Boston Symphony Orchestra played summer concerts for wine-toting picnickers. By October 9 the concert season was well over, and below the small plane commuter headlights flashed in the intermittent rain.

Sinzheimer called Bradley Air Traffic Control, "Bradley, Grumman Zero Zero Lima at seven thousand feet."

"Roger Zero Zero Lima, current altimeter is zero zero zero," replied the controller, meaning a setting of 30.00. The barometric pressure had dropped but at Bradley airport, between Hartford, Connecticut and Springfield, Massachusetts, the weather was almost calm. The visibility was ten miles, the overcast cloud layer floated at 1,600 feet. The wind had been gusting earlier, but as Sinzheimer flew toward Bradley the winds steadied at about 13 knots, directly off the Grumman's left wing.

The air traffic controller called back, "Grumman Zero Zero Lima, I have a revised routing for you, advise when ready to copy."

"Zero Zero Lima, ready to copy," Sinzheimer replied. The controller was juggling a lot of IFR traffic. It was not surprising that a few planes would have to change routes to stay clear of each other.

"Zero Zero Lima is cleared to Provincetown via radar vectors to Providence, Victor one fifty one to Gails intersection, direct Provincetown."

Sinzheimer read the routing back and then consulted his chart. A minor change for the better, he realized. The controller would give him headings to fly directly toward Providence, Rhode Island. From there, everything was the same as before.

"Zero Zero Lima, turn left heading one two zero and direct Providence when able," announced the controller. It was a slight turn eastward. Sinzheimer would shave a few minutes off the flight by turning early instead of continuing southeast all the way to the VOR beacon at Bradley. He rolled the airplane to the left, turning from his current heading of 147 degrees.

The Grumman was 90 nautical miles from the VOR beacon at Providence. The 120 heading from the controller would keep the plane on-course for a few miles until the beacon came in with a strong signal. Then Sinzheimer would center the VOR needle and fly there by his own navigation, making adjustments to the heading if necessary.

Flying is often described by pilots as being long hours of boredom, punctuated by moments of sheer terror. By that, they mean that landings and takeoffs are the pressure-cooker moments, when things happen quickly and uncomfortably close to the ground. When the airplane is level, flying along its course, there's not much to do. Unlike with a car, the cruising plane will stay fairly level without much handling of the control wheel. To keep from dozing off, lulled by the drone of the engine, pilots look for little cockpit jobs. They hunt around the cabin for loose upholstery screws to tighten. They double-check radio frequencies. They glance ahead of their positions on the maps, preparing for the next turn or descent. They eat snacks. When the weather is bad, they study the approach plates for the instrument landing, getting familiar with the procedure waiting at the end of the flight.

Pilots shooting approaches sometimes get in on the second or third or fourth try, popping out below the cloud layer and spotting the runway just in time. There's danger, however, in trying too many times, pushing the plane a bit lower through the clouds on each attempt as the pilot hunts for the runway, finally plowing into the ground.

NTSB accident reports have documented that trying too many times can tempt pilots to fly too low, so many instrument pilots try to avoid it by setting personal limits for shooting approaches. Some won't even try if the airport weather is at minimums. Another common practice is to try twice, and then, no matter how tempting it is to try again, head for the alternate. It is a tough rule to stick to. Maybe on that second approach the runway peeked through the clouds, but a split-second too late for the dive and the slow, controlled landing. Would one more try do it? The airport is tantalizingly close, friends are waiting in the lobby. Then the pilot remembers how dangerous it is, how tempting it would be to dip too low. Better to turn for the alternate, an hour away. That means shooting another approach there, then renting a car to drive to the final destination. This only works, however, if the alternate's weather is better.

Concord, Sinzheimer's alternate, sounded good at 2:00 P.M., but nobody knew what would be happening there when he arrived, almost five hours later. As he flew along, Sinzheimer planned his "outs," his alternate plans should the clouds hang low at Provincetown. Were there alternates closer than Concord, perhaps Providence or Hyannis? How many times should he shoot the approach at Provincetown before diverting? The weather on the coast is so changeable that pilots often "hold," circling in the clouds, waiting for them to lift enough to shoot another approach. Did he have enough fuel to try that?

As the Grumman droned over Springfield, the controller passed the plane to a coworker who was working a different piece of the radarscope pie. Sinzheimer changed frequencies and contacted the new controller with a routine radio call.

"Bradley, Zero Zero Lima at seven thousand."

"Zero Zero Lima, roger."

He flew along without talking for 15 minutes, just listening to the radio chatter, the flow of other airplanes checking in and getting handed off to other control frequencies. He flew past Springfield and crossed the Connecticut state line, passed over the small towns of Stafford Springs and Woodstock. The little plane dodged in and out of rain showers and the rain banged on the canopy and swept over the wings. Sinzheimer kept his hand on the yoke and his eyes on the instruments.

He liked to fly with his Global Positioning System unit. The little black GPS was not mounted in the panel. It was a hand-held device, about the size of a telephone handset, with a small black and gray moving map that showed the plane's current position. Ahead of the small plane on the GPS screen was a thin black line—the plane's course to Providence, then on to Provincetown.

The hand-held GPS was approved by the FAA as a legal navigational device for visual conditions only, not in actual instrument conditions. Many pilots used it anyway in actual IFR as a backup. It came in handy because it did a lot of things—monitored the plane's groundspeed (factoring in winds aloft), showed the nearest airports and navigational beacons with their radio frequencies, estimated the plane's arrival time and how far it was from the runway. It also gave the airplane's current position. Rather than shuffling through the charts and doing math with vectors from the closest navigational beacon, a pilot could glance at the little map on the GPS. It was just the kind of cutting-edge electronic gizmo that Sinzheimer loved to play with.

And it helped make the Grumman more fun to fly. Compared to the Mooneys, the Grumman was more like Sinzheimer's first airplane, a Piper Cherokee. Both handled sort of like Honda cars. They didn't wow you with responsiveness or speed, but likewise there were not many surprises or sudden maneuvers. The Grumman flew along at about 140 miles an hour, stable, reliable, affordable and easy to fix.

Thank goodness for the GPS because although the instruments in the Grumman worked, they were old and plain. There were none of the fun toys that more advanced planes had—stormscope, distance measuring equipment (DME) which tracked how far the plane was from a beacon or airport, weather radar, an HSI navigational instrument or radar altimeter. The "autopilot," for example, was generously named. It was original to the plane, and was a simple, single-axis system known as a "wing-leveler." It sort of kept the wings straight, could take over in a pinch when Sinzheimer needed to spend some quality time with a chart, glancing up from time to time to give a correction if the wing-leveler slipped a bit.

Not that the Grumman was tricky to fly. It handled well. There weren't many engine gauges or knobs to monitor. It flew slowly enough to give Sinzheimer the luxury of time. In the Grumman he could think through an approach, or map a change in a flight plan without the plane zipping ahead of him.

Transitioning to a new airplane is like learning a foreign language. At first, you form a phrase in English then translate it mentally into Spanish before speaking. You may be quite skilled, but under stress you revert to the most familiar language. When your Caribbean hotel is full and the clerk has lost the reservations you are far more likely to scream out your frustrations in English.

If you practice every day, at a certain point you stop translating. Your brain shifts, the barrier lifts, and the ideas themselves begin to form in Spanish. Sometimes you even struggle for the proper English word to express a Spanish idea. That kind of comfort level is what pilots mean when they talk about proficiency.

Commercial pilots, the ones who fly almost every day, will say that it takes six to eight months to be proficient in a new airplane. They mean that although they have passed the check ride and have mastered the procedures, those procedures are not yet second nature. The pilot has to think about them, remember them. And in times of stress, when the pilot is being blasted with information, he is not as able to handle that thought process.

Granted, a Boeing 767 is much more complex than a single-engine propeller plane, but the basic concept still applies. It takes time to become comfortable in a new cockpit, so comfortable that in stressful situations the new procedures become second nature.

Military engineers and airline managers have spent entire careers studying Cockpit Resource Management, the ways in which pilots handle the workloads of flying. In particular, they focus on the heavy demands of emergency situations, takeoffs and landings.

They have made several discoveries. First, when the workload picks up, the pilot's situational awareness decreases. Being bombarded with an overwhelming amount of information makes the pilot's brain less able to process it. It is like being in a crowded room of people, each one shouting for attention. The brain cannot hear them all at once, can't handle the big picture. "Calm down," it says. "Let's take you one at a time."

When that happens and pilots enter a stressed state, they tend to revert to familiar habits. Often without realizing it, pilots fall back on the procedures they have performed hundreds of times before.

This is why airlines love simulator training. Run pilots through enough simulated emergency situations and they should react to the real thing with smooth and confident actions. NASA trained the first Mercury astronauts the same way. By the time Alan Shephard blasted into space the experience was almost anti-climactic, he had done it so many times before in the simulators.

If a pilot could recognize his stress level, most of these issues would not affect him. The pilot under stress could cancel the flight, land or ask for help. Unfortunately, people are notoriously poor predictors of their own physical well-being. If you are tired, by time you figure that out you are over-tired. The same goes for dehydration, hunger or being overwhelmed by events. By the time a pilot realizes that he is swamped, the ship is on the verge of going down.

As the Grumman flew over Woodstock, Connecticut, the controller at Bradley handed him off to the next radar facility.

"Zero Zero Lima, contact Providence on one three five point four."

"One three five point four, Zero Zero Lima," Sinzheimer responded. He tuned his second communications radio to the new frequency and switched over.

"Good evening Providence, Grumman Zero Zero Lima with you at seven thousand," he checked in.

"Zero Zero Lima, altimeter zero zero three," the controller responded.

Sinzheimer checked the setting in the tiny window on the face of his altimeter: 30.03. Each of the four tiny tick marks between 30.00 and 30.10 represented two hundredths of an inch in mercury pressure, each marked 20 feet in altitude.

At night, bumping around in the clouds, a pilot dialing in the proper altimeter setting is pretty much making a quick stab in the general area. The range between 30.00 and 30.10 is barely a quarter of an inch. It's further divided by four little white lines. Hitting a setting of 30.03 means aiming for the miniscule space between the first and second tiny lines. Those lines swim together as you bump around, scanning half a dozen other gauges. "It's about a third of the way," you think, and spin the dial so the arrow marker bisects the quarter-inch space at its first third. Later, when you land, you may examine it and realize that you've dialed in something more like 30.05—a difference of 20 feet.

The number represents barometric pressure in inches of mercury. That tells the instrument what the current air pressure is at ground level. But the airplane is usually above ground level, where the air is much thinner. The altimeter measures the difference between ground level air pressure at that moment—the setting given by the air traffic controller—and the ambient air pressure in cruise, then deduces the proper altitude above sea level. If the altimeter reads 75 feet lower or higher than the airplane is, that is considered accurate enough for flight use.

The air pressure changes as the plane zips along. It's most changeable when high and low pressure systems fight each other along a front. In Albany, the setting had been 30.09, by Bradley it had fallen to 30.00, a difference of 90 feet. Without the new altimeter setting the altimeter would indicate 90 feet higher than the plane's actual altitude.

The changing altimeter can become problematic when an airplane flies from east to west. There, pilots face a double whammy altitude problem: the rising terrain of the Rocky Mountains and areas of lower air pressure. Falling air pressure tricks the airplane into thinking that it is farther from the ground than it really is. Meanwhile it gets closer and closer to rising terrain. An airplane out of radar coverage, in the mountains, with an improperly-set altimeter is at high risk for a ground collision. The preventive measure is to reset the altimeter as often as possible.

Air traffic controllers are required to give current altimeter settings at least once to each plane within their jurisdiction. In return, the pilot is required to state the plane's indicated altitude, as a sort of cross-check of the altimeter.

"Providence Approach, Zero Zero Lima is at seven thousand," announced Sinzheimer.

"Zero Zero Lima, current altimeter zero zero three," answered the controller. The pilot was saying, "Hi, I'm in your airspace and my plane thinks it's at seven thousand feet." The controller answered, "Welcome to my airspace, here's what our ground pressure is and you're pretty close to seven thousand feet according to my radar." If the controller noticed the plane to be at, say, 6,000 feet, he would say something like, "Check altimeter setting of zero zero niner, my radar shows you at six thousand." If the current altimeter setting didn't correct the error the pilot would assume that his altimeter wasn't working. He would ask the controller to announce the plane's altitudes for the rest of the flight and descent, and then have the instrument checked on landing.

Combine the 75-foot acceptable instrument error with a 10- to 20-foot error in dialing in the new altimeter setting and it is easy to see that the instrument can be off by a hundred feet. Pilots know this. That's why they sit up and pay attention at low altitudes. Dipping a wing at 6,000 feet is playful indulgence, doing it over the runway is suicidal.

The best and most accurate way to measure distance from the ground is with a radar altimeter. It uses radar signals bounced off ground objects to continually measure the plane's exact altitude. Sinzheimer had one in his Mooney but not in the Grumman. Few small airplanes have them because they cost $4,000-$7,000 to purchase and install, and they do not replace the traditional altimeter. They work as

71

more of a backup system. Pilots set the radar altimeter to sound an alarm when reaching a certain altitude, like the minimum height on an instrument approach.

Eight more minutes of radio silence in the Grumman cockpit, the steady instruments lit by a dim glow. It had been raining off and on in Providence, Rhode Island all day. The visibilities and cloud cover rose and dropped and rose again as the unstable air swirled in from the coast.

At 6:53 P.M., Sinzheimer was 15 nautical miles northwest of Providence, bumping around a bit in the plane. Pilots get used to turbulence. They barely notice the jolts that make passengers gasp and grab the armrest. As long as the wings stay level, pilots don't sweat a few updrafts and downdrafts.

Sinzheimer knew that he would fly over Providence in a few minutes. Then he would turn left for the 20-minute flight over the bay to Provincetown. Time to start a descent and get the Grumman a little closer to sea level.

The controller was thinking along the same lines, "Grumman Zero Zero Lima, descend and maintain six thousand," he announced.

"Down to six," Sinzheimer answered and pushed on the yoke, scanning the instrument panel to make sure everything agreed on the descent—airspeed picking up a bit, vertical speed indicator on a downward trend, altimeter needle falling.

At the same time, the VOR needle started its little dance, becoming unreliable for the moment because it was right over the beacon on the Providence airfield. Sinzheimer had two things to watch: a descent and a heading change. Keep an eye on the VOR needle, watch the flag for the flip once it passes Providence, monitor that airspeed, pull the nose up a bit to slow the plane down. Has the VOR needle flipped yet? What about that altimeter? Don't blow past 6,000 feet. Double check the Attitude Indicator, make sure the plane isn't turning until after the needle flips.

The Grumman leveled off at 6,000 feet just in time for the next step down.

"Grumman Zero Zero Lima, descend and maintain five thousand feet," called the controller.

"Out of six for five," Sinzheimer said. He pushed the yoke down for a minute to hold a 500 feet per minute descent, then leveled off at 5,000 feet. The plane crossed Providence's Green State airport, the VOR needle flipped, and Sinzheimer rolled the plane to the left, toward the new heading of 93 degrees on Victor 151. Ten minutes of instrument maneuvering, entry-level stuff compared to an approach.

The Grumman was established on Victor 151. Ready for the last descent to 3,000. Next, Sinzheimer would get the handoff to a controller at Cape TRACON, who would set him up for the landing approach.

He was directly over the busy VOR beacon at Providence, Rhode Island's T.F. Green. It serves as a navigational fix for 22 instrument landing approaches, nine Victor airways, and one hold. The frequency is 115.6. The pilot dials the frequency into the plane's navigational radio, and a needle on the gauge points to the beacon. On the charts, each beacon like the one at Providence is at the center of its own compass rose. Using that, the pilot can calculate the airplane's position even when it is buried in clouds.

The calculation works like this: Dial in the frequency, center the gauge's needle and note to which heading it points. Whip out the chart and mark that heading on Providence's compass rose. Draw a line from the center of the beacon through that heading and extend it the distance the airplane is from the beacon. A plane 22 miles from Providence on a 114 degree heading is smack over New Bedford.

Busy as Providence is, the beacon is not on the East Coast's aerial superhighways. Victor 16 and Victor 1 are the routes planes take up and down the East coast between New York and Boston and points beyond. Nonetheless, all planes flying to Cape Cod, Martha's Vineyard, Nantucket, or Block Island from points west cross Providence. They pass between the approach paths for Boston's Logan and New York's LaGuardia and Kennedy airports.

Sinzheimer crossed it at 5,000 feet because he was flying east. Westbound airplanes fly at even altitudes, lowering the odds that two of them will whack into each other head-on.

He rolled to his new heading on Victor 151, tracking away from the Providence VOR signal on the 93-degree radial. He was getting close to the coast. It was time to get a weather update.

As he turned, Sinzheimer dialed in 123.8, the frequency for Hyannis's continual weather broadcast, updated every hour. He tuned in just in time to hear a "special." The weather had changed significantly in the past 20 minutes, so the briefer filed a new report rather than waiting the standard full hour to elapse. The recording droned in a monotone voice.

"Hyannis automated weather special information Sierra: Ceilings five hundred overcast, visibility eight miles, winds zero five zero at five knots with light rain. Temperature fourteen Celsius, dew point fourteen Celsius. Hyannis automated weather..." Sinzheimer flipped the radio off as the broadcast started repeating.

Hmmm. Five hundred overcast was high, even with Hyannis's approach minimums of 294 feet. He would have no trouble getting in, would break out of the clouds far above the runway. Was it better to divert to Hyannis now? Better check the weather at Provincetown.

Sinzheimer tuned the radio to the automated weather. He picked up a scratchy signal, strong enough to catch that the ceilings were still low, hovering around 200 feet.

He thought about the two options. Over the past ten years, he had gotten into Provincetown a few times in bad weather. There was that flight with Bill Newman, five years earlier in the Mooney. The clouds had been low, but that hadn't bothered Sinzheimer. There was not much in the way of obstructions near the airport. Just the lighthouse a mile past the end of the runway at 129 feet. He wouldn't hit anything by dipping a bit lower than the 208-foot decision height for the approach. He had pushed lower and broken out at 150 feet above the ocean, lined up with the runway. They landed. Sometimes taking a chance pays off.

As Sinzheimer flew over Providence just after 7:00 P.M., the city's weather hit its lowest point of the day. Visibilities dropped from eight miles to around two. The scattered clouds at 600 feet had closed to an overcast layer. Fifteen minutes later the fickle weather would be up again, with three miles' visibility and a broken layer of clouds at 700 feet. The whole New England coast had see-sawed up and down all day. Maybe Provincetown would be up by the time he got there.

There is no VOR beacon at Provincetown. Instead, it has a different type, a "non-directional beacon," or NDB. They are usually weak but the NDB signal at Provincetown is strong. Pilots can pick it up once they cross the coastline, adding the Automatic Direction Finding instrument, or ADF, to their panel scan. The ADF needle points straight to the NDB beacon.

One of the other navigational instruments, linked to the radio, was still tuned to the Providence beacon and aligned with the airway that headed out over Cape Cod Bay. That left the other VOR instrument free until Sinzheimer was ready to tune in the landing approach frequency. An extra navigational instrument has a lot of useful possibilities. Sinzheimer could use it to stay a step ahead of the airplane, tuning it into the next beacon along the flight path. He could tune in two nearby beacons at once and triangulate his exact position. On the approach into Provincetown he could use the second radio/instrument combination for his alternate airport's approach frequency, so he would be ready to turn to it on the go-around. The two communications radios are used in the same way—to talk to ATC and simultaneously monitor weather broadcasts or jump ahead to the next controller's frequency.

Skilled radio work keeps the pilot ahead of the plane. The faster the plane, the more quickly the pilot must flip radio switches to dial in the next beacon, the next communications channel. Because the radios tell pilots where they are, and bring helpful voices into the cockpit, it is tempting to obsess about them. But that is the last thing pilots are supposed to do in tense situations. Nervous chatter, flipping radios to set up for the next procedure without focusing on the one at hand—those non-essential tasks can draw a pilot's attention away from flying the airplane. "Fly first, talk second," the saying goes.

Sinzheimer had the radio thing down cold after years of flying, flipping from one frequency to the next. Counting the hand-held GPS he had four navigational radios to play with. He could dial in the Providence radial, a backup navigational beacon, the Provincetown landing frequency and the frequency for his alternate airport all at the same time.

The alternate. To decide what the alternate would be, Sinzheimer first had to decide where he was landing. Hyannis or Provincetown?

Sinzheimer settled on Provincetown. What harm could there be in trying? The ceilings were not the lowest he had ever run into out there. Hyannis was a solid alternate, Marsha could pick him up in less than an hour. He would go ahead and dial in the Hyannis frequency in the second navigational radio just to be prepared for a go-around.

The plan made sense, but just in case he'd check with Cape Approach and their weather radar. Maybe they knew something he didn't, maybe the controller would say something like, "There's a huge thunderstorm cell headed for Provincetown right now and you're not going to beat it." In that case, he'd take Hyannis.

Theo panted in the back seat. Ron dug around in his flight bag until he found the binder with Massachusetts in it. He flipped through the binder until he found the page for Provincetown, and started studying the approach plate.

"Grumman Zero Zero Lima," the Providence controller called. "Contact Cape Approach on one one eight point two."

"One one eight two," Sinzheimer answered, and switched frequencies.

# Chapter 7

# Cleared for the Approach

"CAPE APPROACH, November Seven One Zero Zero Lima is with you at five thousand with a request," the voice came over David Loring's headset at 7:20 P.M. But it was not a good time for whatever question this pilot had. Loring had a full load of traffic headed into Hyannis. He had to clear one for the approach and hand another off to the tower. Then he could talk to the Grumman pilot.

"Zero Zero Lima, stand by with your request," he said. He chattered into the microphone attached to the black earpiece, wired to the "talk" button in his hand. Get a few planes turned on to final approach, get another one down on the ground. Catch a breather. Okay, now that Grumman.

"Zero Zero Lima, go ahead with your request and make it simple," Loring called back.

"The weather at Provincetown is showing below minimums, sir. Do you have any other suggestions for an alternate on the Cape?"

Loring glanced at the screen above his round radarscope, the overhead screen with weather reports for the airports in his sector. Provincetown's automated weather station was three-quarters of a mile, the minimum to shoot the ILS. The ceiling was 208 feet above sea level, right at the decision height. In saying it was "below minimums," the pilot was probably confused, thinking that he needed 208 feet above *ground* level and not *sea* level. Well, it was only a difference of eight feet, it did not affect the approach.

But the weather at Hyannis was better—eight miles and 500 feet. The decision height there was 294 feet, so everybody was breaking out at 500 and getting in.

Loring thought about pushing Hyannis.

"Ah, yes sir the Hyannis airport is available," he floated the idea. "Advise when you have weather for that please." Maybe the pilot would jump on it, would sound relieved at the option.

The pilot called back immediately. "I do have weather for Hyannis," he said. "Let me try the approach into P-town and then Hyannis if I can't make it, sir."

If the guy had Hyannis weather already, what was he doing asking for an alternate? Loring tapped his pen on the counter in front of the radar screen. He wondered if the guy was nervous, just checking in for another opinion to make sure his plans made sense. Pilots did that sometimes when they felt too alone in the cockpit.

He hesitated for a second, thinking it over. The pilot seemed set on Provincetown. He sounded confident, was clearly working ahead on the radios since he already had the weather report.

Oops, almost missed that last call from the Cessna heading into Hyannis. Better hand it over to the tower, quick.

Loring decided to leave the Grumman well enough alone. It was the pilot's decision, after all. The controller couldn't climb up there and fly the plane for him.

Actually, Loring was a little relieved. The Grumman was inbound from the west and could head almost straight in to Provincetown. That made the job easier than trying to sequence a new arrival into Hyannis, behind the half dozen other planes landing there. Just give this guy a little right turn once he hit the fix at Phony intersection, then he'd have a straight-in approach to Runway 7.

"Grumman Zero Zero Lima, roger. Fly your present heading to join the ILS for Runway Seven final approach course, proceed inbound."

"Zero Zero Lima," the pilot confirmed.

Better get the Grumman down, Loring thought, he was getting close. "Zero Zero Lima, descend and maintain three thousand," he called out.

"Down to three, Zero Zero Lima," the Grumman pilot answered.

Loring worked his Hyannis traffic and eyed the scope, watching his lined up blips disappear, one by one, as they each landed. A few minutes later the Grumman was nearing a position 15 nautical miles west of Provincetown. It was the point where Loring usually gave clearance for the plane to commence the landing approach for Provincetown.

"Grumman Zero Zero Lima is eleven miles from Phony, cleared ILS Runway Seven approach."

"Zero Zero Lima is cleared for the approach," the pilot acknowledged. A brief readback, but Loring didn't think much of it. Pilots didn't always read back the full clearance, especially if they were busy setting up for the approach.

At the Clearance Delivery desk behind Loring's seat at the scope, the Flight Data controller picked up a radio call from one of the Cape Air planes on the ground at Provincetown. Dan Duda was looking for his takeoff clearance—the heading and altitude to fly right after takeoff. Now the props were turning and he sat at the end of the runway, ready to depart.

Uh, Clearance, Care Nine Eleven IFR to Boston.

Care Nine Eleven, standby on takeoff, we've got one inbound on the ILS, radioed the Data controller.

Care Nine Eleven standing by, Duda answered. The Flight Data controller had seen the strips, knew that pilot Pete Kacergis, Cape Air flight 685, also sat waiting to depart right behind Cape Air 911. But now that Loring had issued an approach clearance for the Grumman, everyone else had to wait their turn. Sorry.

Loring also noticed that suddenly Provincetown was lousy with planes. Here came another inbound. Loring saw the flashing blip on the left of his screen, a handoff from Boston Approach. He trackballed his screen's cursor over to the data tag next to the blip and typed in an "I," the designator for his radar sector. On the radar screen in Boston's radar room, the controller would see the "I" appear and know Cape had accepted the handoff. A few seconds later a crisp British voice came over Loring's headset.

Evening Cape, Care One Seventy-Seven at five thousand, Alan Davis announced.

Care One Seventy-Seven, expect ILS Seven for P-town, we've got one other going in before you, Loring answered.

Roger, ILS Seven, number two, Care One Seventy-Seven, replied Davis.

At 7:37, the Grumman was almost to Phony. Time to cut him loose for the approach.

Loring made the announcement, "Grumman Zero Zero Lima is four miles from Phony, frequency change is approved, report cancellation as soon as possible on the ground on one two zero point six five, have departure traffic waiting." The Grumman would leave Cape's frequency, the pilot would switch to the Provincetown frequency and announce his position.

"Zero Zero Lima," Sinzheimer acknowledged. It was the kind of short call-back that pilots use when they're busy.

Weather is the fickle mistress of pilots everywhere. Crystal-blue skies full of sun beckon pilots out to play. Then a few clouds creep over the horizon, chasing the plane with teasing little bumps. Suddenly they get serious, exploding into thunderstorms that bury the plane in dark turbulence, threatening to tear the machine apart. Who knew? Half the time that was not in the forecast.

All weather forecasts originate from data gathered by instruments installed at the nation's airports. When Charles Lindbergh was flying the overnight mail, knowing the weather at the airports along the way told him whether to prepare for a starry sightseeing flight or a night of punching through clouds filled with ice. Until then, nobody needed hourly weather information. Farmers and fisherman, who relied on weather data more than most, made do with daily updates on freezes, storms and rains. Only pilots, whizzing through the air at spectacular new speeds, needed the constant stream of weather data. The operation of their machines, their very lives, depended on knowing the conditions from one hour to the next across the nation's varied regions.

In an attempt to forecast, pilots have always studied the tendencies of their particular microclimates. The coasts have fog, the deserts and plains have overbearing heat, mountains generate dangerous turbulence and pop-up afternoon thunderstorms.

In the Great Plains and Deep South the bright sun heats the air until it expands and grows very thin. Airplanes struggle to take off and fly in such thin air. It is worse at high altitudes which is why the runways out West are so long. The engine chokes on a too-rich fuel/air mixture, which must be leaned by turning a knob in the cockpit.

Pilots who fly out West pay attention to "density altitude" numbers reported by the local airports. A density altitude of 8,000 feet means that although the airport elevation might be only 4,000 feet, the air is so hot and thin that the airplane will perform as if it were at 8,000 feet, and the pilot must further lean the engine and expect a longer takeoff roll.

The air tumbles over the sharp Rocky Mountains, becoming more violent as the sun warms it during the day. Afternoon clouds quickly form into sharp thunderstorms which blow quickly across the sky. Pilots who fly in the Rockies tend to do it early in the morning, and through the lower-altitude passes, before the afternoon air heats up. A pilot facing a thunderstorm can usually see well enough through the surrounding dry, thin air to go around, or land and wait an hour or so for it to pass.

The coasts tend to "sock in," meaning that low clouds move in and cover entire states. The thick, dense air does not heat up much and so it holds a lot of moisture for a long time, slowly squeezing it out in the form of clouds, fog and mist. Fronts stall out at the ocean's edge, camping out and making rain or snow for days.

The seasons throw their characteristics into the mix. Winter is full of snow and ice. Spring brings rain and bumpy little breezes. Summer's heat generates fog and thunderstorms. Fall is usually glorious, full of crisp, clear air and spectacular scenery below.

It is anybody's guess how conditions will change over time, especially in the air. Clouds cling together, then spread apart. They rise, cool, and release "virga," rain that never makes it to the ground below but can stick to a cold airplane and turn into ice. Air is a fluid, and it flows over the contours of the ground just as water flows over a riverbed. When the air moves faster, or boils up from warmed ground, the "rapids" get bumpier.

Pilots try desperately to anticipate these myriad factors and then predict whether or not clear skies will hold, or rain will sweep quickly past a destination. For this they rely on two tools: The Weather Channel and Flight Service.

The Weather Channel is the starting point. A few days before a flight, the pilot watches the frontal lines and green blobs of precipitation sweep across the continent and gauges the likelihood of dodging them. That is the macro view. For micro data, the pilot turns to Flight Service—available both on the ground and over the communications radio in flight. The reports are detailed, including wind speeds and temperatures at altitude, cloud altitudes and percentage of the sky that is overcast. Flight Service briefers focus the information for the pilot's route of flight.

Pilots, then, become minor meteorologists, eyeing the skies and measuring the conditions against what happened on previous flights. They weigh the data from Flight Service and make "go/no-go decisions." A pilot in bad weather ends up evaluating the conditions along the entire route of flight. Every minute brings a new bump, more rain, darker skies. Should the pilot use the "out," the path toward more gentle weather and a clear runway? Or is it wiser to press on, chancing that the whole thing will improve?

The airspace around Provincetown belonged to the Grumman once it was cleared for the approach. Nobody could move at P-town until the plane touched down and the pilot radioed Cape Approach to say he had arrived.

On the ground, Pete Kacergis sat in the cockpit of his twin Cessna parked by the small airport terminal at the approach end of Runway 25. He was monitoring the Provincetown frequency and Cape Approach. When he heard Loring clear the Grumman for landing he cranked his engines one at a time, turned his airplane and taxied along the runway to the opposite end, Runway 7, where the Grumman would land and then Kacergis would depart behind the other Cape Air flight.

He parked far back on the taxiway. Give this guy plenty of room, he thought to himself. He's not a professional pilot, not used to flying in this kind of weather. He's probably going to be all over the place when he breaks out of the clouds.

Kacergis switched his second radio over to the Cape Air operations center at Hyannis. He radioed them, asking, Where's Alan Davis?

Davis came on the frequency himself. What a pisser, he cursed. I'm stuck holding out here just past Drunk intersection. Let me know when that Grumman gets down and I can land, will you?

Sure thing, Kacergis answered. He switched one of his radios to Cape Approach's Clearance Delivery frequency, waiting for his takeoff clearance. Davis was put out, but Kacergis was not bothered by waiting for the inbound plane. He could make up any time he missed on the ground by edging the throttles forward in flight. No big deal.

He tuned his second radio to Provincetown's frequency to listen for the pilot to announce his position. As he waited, he keyed his microphone five times to turn on the pilot-controlled runway lights. He doubted it would help the guy. Kacergis guessed the ceiling was at about 100 feet. Even with the lights the Grumman probably would not see the runway and would have to do a missed approach, climbing and circling around to its alternate.

Davis continued to hold in the sky northwest of the airport. The Grumman was inbound from the southwest. It shadowed the glide slope, hanging a hundred feet or so below it. It crossed Phony a bit low—at 1,800 feet instead of the 2,000 the approach plate mandated. From there it descended through 1,700, 1,600, down to 1,000 feet four miles from the runway.

On the ground, Kacergis waited. He shut down the engines and listened to the Provincetown frequency for the position call that never came. Where was the Grumman? Shouldn't he be able to see its lights by now, fuzzy through the mist? After a few minutes, he climbed out the door at the back of the airplane. The rain had stopped and the winds were calm. Kacergis stood scanning the sky for airplane lights. He could not see the beacon of the lighthouse, less than a mile away.

Four miles out, the Grumman descended through 900 feet, then 700, all the while staying below the glide slope. It flew along the runway heading and nosed even lower, past 700 to 400 feet. It was almost three miles from the runway, at a point where a plane on the glide slope would be at 800 feet, when it dipped to 100 feet. Twelve seconds later, on the second radar sweep, it was still at 100 feet. By the third radar sweep at 7:43 P.M., it was gone.

Controller David Loring didn't notice. Not that he wasn't paying attention, but Cape Approach's radar loses coverage below about 1,600 feet. Loring did not realize that the Grumman was dipping below the glide slope because it was no longer on his radarscope. The radar facility tracking the plane was Boston Center, miles away in Nashua, New Hampshire.

Cape Cod is flat but on the north side of the upper Cape, near the mainland, is a glacial ridge. It was formed 25,000 years ago during the last great ice age, the Pleistocene Epoch. Ancient glaciers bulldozed sand and gravel from Canada down to the Cape, forming a sturdy ridge called a moraine. Route 6, the Cape's main highway, runs along the moraine from the Sagamore Bridge to Hyannis.

Much of the Cape is 20 feet above sea level, but the ridge runs as high as 80 feet. It is high enough to block Cape TRACON's radar coverage of the Chatham and Provincetown airports.

Loring watched the radar blip on the right half of his screen, saw it start flashing the "ZZ" tag as it descended below 1,600 feet. For the next few sweeps the radarscope painted the plane on a reasonable descent—a projection based on its previous flight path. Loring had no idea that the plane was steepening its descent.

If he had known, he would have made a radio call telling the Grumman pilot he was low, reminding him to stay on the glide slope. But from what Loring could see, it appeared to be a typical instrument approach. He expected that the pilot would shoot Provincetown once, not break out in time to see the runway, then go around. Loring sat in the radar room and waited to talk to the pilot on the missed, and vector him into Hyannis.

As he waited, he focused on his Hyannis traffic. They were bouncing all over the glide slope as the winds shifted again, now out of the north.

At 7:42, five minutes after the Grumman had been cleared to land, the pilot still had not radioed to say he had arrived. At the Flight Data desk, the controller was getting antsy. With one plane holding in the air and two more waiting to take off, he was ready for the Grumman to land and free up Provincetown. Surely by now the guy had landed and forgotten to call and cancel. No biggie, happens all the time.

The controller pressed the "talk" button on the hand-held microphone. Distracted, he botched the airplane's call sign, "Grumman One Zero Seven, Cape Approach."

No answer.

The Flight Data controller knew that the two Cape Air pilots were monitoring his frequency, waiting to be released for takeoff. He called the one parked at the end of Runway 7, "Care Six Eighty Five, have you seen anybody land yet?"

"Ah, we're looking down there," Pete Kacergis replied. "Not yet." Kacergis could barely make out the dark line of scrubby trees on the other side of the runway.

Loring watched the scope as the Clearance Delivery controller worked the radios to find the plane. Maybe the pilot was on the missed approach, busy cramming the throttle full forward and making the climbing left turn to hold at the Provincetown navigational beacon. In a few minutes they would see him pop up on the screen. Then he would call in, announcing the missed and asking for Hyannis.

The controller broadcast again on the Clearance Delivery frequency with the wrong call sign, "Grumman Seven Zero Lima, Cape Approach." He stood and drummed his fingers on the table, burning off the uneasy tension.

Nothing.

One more time, the controller called, clearly and deliberately reciting the airplane's full registration number, including the "N" prefix that all airplanes use. "November Seven One Zero Zero Lima, Cape Approach."

Quiet.

"Care Six Eighty Five," he called Kacergis again. "Have you seen a Grumman land yet? I'm going to keep asking you until he calls."

"Yeah, I haven't seen him land," Kacergis repeated. "And he hasn't made any calls on the advisory frequency. I don't know if he's coming in without letting anybody know. We've been listening for him and calling him and we haven't heard him."

"Thanks," the controller said.

It was 7:49 P.M., 11 minutes after the Grumman had been cleared to land—more than enough time for it to have flown the ten miles to the runway, touch down, roll out and taxi back to the ramp. David Loring grabbed a pen and made a mark on the scope's glass screen—"LKP" for the Grumman's last known position on TRACON's radar.

It was strange that the pilot hadn't announced on the Provincetown advisory frequency that he was coming in for a landing. It was standard procedure on an instrument approach, something pilots do right after receiving the landing clearance. Loring was starting to feel the hair on the back of his neck rise.

He called over his shoulder: Need a supervisor over here.

Within seconds, the supervisor was standing behind the chair, listening to the story and watching as Loring pointed to the pen mark.

Both Loring and the supervisor had seen their share of false alarms. Ninety-nine percent of the time the pilot had landed, shut down the engine and turned off the radios before remembering to call in. Nobody at Cape TRACON was sweating, yet. But the jokes had stopped as the other controllers pricked up their ears to hear how it all turned out.

Okay, you know the drill on lost aircraft, the supervisor said. I'm supposed to relieve the controller. You're off the scope but stay and help us out on Flight Data.

Loring stood up, pulled the tiny earplug out of his left ear and removed the earpiece as the supervisor motioned to the other controller to swap stations. Loring walked across the room to the Flight Data desk, where he would pull and pass out the flight-plan strips and work Cape's Clearance Delivery frequency.

The supervisor headed back to his desk for step two of the procedure: Call the Cape Air desk clerk at Provincetown to see if she had seen or heard anything. With no sign of distress from the plane—no emergency radio call, no signal from the emergency locator transmitter, or ELT, and no weird radar movements, the rule was to check on the ground to see if the pilot had landed there. The guy was probably on the missed approach, flying toward Chatham or Hyannis. When they found him they would give the irresponsible bozo a good lecture about forgetting to radio in.

Marsha Sinzheimer sat stewing in the house in Truro, ten miles from the Provincetown airport. Ron was late. He had gotten tied up at the law firm and forgot to call and tell her. Yeah, that was it, Marsha told herself, and felt frustrated because he was ruining their dinner plans. She stomped into the kitchen and got a Dove ice cream bar. To hell with the calories, she thought, as she ate it and half-watched the ballgame on television. It was game three of the American League Championship series, and she was rooting for Cleveland.

She ate the ice cream to get back at him. "I couldn't wait any more," she planned to say. "I had an ice cream, so forget about dinner. We'll just eat something at the house and watch the game." He would have to make it up to her, maybe cook dinner. He would cheer for the Yankees and she would yell for Cleveland, and then when the game was over she would show him the new nightie she had bought that morning, and they would make up.

An inning later, by 8:00, Marsha's annoyance was tinged with worry. She called the Provincetown airport. He must be close, must have at least announced that he was on the way in. A clerk answered the phone.

Marsha knew Ron's call sign, she asked: Has Grumman Seven One Zero Zero Lima landed yet?

She got the answer she had dreaded for the past 22 years.

Not yet, we're looking for him right now, said the ticket clerk for Cape Air. Have you heard from him?

No, Marsha said, flustered. What's happening?

We're not sure, the clerk answered. And I have to keep the phones clear in case Air Traffic Control calls. That's all I know, I'm sorry.

Marsha hung up and stood for a moment by the wall phone in the silent kitchen. What was that all about? Where was Ron? Why didn't they know anything? She could feel herself panicking. Ron hadn't nick-named her the "Queen of Hyperbole" for nothing. Marsha's reactions were extreme, things were either the best or worst.

The house was empty, the dark windows shiny with rain. Ron was never late. What was going on? Doesn't somebody know something? Who am I supposed to call? Her brain started screaming, looking for something to latch on to. No way could she handle this alone. Marsha picked up the phone and called her closest neighbor, Bob Corey.

Bob, it's me, Marsha. Ron is missing. Like, seriously missing. Can you come over?

I'll be right there, he said. Didn't even hesitate.

He lived next door. A few minutes later the bell rang and Corey stood there, a little older than Marsha, slightly stooped with gray hair. He was a kind and helpful neighbor who had become a friend and walked over frequently to visit Marsha during the summers.

What is it? What's wrong? He hugged Marsha and held her hand.

Marsha was shaking—her hands, her voice, her guts. She couldn't stop.

I called the airport, Ron was late. They said they were looking for him, that he hadn't landed yet. They don't know where he is. Her eyes darted around the room and her breath came in short bursts.

Suddenly, Marsha's stomach turned as she had a terrible thought. Oh God, Andrew! Ron said he might bring Andrew with him! She ran to the kitchen, grabbed the wall phone and dialed the Albany house. Pick up, pick up, she said as the phone rang. Oh God, please be at home. Then the answering machine.

She didn't bother to hide the panic in her voice: Andrew, it's Mom. If you're there, call me. Call me immediately, it's urgent.

Friday night, she reminded herself as she hung up. He's out with his girlfriend. He must be out with his girlfriend.

She stood in the kitchen, crying, looking at Corey.

What about the airport where he took off? Corey suggested calling, maybe they would know if Andrew was in the plane.

Marsha dialed Signature Aviation, spoke with a shaky voice through chattering teeth. Hello, this is Marsha Sinzheimer calling about Ron Sinzheimer in Grumman Seven One Zero Zero Lima. He's... I'm out here on the Cape and he hasn't landed yet. He's missing. Did he take off earlier?

The clerk had a calm voice. Yes, he did take off earlier, but don't worry. He may have diverted for weather, or maybe ATC has him holding somewhere. It's not uncommon in bad weather like this.

Marsha only half-heard the clerk's attempt to comfort her. She had another question: Was he alone? Was there someone else with him when he left?

I'm not sure, the clerk said. I didn't see anyone else.

Marsha hung up and looked at Corey. They don't know, she said. Maybe Andrew was with him.

"Grumman Zero Zero Lima, Cape Approach," Loring called from the Clearance Delivery desk. When there was no answer, he radioed Dan Duda, Cape Air number one for departure from Provincetown.

"Care Nine Eleven, I'll be able to get you off shortly, after I find out what happened with this Grumman," Loring said.

Duda and Pete Kacergis sat in their airplanes, switching from frequency to frequency. They tuned in 121.5, hoping to hear the Grumman's Emergency Locator Transmitter, or ELT. On impact it should have sent out a sharp screech, a beacon of noise that would light up communications radios all over New England. It was silent.

"We just called him and haven't seen him go by or anything," Duda announced over the frequency. Pete Kacergis was also taxiing up and down the runway, eyeing the planes parked on the tarmac.

"Just thought I'd let you know we've been listening to one twenty one five and nothing happening," Duda radioed. He spoke in a dull monotone. "No smell . . . no hear . . . no see . . . no nothing."

Loring felt goosebumps rise on his arms and at that moment gave up hope that the pilot was on the ground somewhere—in the bathroom at Provincetown, or driving home in his car. Sixteen years without a lost plane, he thought. Dammit.

"Okay, thanks," Loring answered.

Behind him, at the supervisor desk, the call to Provincetown was fruitless. No Grumman or pilot on the ground there.

At 7:59 P.M., the supervisor made the standard procedural call to Boston Center. As the overseeing facility for New England, Boston would issue the Alert Notice, or ALNOT, to all airports along the Grumman's flight path, asking them to search their area for the missing plane. Boston would call in the search and rescue forces.

With Boston duly notified, Cape TRACON's job was done. But the controllers and the pilots on the ground at Provincetown still kept looking for the Grumman.

An unknown voice came over the Provincetown frequency. Another pilot, maybe, or someone on the ground listening with a handheld radio. "Haven't found him yet, huh?" Nobody answered, and the frequency was silent for three long minutes as the pilots taxied up and down the parking ramp.

Dan Duda called back, "Cape, Care Nine Eleven."

"Calling Cape, say again please," Loring had been talking to the controller who replaced him on Provincetown. Cape Air pilot Alan Davis had been swinging his Cessna around in a holding pattern west of the field and had begun to run low on fuel. He could not continue holding, and the controller checked with Loring about opening the field. FAA regulations required that Cape close the runway for half an hour. Nobody could come in or out, just in case the Grumman was up there holding somewhere, below radar coverage and waiting to smack into a departing airplane. Davis had decided to divert to Hyannis where Cape Air would bus his passengers to Provincetown.

"What's the number of the plane?" Duda asked. "We're up and down the taxiway here looking at all the airplanes. Grumman what?"

Loring didn't remember, "The last three are Zero Zero Lima, let me get the full call sign for you." He had to find the strip. A minute later he called back, "Okay it's Grumman Seven One Zero Zero Lima, a Tiger." He assumed the Grumman was the more popular model, a Tiger, instead of the Traveler.

Duda called back, "I'm halfway down the taxiway looking. We've been sitting here and haven't seen anything come in, so unless he came in with his lights off and sneaking in, he wasn't here. But I'll have a firm answer for you in just a second." Loring knew the chances of a pilot landing with no lights in 200-foot ceilings and half-mile visibility were microscopic. But Duda and Kacergis kept checking.

"There's nothing on the ramp. I'm going to go ahead and take a run down the runway, but I don't believe there is anything there either. I'll call you back with a runway sweep," Duda announced on the frequency.

"Okay, thank you sir."

Loring waited while Dan Duda taxied up and down the runway. His callback was what Loring expected.

"And Cape, Care Nine Eleven confirm runway sweep is clear," Duda finally said. "We went down to the end there, there are no engines out there, there's no smell of any kind, no nothing. We've also listened on one twenty one five and there is no ELT at all."

"Roger," Loring said.

A minute later, the ticket clerk for Cape Air called on the frequency. "Cape Approach, this is Provincetown calling. The person that was picking up the Grumman called and said they've not heard from him yet either."

**Chapter 8**

# Possible Downed Aircraft

THE GRUMMAN DISAPPEARED from David Loring's radar at about 7:40 P.M., but it stayed on Boston Center's scopes for 12 more sweeps, until 7:43. Boston Center owned the airspace from Long Island through most of New York State, over the ocean and up to the Canadian border. It had several radar antennas that created a mosaic image on the radarscopes, made up of feeds from whichever antenna has the best coverage at the moment. Boston's radar followed the Grumman down to 100 feet off the water.

Not that anybody noticed.

In the darkened radar room in Nashua, the Center controllers tracked their blips. If for some reason a controller had wanted to see the big picture and set his scope to show all planes in the coverage area, he might have noticed the Grumman with the tag identifying it as a Cape TRACON plane, inbound for Provincetown. Out of the corner of his eye he could have glimpsed it descending, then disappearing at 100 feet. If he bothered to think about it, his attention wandering from his own planes to process a few sweeps of the two-digit altitude information buried in the Grumman's data tag, he would have assumed that it landed.

It is far more likely he would not even have seen it. A controller working jets at 18,000 feet doesn't need to clutter his scope with little planes messing around down on the deck. Most controllers like to filter out all the blips but the ones they are working.

Radar coverage works by radio waves. They are transmitted into the air and then received back, reflected by objects in the path of the beam. Distance to the object is determined by the time it takes the waves to make the round trip. Radio waves can be affected by a couple of natural phenomena. Dense rain showers, heavy clouds, or temperature inversions can bend the waves, rendering the signals unreliable. High terrain can stop the waves cold, reflecting them back and blocking out entire segments of radar coverage. Some mountainous areas of the United States have very little low-altitude radar coverage. In those cases, controllers depend on the pilots to radio their airplanes' positions so that the controller can key the data into the tags on the scope.

Cape TRACON's coverage is blocked by the ridge to the northeast. One of Boston's radar antennas is in Truro and provides Cape coverage nearly to the ground. Since Boston has better radar coverage, why can't TRACON use that to work their traffic? It would seem like an easy thing to put the two together, but it isn't.

Can't Boston's radar feed be sent down to Cape TRACON? No, because Cape's system isn't compatible with Boston's. Also, and more importantly, it only sweeps every 12 seconds. TRACON works with radar that sweeps about every four seconds. This is critical for working planes on approach and departure. TRACON's planes make tight turns, descending and climbing close to the ground. Those planes are close together, with three miles of separation instead of Center's five. Center's far-apart planes fly in straight lines at fixed altitudes and don't need four-second radar sweeps.

Cape is slated for the next wave of air traffic control updates. Its system will be "multiplexed" so that computers will take feeds from several area radar sites and create one mosaic image for the scopes. The FAA began the upgrades around the country in the early 1990s. Ten years into the project, Cape TRACON was scheduled for 2008.

At 7:59 P.M. on Friday night, Cape TRACON's supervisor made the standard procedural call to its overlying facility, Boston Center.

Boston, we have a possible downed aircraft, lost on the ILS to Provincetown, he said. It was the flat, neutral language of bureaucracy: "possible downed aircraft," instead of something more urgent like, "Hey guys, get moving, we think we lost an airplane!"

The response was similarly low-key: Thanks, Cape, we'll take care of it.

Then for 35 minutes, nothing happened.

It was a call that Boston got countless times that summer whenever anyone forgot to cancel a flight plan. The procedure was to take each and every call seriously, but the controllers all knew it was probably just another case of the pilot landing and forgetting to radio in. They would handle it, but there was no reason for anyone to leap out of a chair and barrel through the hallway screaming.

Boston might have been too busy to deal with it right away. They were working a sky full of traffic—it's not like a controller could just stand up and walk away from the scope. A reliever must be found to do the job, someone pulled away from the break room, maybe, or a newbie who was still in training. Someone who could be spared.

The supervisor may have spent time gathering information on the plane, grabbing a rookie controller to dig through the flight strips to see if Center had worked it. That would have taken a few minutes, digging through the storage piles, but wouldn't have turned up anything. Grumman 7100L had not talked to any Center controllers.

Maybe the supervisor asked around until he found someone who could run the National Track Analysis Program, or NTAP. The controller could play back the radar feed, recreating the Grumman's flight path. Not every controller knows how to run the program. It would have had to be someone who knew how to work the computer terminal in the radar room, reviewing the radar data tapes that recorded every airplane passing through New England airspace. He would have replayed the tapes, searching for N7100L's beacon code, focusing on the general time and location Cape Approach gave for its last position. He would have tried to determine if the blip dropped from the scope, or instead circled low and headed back inland.

Finding someone to run the tapes may have taken a while. But the process itself takes only a few minutes. The computer zeroes in on the target's last known position, weeding out the other blips and running the data until the blip squawking 7100L's transponder code showed up. Every 12 seconds would show a hit as the blip dropped down to 100 feet and then disappeared.

Whatever Boston spent the time doing, they kept it to themselves. Boston Center's supervisor called the Coast Guard at 8:35 P.M. That was 36 minutes after Cape Approach first notified Center. The Boston supervisor mentioned NTAP to the Coast Guard but did not pass along the Grumman's last known position coordinates. Perhaps Center had just gotten around to reviewing the tapes. Or they had not yet zeroed in on the exact latitude and longitude. Or maybe they had and just didn't offer it. Boston Center pointed out later that they were not required to provide an NTAP unless it was requested.

At Otis, David Loring left the dark radar room and stepped into the blazing fluorescent light of the hallway. He headed down to the break room where he stepped out the door into the damp darkness, lit a cigarette and took a deep drag.

He was trying to relax. TRACON had passed the ball to Boston Center, who would call the rescue teams. Nothing else for Loring to do but wait. There was a Coast Guard station right in Provincetown Harbor, Loring reassured himself. They would get a helicopter or boat out there right away.

His brain ran over the events of the past hour. How had he managed to lose his first plane? Loring knew he hadn't made any mistakes. He had listened to the tape of his voice talking with the pilot, and it was all very straightforward and correct. Standard instrument procedures, not even any of his usual joking around, which he was happy to hear. He sounded very professional.

But the tape had gotten to him. Did he have to sound so curt, telling the pilot, "stand by with your request"? Should he have pushed Hyannis a little harder when the pilot asked about it?

Loring knew that he was faultless. But he wondered if he could have prevented the accident nonetheless. Maybe when the pilot asked for alternates he should have pointed out that it was a crappy night at

Provincetown. There was such a hell of a crosswind there. He had known it would be a tough approach.

He had to remind himself what a controller's job was all about: The pilot flies the plane, I tell him where to put it. It was not my fault that the pilot decided on Provincetown, he told himself. It was his choice to make, not mine. He had to admit that was small comfort when the poor guy was probably downed somewhere.

Loring looked across the runway. On a clear day he would have been able to see the Coast Guard's barracks and hangar. Today it was too misty, but he knew the bulky orange and white helicopters were there and would launch any minute. It seemed kind of silly to be on the same runway and not just phone down there himself. A few years ago he would have. Loring called the Air Station when one of his planes reported engine trouble over the bay. The Jayhawk launched right away, following the pilot just in case he had to ditch. That one had a happy ending: The plane made it to an airport.

That was before the Coast Guard budget cuts, when they told TRACON not to call the Air Station directly anymore. Now Cape called Boston Center, who was supposed to gather information and then contact the Coast Guard District headquarters in Boston. The District made the centralized decision of which station to contact, whether or not to launch and what equipment to send.

Loring tossed the cigarette butt and stepped back into the break room. The supervisor poked his head out of the radar room door and called to him down the hall: Paperwork.

The cube of a conference room was bright with fluorescent light. Loring pulled up a metal chair and sat down at the plain table. His supervisor followed with a piece of paper.

Just write down what you remember and sign and date the bottom, he said, handing Loring the form.

Loring had seen the FAA's Personnel Statement form. He had handed it out as a supervisor himself. Years ago he had even filled one out when a plane he worked just after takeoff crashed at the end of its flight, far from Cape TRACON's airspace.

He read the form's instructions all the way through, not wanting to miss anything: "Much of the information concerning the circumstances surrounding this accident/incident can be retrieved via some sort of recorded data source . . . the purpose of this statement is to provide any facts within your personal knowledge that you believe will provide a more complete understanding . . . speculations, hearsay, opinions, conclusions and/or other extraneous data are not to be included."

Loring had listened to the tape. He had done his job correctly and thoroughly. But he had always prided himself on the extra skill he brought to his work—his rapport with his pilots. Maybe he shouldn't have been so abrupt with this one, asking him to be brief with his request. The guy might have opened up, might have expressed some doubts about the weather situation.

Well, there is something that will provide a "more complete understanding" of the situation, thought Loring. He wrote evenly, in block letters, mentioning that the pilot sounded confident. That he, Loring, had decided not to stress Hyannis because there was no sign of concern from the pilot. That he had been very busy handling a lot of other planes at the same time. He was hoping that might explain why he sounded short on the tape.

When Loring handed his statement to the supervisor, he read it and shook his head.

Do it again, Dave, he said. Take out this stuff about the pilot sounding confident.

But it's my statement, Loring argued. This is what I want to say.

Nope. Just the facts. You did your job and that's all you should say. Write it again.

Loring wrote it again.

Sinzheimer's friends were shocked to see Ron's face on the evening news report. What could have happened? For pilots, the accident quickly became a sort of Rashomon. Each person had a different version of what must have happened, the stories dependent on each pilot's particular experiences.

In the media frenzy that followed the accident, Albany attorney Tom Wiltshire became a primary source for reporters, appearing on television and being quoted in the newspapers. Wiltshire quickly formed an opinion of what must have happened. As a fellow pilot, his perspective focused on a skilled pilot's ability to control his craft.

"He would have survived landing at sea," Wiltshire said. "I think of somebody who is very calm and collected in an emergency situation, does not lose their head. He would never give in to panic. If I were going to be flying with someone in challenging conditions, he would be someone I would have complete faith in."

Wiltshire believed that Sinzheimer must have experienced some sort of mechanical trouble, then set the plane down on the water in a skilled emergency landing. "He would have flown the plane right down, rather than having his muscles lock up and terror take over. He would say, 'I have a major problem, I've got to land it in water.' He would be thinking three or four steps ahead, thinking about canceling his dinner reservation."

Chris Albright was an acquaintance of Sinzheimer's who worked Albany TRACON. Over the years he had frequently chatted with Sinzheimer on the frequency and occasionally ran into him in person. Albright studied the information on the plane's position during the approach and immediately thought of a story Ron had told him.

"One time he flew down south in the Mooney. He was IFR and picked up so much ice he couldn't maintain altitude. It was a scary situation for him, in icing when he shouldn't have been. I got the impression he took chances.

"Some flights back and forth to the Cape had thunderstorms. I think he knew the Provincetown approach really well, almost too well for his own good. Something happened on two-mile final. What, I don't know. A failed magneto?

"It sounds like he's flying, he realizes where he is, knows nothing is out there, starts to descend. He's taking a calculated risk, he's done this approach tons of times. He did this approach every week all summer. He knows it's a low ceiling, the only way to get in is to get below it."

Perry Sporn was an Albany lawyer and acquaintance of Sinzheimer's. Sporn was spending the weekend shooting practice instrument approaches in Nashua, New Hampshire. He and an instructor were flying Sporn's twin-engine Beechcraft Baron at an airport about 70 miles northwest of Provincetown.

On Saturday, Sporn struggled to hold the big Baron on the glide path for the instrument approach. "It pushed the limit of what I was comfortable with in my plane," Sporn remembered. "It was very gusty, hard to hold a heading. I was getting blown all over the place on the approach."

At one point, the instructor suggested that the two take a break because the turbulence was worsening. On the ground, Sporn learned that Sinzheimer was missing. Sporn was the pilot of a powerful and capable twin-engine airplane, so it is not surprising that he found fault with Sinzheimer's little Grumman.

"He was flying in something that was a trainer-type plane. He hadn't had it long enough to have confidence in the approaches. Flying a little aircraft like that and to make that type of flight, he should have been daytime in beautiful weather, that's it. He owned a more capable plane in the past and certainly knew the differences. I think he got too confident.

"I heard him tell [an instructor in Albany], 'I just need something cheap to get back and forth in.' Maybe he was not looking at what he really needed to fly the approach."

Sporn sometimes ran into Sinzheimer at the airport, and also knew him from Albany's legal community. "My impression was he was a bright guy, seemed to be on the ball," he remembered. "My friends who worked with him said he was confident. These types of things can happen. Your confidence and intelligence can put you in a situation where you're working hard to minimize the risk."

Coincidentally, Sporn's instructor that weekend was Itzhak Jacoby. Jacoby was a legendary Beechcraft instructor with over 5,000 hours. He had years of experience teaching in the Beechcraft Pilot Proficiency Program for which Perry Sporn had signed up.

A year after Sinzheimer's accident, Jacoby himself would make headlines in a mysterious crash. On the rainy Friday morning after Thanksgiving, he departed Linden, New Jersey in his Beechcraft Bonanza with his wife and daughter aboard. After takeoff the controller gave Jacoby a heading to fly, then corrected himself and offered another, then another, but the pilot didn't respond. The controller called several more times, and Jacoby finally answered, reporting that he had a problem with one of the gyroscopic instruments.

The gyroscopic instruments—which give the airplane's heading and its attitude on the three axes—are critical. Where many pilots make a mistake is in not recognizing that the instruments have failed. They keep relying on them, eventually flying them right into the ground. Jacoby recognized that his had stopped working. As an experienced instrument-rated instructor, he would have known how to compensate by eyeing other instruments instead. That is standard practice in instrument training.

And yet, Jacoby was unable to control his airplane. It made many meandering turns. Minutes after takeoff it crashed into a residential area in Newark. Several buildings burned and everyone aboard the plane died.

When the news of that accident flashed through aviation circles, pilots marveled that the great Itzhak Jacoby had been unable to recover from a fairly straightforward instrument failure. It was the type of exercise he had frequently simulated with his students, and a situation that instrument pilots like to think they could fly out of.

Word of Sinzheimer's accident started passing through the flying community. Pilots, mechanics and airport managers all pricked up their ears: Grumman 7100L crashed, did you touch it? Better watch yourself because the NTSB, the FAA, and who knows who else will come calling. What was the guy's name, Sinzheimer, right? He was a lawyer.

Providence TRACON heard the news when the Coast Guard called to see if the Grumman had for some reason headed back to Rhode Island. The controller who talked to Sinzheimer took a break and pulled the voice tapes. He listened to the dialog and double-checked his bed-side manner to make sure he hadn't given the pilot any bad steers. Did the pilot sound scared, had he mentioned any trouble? Nope, every-thing looked clear.

Controllers at Bradley and Albany TRACONs also pulled their tapes, listening and making sure nothing they had done could have contributed to the accident.

In Albany, the desk clerk at Signature Aviation got the frantic call from Marsha. After hanging up, the clerk dug Sinzheimer's fuel receipt out of the day's pile of paperwork. Was there anything unusual? At 4:32 the fuel truck pumped 14 gallons into the Grumman. The slip was marked "100 LL" for low-lead airplane gas, so nobody had slipped jet fuel in by mistake. Everything looked safe. Better call the manager though, just so he would know that a tie-down customer was missing.

The name rang a bell for Steve Vosburgh. Sinzheimer. It was an unusual name. It had to be the same guy who bought the Grumman in May. Vosburgh remembered the first phone call, a lawyer wanted to buy the Grumman advertised in Trade-A-Plane for $25,000. The guy had driven out to Plymouth, looked at the plane and wrote a check. It was a typical purchase. Vosburgh wouldn't even have remembered it if it weren't for the hairy flight to Provincetown a few months later.

As part of the sale, Vosburgh had agreed to let Sinzheimer take the plane in May, then return it for the annual inspection—routine yearly maintenance that Vosburgh would pay for.

Sinzheimer had picked Vosburgh up in Chatham, at the tip of Cape Cod's elbow. They had flown straight up the Cape's arm to Provincetown to drop Sinzheimer off. Vosburgh was to fly the airplane back across the bay to Plymouth for the annual.

On the flight from Chatham to Provincetown, Sinzheimer had been at the controls, his tennis partner in the right seat. Vosburgh rode in the back, comfortable at first but increasingly nervous as the plane flew in and out of clouds. There was no intercom jack for the back seat so Vosburgh could not plug in his headset. He strained over the engine noise to hear Sinzheimer talking to Cape Approach. From what he could tell, the guy hadn't filed an instrument flight plan. Apparently he was punching in and out of the clouds illegally, not even telling the controller that he was on instruments.

As Vosburgh thought about the flight he took off his big square reading glasses and rubbed his hand over his long, boxy face that was getting a little jowly at the corners. A shame to lose such a nice little airplane in a stupid accident, he thought. The fleet was shrinking. Years ago Vosburgh had two offices full of employees selling airplanes from the Plymouth airport. Now most of the new planes went to Europe, and it was just him in the office, scraping by on a handful of sales each year. He hated to see another one crumple up.

On the ground in Provincetown Sinzheimer had laughed the unexpected clouds off, saying the flight was more "interesting" than he thought it would be. Yeah, right. Vosburgh pulled himself heavily out of the back seat and complained, loudly and right in front of the wife who had arrived to pick up the tennis players. He ordered a load of fuel before taking off and swore he would never again ride in the back when delivering an airplane. It did not surprise him that the guy had splashed in.

The accident was all over the evening news and morning papers, and had mechanics across New England checking the tail number: Grumman N7100L. Did I work on that plane? A mechanic who signs off on an engine or airframe logbook is bound to that plane for life, eternally responsible for any failure related to the job. Mechanics have nightmares of missing something, some miniscule, life-threatening detail. The Grumman that crashed, was it a mechanical failure? It wasn't my plane, but was the problem something that I could have missed on one of the other Grummans I've worked on?

When Vosburgh called, Pete Conner was in his shop at the airport—he lived off the end of the runway so he sometimes came in on weekends. The phones rang at the handful of desks in the large mauve and cream office on the other side of the hangar. Conner punched line one and picked up.

Pete, Vosburgh said. You know that Grumman that's missing out at Provincetown?

Yeah, Pete had seen it on the news. They hadn't said the tail number though.

Well I have a friend at the FSDO, he says it was that guy, Sinzheimer. Remember him? The one who couldn't stop talking about his Mooney? You did the annual inspection.

Conner swore under his breath. His plane. He had worked on it. He remembered it all right—the Grumman Traveler, the AA-5 model with the small tail.

Did they say what the cause was? Any clues?

Vosburgh didn't know. Probably pilot error, but you may want to pull the records from the annual just in case.

Thanks, just what I need, Conner said. Have you heard anything from the NTSB?

Not yet.

Conner hung up and opened his filing cabinet. When had that annual inspection been, July, August? Where were those files, had he moved them to boxes yet? He dug around and found the file at the back of the drawer. Not much there, invoice and checklist for a routine annual: opening the panels, inspecting the control cables, gapping and replacing the spark plugs, setting the engine timing. Each system—fuel, power, controls, electrical, landing gear—had a checklist of items to be evaluated each year. Annuals took a week or two, depending on how complicated the airplane was and what needed to be fixed.

Vosburgh had introduced Conner to Sinzheimer in May, the day he had bought the plane. Conner recalled the tall guy from Albany. They had chatted briefly. He had wanted to schedule the annual during his vacation in July, when he would be out on the Cape.

Conner remembered the Grumman model AA-5 with its small, 150-horsepower engine and small tail. It was called a Traveler, and in

Conner's opinion, it had not been well designed. The lessons he had given in them left him underwhelmed by the plane's performance on takeoff and at slow airspeeds. The original, smaller tail tended to run out of elevator. You would be pulling back all the way on the yoke and the plane would take forever to lift off. Grumman improved the design when they stuck a bigger tail and engine on and renamed it the Tiger. That was the model which Conner preferred.

Still, all of them were nice little planes, Conner thought. Designer Jim Bede made the thing out of steel tubing—one fat one running through the center of each wing that served as the wing spar and also, on some models, the fuel tank. Long concentric tubes, called "torque tubes," ran along the backs of the wings and tail. They ingeniously moved the flaps and control surfaces. The fuselage walls were of aluminum honeycomb, which was far stronger than the standard sheet metal of other airplanes. All in all it was sturdy, cheap transportation, easy to repair and keep running.

Well, nothing he could do about 7100L now, Conner thought. There was no reason for the NTSB or the FAA to call him unless there was mechanical trouble, and he felt certain he had given it a good annual. He stuck the file back in the drawer, put the Grumman out of his mind, and went back to his paperwork.

The news of the accident would begin to flash through the Grumman owners' associations, those tightly-knit groups that held regular meetings and sent out newsletters full of news about Grumman fly-ins, repairs and crashes. Across the country, their ears would prick up. A Grumman, you say? What was the cause of the crash? A mechanical failure? The unasked question would be, What can I do to prevent it from happening to me?

Word would ripple through the East Coast flying community, the gossip flying along with the pilots themselves from Hyannis to Wilkes-Barre to Atlanta to Richmond to Boston.

Pilots obsess over accidents. They study the FAA and NTSB reports, attend safety seminars that dissect accident causes and subscribe to *Aviation Safety*, a newsletter devoted to post-mortems of small aircraft crashes. It's not morbid curiosity, it's self-preservation.

The pilot's license, it is said, is a license to learn. It means that pilots start figuring things out when they get up there and begin buzzing around, logging flight hours. Experience is the best teacher. And reading about someone else's crash experience is better than crashing yourself. If I can figure out what happened to those poor saps, a pilot thinks, then I can prevent it from happening to me.

I'm never going to see him again.

That had been Marsha's first thought when she called the Provincetown airport. She faced the horror head-on, never the type to shy away from her emotions. Everyone she talked to on the phone had tried to calm her, saying that it was probably just a delay. But Marsha was not pacified. She had been picking up her husband at airports for 20 years. She knew the fact that he had been on the approach but hadn't landed yet was very bad news.

She was still standing in the kitchen, next to the house's only phone. Bob Corey sat on a barstool at the counter. It was 8:30 P.M.

Who to call? What could she do? Marsha assumed that the airport people had things under control. All she could do was sit and wait. But that was horrible and she could not do it alone, or even with Bob. She needed family. She picked up the phone and called her sister in Albany.

Trudy, Ron is missing. They can't find him. He was flying in tonight and his plane is missing. Andrew might be with him.

Oh God, Marsha. We'll come out right away. I'll tell Eric and we'll drive out right now.

Thanks, and please be careful, the rain here is really bad.

She hung up. Six hours from Albany to Truro, that meant they would arrive well after midnight. She hung up and turned to Bob, her hands shaking.

My sister and her husband are coming, but they won't get here until late tonight. Do you mind staying?

Of course not, just tell me what you need.

Just then the phone rang. Marsha turned and picked up, her voice short and excited: Yes?

It was Pat Cook, the dispatcher at the Coast Guard.

Hello Mrs. Sinzheimer, this is Coast Guard District One in Boston. We're calling about the aircraft. Is the pilot your husband?

Yes it's my husband! What's happening?

I just need to confirm that you haven't heard from him, that he's missing.

Of course he's missing! It's been over an hour, what are you guys doing?

Yes ma'am, we're trying to get crews out there now. We're going to request a cutter from Gloucester that should be here in three hours.

Three hours? Marsha was incredulous. Wasn't anything out there right now?

We're moving as quickly as we can, ma'am. I have to go coordinate the mission, but please call me back if I can answer any questions or anything.

Marsha put down the phone and turned to Corey. Three hours, he said! They're sending a boat but it will take three hours! You have to answer the phone, Bob. I can't deal with this.

Tears flooded her tanned face as she fled across foyer into the bedroom. She curled up on the bed, hugging her knees drawn up to her chest. She was still wearing the pants and shirt she had put on for dinner with Ron, her dark brown hair pulled back in a stubby ponytail.

As Marsha rocked on the bed thinking of Ron, she also worried about her son. Was he in the water, or safe in Albany? It was possible he was at home, she decided, even probable. But Ron, she knew, had been in that plane and was now out there somewhere in the dark rain.

Maybe, at this moment, he was clinging to a tree branch. Or floating among debris in the waves, striking out for the lights along the shore. Was he hearing the helicopter overhead? That would be interesting, she thought. Ron being a character in his favorite book, *The Perfect Storm*. Author Sebastian Junger's father lived just down the street, and Ron was fascinated with his book. He particularly liked the helicopter rescues. Maybe at this moment he was waiting in the water for the helicopter to drop the rescue basket and winch him up. She figured Ron would like that kind of adventure.

He was a strong swimmer and very comfortable in the water, she reminded herself. That time in Cancun, he had windsurfed out past the shallow waters and drifted out to sea. Marsha had watched as his tiny sail disappeared into the horizon. She wasn't worried. They had taken windsurfing classes together and she knew that he was strong and confident.

He disappeared for two hours. Marsha eventually saw the small sail zigzagging its way back, working across the waves. When Ron finally walked through the surf to the beach, he was exhausted. The winds had made it difficult to tack, he explained.

On another vacation, in Acapulco, she had fallen asleep in her beach chair while Ron was out swimming. When she woke up she saw a crowd by the shore. Ron wasn't next to her. She sat up, panicked, just in time to see Ron push through the crowd and walk toward her, his chest scratched and bloody. A man had been drowning, he said. He had swum out and grabbed him, but as drowning men often do, the victim had struggled and fought, scratching Ron. He had towed the man to shore in a rescue grip, had given him mouth-to-mouth resuscitation.

A few minutes later a swarthy man had walked up to their beach chairs and blurted out a string of words in a foreign language Marsha did not understand. He had bowed his head, gesturing with his hands. Ron nodded and smiled back and the man walked away. That's him, Ron said.

Just another one of Ron's adventures. He was the man to whom people always turned and asked, "So, what are you up to these days?" just to hear the answer. Buying a new Ferrari, installing a Jacuzzi, flying to Disneyworld. It seemed like everything Ron did was exciting, and everything he touched worked.

At the house in Truro, Marsha alternated between hopeful visions and more fatalistic ones. But neighbor Bob Corey sat on the bed next to her and waited, expecting Ron to walk through the door with his blue eyes flashing and his hands jerking excitedly in the air, ready to talk about his latest adventure.

Marsha and Ron Sinzheimer on their wedding day, September 21, 1977.

Ron pictured with his previous plane, the sporty Mooney.

Ron's father Hans, Ron, and son Andrew at Andrew's high school graduation, June 1977

Theo, the chow puppy who accompanied Ron on his final flight. Theo's body washed ashore near Sandwich, Massachusetts, at the base of Cape Cod.

David Loring

Cape TRACON controller David Loring had worked Cape Cod traffic for 16 years without losing an airplane. He prided himself on his "sixth sense" when working traffic.

Author's Collection

The 36-foot U.S. Coast Guard boat at the Provincetown station. This small boat was not able to stay out long in the rough seas off Provincetown the night of October 9, 1988.

The Coast Guard Jayhawk helicopter from Air Station Cape Cod that searched for Ron. Scott Womack and Robin Tarrett piloted the helicopter during the search-and-rescue mission.

The wreckage of Ron's Grumman Traveler as it is dragged into port by the fishing boat *Carla Bee*, November 1, 1998. The *Carla Bee*'s whiting net snagged the plane.

The wrecked Grumman sitting in a hangar at Provincetown Municipal Airport, ready for inspection by the National Transportation Safety Board (NTSB). Although the wreckage barely resembles an airplane, NTSB investigator Bob Hancock considered it "fairly intact" because the engine, instrument panel, and main fuselage were still in one piece.

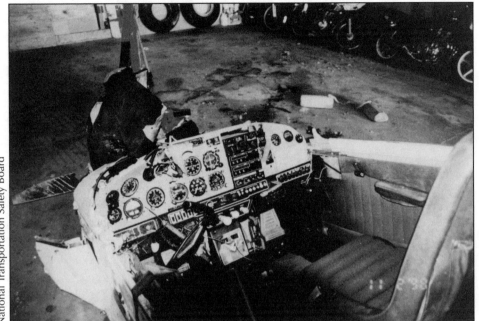

The Grumman's mangled cockpit. A fishing vessel recovered the broken passenger side control yoke, but the pilot's seat was never found. Note the severed cord and adapter plugged into the cigarette lighter, where pilots commonly fit a hand-held Global Positioning System unit.

The unusual navigational radio settings of 114.05 and 115.6
are clearly visible on the Grumman's instruments.

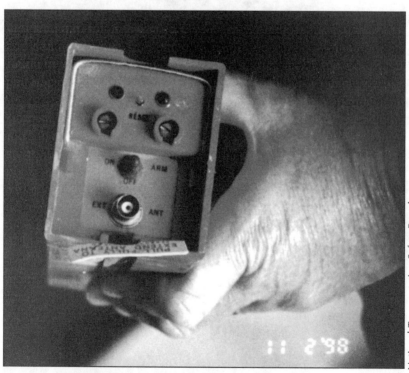

The Grumman's Emergency Locator Transmitter, which is
designed to automatically broadcast an emergency signal
on impact, was found in the "off" position.

# Chapter 9

# Two Hours

*(8:35 P.M.)*

The phone rang at the Coast Guard District in Boston. Chief Petty Controller Pat Cook answered, and grabbed an Incident Report form from a file drawer in his desk. Possible downed aircraft, he wrote as he listened to the supervisor at Boston Center. Cleared on approach into Provincetown at 7:37 P.M.

Last known position?

Boston Center wasn't sure. They were reviewing their radar tapes.

Cook wrote down the controller's strange acronym, "NTAP." He was not sure what it meant but apparently it had something to do with the radar.

Any mayday or ELT signal?

No, we didn't pick up anything here in Boston. Cape Approach was the facility working him, try them.

That was a little odd, Cook thought. Normally Boston called with more detail, could at least confirm that the plane was missing. Or somebody would have heard an ELT signal.

Cook wrote down Cape's number and hung up. He looked at his notes. The plane disappeared at 7:37? Why had Boston waited so long to call? This plane had been missing for an hour!

Cook knew the urgency of getting rescue equipment to the site immediately—every moment that passed was one more moment in which hypothermia could set in, particularly in the 55-degree water of Cape Cod. What had taken so long for this call to come through? The window for immediate response had already closed.

It was closing further. Cook couldn't launch rescue crews until he knew it was more than a "possible" downed airplane. He needed confirmation before he sent boats and helicopters out to search the bay, especially in this weather. He might be risking their lives while the pilot was parking his plane at an alternate airport.

Better wait until he had something he could hang his hat on.

When he first rang Cape Approach, the number was busy. The second time he got through.

(8:42 P.M.)

Hello, this is Coast Guard District One calling about a reported possible downed aircraft. Do you have last known position?

We had him ten to thirteen miles west of the airport before we lost him on radar.

Any signs of distress?

No, nothing.

The supervisor explained that this happened a lot at Cape Approach, airplanes sometimes landed or diverted to other airports without radioing in.

The supervisor did not mention the fact that someone had called the airport looking for the pilot, had reported him late. It was unfortunate, because that call was the kind of confirmation that Cook was looking for.

Perhaps the controller who got the report of the call from the Cape Air clerk didn't tell the supervisor. Or perhaps the detail didn't seem important, in the fact of the FAA's official machinery grinding through official channels. There was more technical data to report, procedures to follow.

Cook tried another tack, asking, Where did the plane come from?

We got him from Providence Approach. The controller gave Cook the number before hanging up.

Ten to thirteen miles west of the airport—it was enough of a fix to launch to the site, but Cook still could not get confirmation that the airplane was down. Who had ownership of this airplane, anyway? Cook just needed someone to say that this guy was missing. Maybe Providence would know whether or not the pilot was late.

*(8:45 P.M.)*

Providence wasn't much help either. The plane had passed through their airspace with no problems, they had picked it up from Albany.

Cook was getting frustrated. Wasn't anybody going to confirm that this plane was missing and let him launch the mission?

Providence gave him Albany's number.

Hello, Albany, Coast Guard calling about a possible downed aircraft. We need confirmation that the plane is late at its destination.

We wouldn't know about that, it took off from here with no problems. The controller suggested calling the contact number on the flight plan.

Almost before he finished scribbling the number down, Cook was punching the telephone keys. A recording answered, "The number you have dialed is out of service." That was strange. Maybe he had dialed it wrong.

Cook tried again and got a busy signal. That was more like it. He waited a minute and tried again. A woman's voice answered.

*(8:55 P.M.)*

She sounded almost hysterical, her voice rising as they talked.

Of course he is missing! He always calls me when there is a delay! It has been over an hour now, she demanded, what were they going to do?

Okay, now we're getting somewhere, Cook thought. He tried to reassure her.

Yes ma'am, we're doing everything we can. In fact I have to get back to the mission. We're going to try to get a cutter from Gloucester. Here's my number, please call me if you have any questions. Anything at all.

He hung up and commenced launching the Coast Guard.

Cook's job was to coordinate the incoming calls to Coast Guard District One, based in Boston's inner harbor. Below the District level were the Groups, including Group Woods Hole at the base of the Cape. The Group directed the Stations, which on the Cape were at Cape Cod Canal (near the mainland and covering the northeast half of the bay), Chatham (at the Cape's elbow, covering the Atlantic to the south and east) and Provincetown, a substation of Chatham that covered the southeastern side of the bay.

The plane had gone down off Provincetown, at the tip of the Cape. That put it in Group Woods Hole territory. Cook called them first and handed over control for the mission. Woods Hole, at the base of Cape Cod's upper arm, would be SMC, or the Search and Rescue Mission Coordinator, in charge of launching and commanding the boats from the stations.

At Station Provincetown, closest to the search area, was based a 47-foot boat. But that was too small to stay out in bad weather for very long. Crews grew fatigued, especially if they had already been on duty for a while and had already run a mission. What this mission wanted was a cutter—a 110-footer that could stay at sea in bad weather for days. The closest one was in Gloucester, three hours north and under another group's command. Cook would call and see if it could be released.

Although the Group would run the mission, it had no authority over the Air Station. The District would command air crews, coordinating with the Group. The Duty Officer at Woods Hole asked for a helicopter; Cook said that he would call the Air Station to request one.

As Woods Hole began calling the stations to coordinate boats and crews, Cook sent out an Urgent Marine Information Bulletin, alerting all boats in the area to keep an eye out for the airplane. The alert would broadcast every fifteen minutes over Channel 16, the "calling and distress" frequency that all commercial vessels monitored.

Cook still didn't have an exact "last known position" to pass along to Woods Hole, but crews could begin searching the beach and off the end of the runway until the radar data arrived. The important thing was to get equipment out there before tides and currents widened the search area further, and while chances of survival were at their best.

*(8:57 P.M.)*

At one end of the flight planning room at the Air Station, Scottie Womack was tethered to the wall phone by the receiver cord. He nodded as the Flight Service briefer outlined the weather conditions along the Cape. Across the room, Robin Starrett scrolled through computer screen images, studying the green Doppler radar that painted the local rainfall.

Womack hung up and stepped over to the giant square table in the middle of the flight planning room. Okay, Robin, what are you thinking?

Starrett stood up and ran his finger along the map under the table glass. I say we file for the approach, take off here and fly out to Provincetown. Then we can backtrack on the localizer and run the coastline—his finger slid back and forth along the westernmost edge of the hook.

It's pretty nasty out there, Womack said. We're going to be right on the deck. But we have some good recovery spots. Conditions are above minimums over here—Womack tapped Hyannis—chances are good we could also recover back to Otis. Womack wanted to be sure of his options. He didn't buy that old Coastie slogan, "You have to go out but you don't have to come back." If it looked like he couldn't get his crew home again, he didn't launch.

New England weather was similar to Alaska, where Womack had transferred from a year earlier, and Starrett just a month ago. In either place the ceiling could slam down to minimums within minutes, fog and haze appearing from nowhere, low-pressure systems dumping rain and ice all over the place.

But if the sky were like this Alaska, Womack knew he would think hard about taking off. Once the helicopter left the 177-mile island of Kodiak and headed south along the Aleutian island chain, it was on its own. No air traffic control, no other airports for emergency landing sites.

New England was different. In his year at Otis, Womack had discovered that if he zipped up and down the coast he would almost always find a hole, somewhere clear to land. If he were stuck in the clouds he could call an air traffic controller for vectors around thunderstorm cells, or for headings to one of the many nearby airports. He could always get some help.

Starrett glanced at his watch. Womack looked up at the wall clock and realized that it had been over 20 minutes since the call had come in. The helicopter was supposed to launch within half an hour of the initial call from District, but they still had to meet up with the rest of the crew, suit up and preflight the Jayhawk. They had better document the delay. Starrett had seniority, he made the call. He stuck his head into the control room, next door, and caught the eye of the operations duty officer.

We're not going to make it in half an hour, he said. Extra flight planning because of the weather.

*(9:00 P.M.)*

After a few years of budget cuts, Station Provincetown had been reduced to a substation of Chatham, called a "station small." There was no Operations Duty Officer to coordinate incoming calls and launches. Instead, Coxswain Troice Hudnell was holding a cordless phone as he sat upstairs in the break room, watching a football game with the crew.

The phone rang, Group Woods Hole calling. There was a downed aircraft off the end of the runway out at the Provincetown airport.

Hudnell and the three other crewmembers were already heading downstairs to the map room. He nodded and talked into the phone. The 47-footer was down for maintenance, he said, but they could take the 36-footer.

Go, said Chatham.

The 36-foot boat was on loan from Chatham, and was not the best piece of equipment for the job. The 47-footer would have been better, with a high, closed cockpit from which to scan the seas. The crew would have had bathrooms. The 36-footer had an open cockpit, no bunks or toilets. The crew would only be able to stay out for a few hours.

They jumped into their one-piece, bright orange survival suits and spent a few minutes poring over the giant table map of Cape Cod Bay in the radio room. Then they ran out of the building, hopped into Hudnell's car and drove the quarter-mile pier out to the boat, leaving on the lights at the empty station behind them.

*(9:05 P.M.)*

The phone rang and Pat Cook answered. It was the spouse. She sounded like she was crying.

It was the toughest part of the job, talking to loved ones. Cook heard the fear and hope all mixed up in her voice as she asked about her husband.

What's happening out there? Do you think you'll find him? What are the chances?

He chose his words carefully, knowing it had already been over an hour, and would be close to another hour before crews got out there.

Well, we hope he's fine. But we have to remember that it is cold water, and at night. The weather conditions aren't good.

It was a crummy thing to have to say, even worse over the telephone. Cook would much rather be directing crews, launching boats, jotting down notes. He tried to change the subject.

Can you give me some more information? About your husband? How old is he and is he in good health? Cook wanted some guidelines to start pinpointing the pilot's expected survival time in the water.

He was forty-nine and healthy, she said. But then she asked again about his survival chances. She wanted it straight. How likely was it that they would find her husband alive?

Well, ma'am, it's hard to say. But in these weather conditions, and with the time that's gone by, we have to start preparing ourselves for the possibility that things might not turn out okay.

*(9:33 P.M.)*

Troice Hudnell throttled forward into the murk, steering the boat away from the concrete pier and into the misty soup that blanketed Provincetown harbor. The 36-foot boat was jet-powered, with a water intake tube that propelled water out the back end. It was powered by a single diesel engine that sat aft of the cabin. Compared to a propeller-driven boat it was jittery. Since there was no rudder, there was no centered position for the wheel. To hold a heading Hudnell had to nudge it constantly, jigging the wheel back and forth like a car driver in a hokey film scene.

Instead of skimming over the waves like an action figure, Hudnell had to poke along in the dense fog and drizzle, edging the throttle forward to make 10 knots when he could. He watched the GPS and strained to see the channel buoys as the boat headed out of the harbor.

Every few minutes he took a hand off the throttle lever and sounded the air horn, just in case some fishing vessel was nuts enough to be out in the dark fog. He kept an eye open for the green beacon that marked the tip of the hook.

Vessel 36501 is underway, he radioed to Chatham. We're making just under ten knots, we've got zero visibility here in the harbor.

Roger, Provincetown. Station Cape Cod Canal is standing down on their launch until you're ready to be relieved. Advise conditions when you reach the search site.

*(9:45 P.M.)*

Womack and Starrett rushed downstairs, across the ramp to the next hangar over. They grabbed the orange inflatable survival vests out of the lockers by the door and tossed them around their necks. Around the corner from the hangar door, in the maintenance control room, Womack paged through the maintenance book for helicopter 6021, reading all of the mechanic's notes for the day and studying what they had tweaked or fixed. Starrett briefed the rescue swimmer and flight mechanic.

Outside, the ceiling hovered at 150 feet and it had started raining. Their shoulders squared, the orange-clad crew headed across the ramp to the helicopter, striding evenly under the heavy loads of survival gear. Womack didn't notice the sky or rain. He saw nothing but the aircraft, and ran a practiced eye over its orange and white body, checking and confirming that it looked ready to go.

The two pilots grabbed the doorframes and pulled themselves up into the cockpit. The flight mechanic walked around the helicopter performing a quick preflight check, then gave a thumbs-up and climbed through the side door. In the pilot's seat, Womack hit the switches to start turning the giant overhead rotor. The blades slowly huffed to life as the turbine whined. The flight mechanic and rescue swimmer strapped into the back and adjusted their night vision goggles.

Clearance Delivery, Womack announced on the radio as he taxied on the Jayhawk's wheels out to the end of the runway. Coast Guard 6021 is IFR to Provincetown.

Roger, came the quick response from Cape TRACON. Coast Guard 6021 is cleared IFR direct to Provincetown. Good luck, guys.

*(9:55 P.M.)*

Troice Hudnell looked every bit the rescuing hero. His sturdy arms and strong hands could have swung a drowning man out of the water in one swipe. Under his efficient buzz cut, Hudnell's contrasting baby face and soft chin made him look wholesome, as if he bought the complete Mom, apple pie, God and country line. He was 25 years old, had been in the Coast Guard for seven years, and this was his first airplane search.

Hudnell had sortied for plenty of emergency boat signals before. EPIRBs, the marine emergency transmitters, were notoriously sensitive to water or changes in position. You would get there and board the vessel, only to find a crew of surprised partiers who had no clue that the beacon was transmitting.

Downed aircraft were different, more serious than boats somehow. The Coast Guard took every emergency signal seriously, of course. But the adrenaline rush was higher with a downed aircraft. Partly that was because airplanes sent so few false alarms. Also, they sank faster than boats did, and rarely carried lifeboats on board. A quick Coast Guard response was pretty much a wet pilot's only hope.

A voice from Chatham crackled over the radio: Okay we've got the last known position from Boston Center radar, you ready to copy?

Hudnell grabbed a pen from his survival suit pocket and spread a piece of paper on the bench seat next to him. The navigator riding to his left grabbed the wheel. Go ahead, Hudnell said into the radio.

Position forty-two oh three oh three north, seventy fifteen fifty-seven west. Hudnell wrote it down and read back the numbers to confirm as the navigator plugged them into the GPS.

The boat rounded the very tip of the hook and Hudnell throttled forward as fast as he dared in the fog, heading west around the southern shore and then curving northwest to the search site. As he left the protection of the harbor and entered the bay proper, the ride got wet. The surf boat scooped up water as its nose dove into the swells, flooding the deck and pouring water into the cabin. Although it was raining, Hudnell rolled up the canvas flaps that acted as walls for the small cabin—it worked out better to just let the rolling water flow right through the cabin and pour back out over the low gunnels. Besides, he wanted to be able to hear.

In the front of the boat, one of the crew members stood next to the storage box on the center of the deck. Anyone riding outside had to hold tight to the railing that ran along the front of the cabin. Hudnell kept an eye out because the waves were high and at night nobody could see them coming, couldn't brace themselves to keep from getting tossed around, beat up or flung over the side.

As the boat turned north it was moving into the Atlantic Ocean, heading into the six-foot waves coming in from the north. The tide was also beginning to come into the bay, pushing steadily at the boat at about half a knot.

Hudnell chattered on the radio with Chatham. He turned the helm over to the navigator and slipped aft to spread his charts out over the engine hatch, under a small cabin-roof overhang. He spread his feet wide and crouched over the hatch for stability. Using his nautical slide rule, he calculated a rough circular pattern in the 180-foot waters off the end of the runway, just south of the bay's riptide line, where the tide was at its strongest. Even in the survival suit, Hudnell was cold and wet. His papers were soaked and the lines were wiggly. The search pattern was not perfectly plotted but at least it was something he could plug into the GPS to get the boat over the area while there was still a decent chance for the target's survival.

The boat plowed through the waves. The crewmembers didn't say much and struggled to keep down their dinners. Coasties are not immune to seasickness. When a boat starts tossing, the fluid in a passenger's inner ear also gets shaken up, but not necessarily in agreement with what the boat is doing—the boat looks stable in relation to the passengers' bodies, but the inner ear fluid is shaking all around. The disagreement between inner ear and eye is what triggers the stomach, for some reason, to barf up its contents. Some people are able to fight off seasickness by getting the eyes and inner ear to agree—for example, by staring at the distant horizon, which moves compared to the steady boat. The crew could not see the horizon—couldn't see further than a few yards.

It was a long 45-minute ride as the small boat tossed up and down. Damn that the 47-footer was down, thought Hudnell. It handled much better in heavy weather, could even roll over and right itself. Hudnell would have been peering down from a higher perch, able to see a bit further.

*(10:15 P.M.)*

The little orange boat rocked as Hudnell peered at the GPS and honed in on the commence point. He shouted out the cabin to alert the crew, swerved the steering wheel around and started driving the boat in a large circle.

Did Chatham have a search pattern yet? He radioed in.

Not yet, we're working on that radar fix. Stick with the Victor Sierra search of the immediate area around the target.

Hudnell was patient, he knew that Chatham was calculating a pattern based on the last known position of the airplane. They factored in time, tides and winds to grow the point into a field where the debris would most likely be scattered. Then they divided the search area into sectors, assigning them to the equipment that was available according to the speed and maneuverability of each craft.

As Hudnell shone the boat's searchlight across the water and aimed it at the shoreline he knew he wasn't looking for anything resembling an airplane. There would be no wings, tail and fuselage floating on the ocean's surface or nestled neatly amid the trees. Crashed planes crumple into nothing. They leave a patch of scorched earth, the glint of smashed windshield or twisted aluminum skin. Hudnell was looking for bits. Shreds of carpet or foam, an oil or gasoline slick.

He wasn't risking his life to recover a wreck. The debris was important only in that it would refine the search area, pinpointing the water movement to show where the survivor might be drifting. People were more difficult to find than wreckage because sometimes they swam away from the accident sites.

In the cabin, Hudnell wedged his large frame between bench seat and the front panel and rocked and rolled with the waves. The searchlight mounted to the roof of the cabin was just bouncing off the fog, back into the eyes of the crew.

It's really bad viz out here, Hudnell radioed Chatham. We need to pop off a flare.

No, hold off on that, Chatham responded. There's a helicopter on the way that needs to get a reference point, don't blind them out.

The boat floated around in circles, the crew only able to scan the waves right next to them. From what Hudnell understood, the pilot didn't even have a life jacket. They were looking for a tiny target, a small dark head bobbing up for a few seconds on the crest of a six-foot wave, then dipping back in the trough in a wicked little game of hide-and-seek.

*(10:20 P.M.)*

A few minutes later, the boat crew heard the helicopter buzz over-head. It popped into view through the mist, an orange and white flash the size of a tractor-trailer truck, hovering so low that the blades beat the water back from around the boat. The white glare from the night sun, bolted to the side of the helicopter, slid across the waves and over the small boat. Then the Jayhawk was gone, off to fly its own, larger search pattern.

Two hours! What the hell was the Coast Guard doing? Marsha wanted to scream, to push the boats out into the water herself. What was taking so long?

At around 9:30 P.M. Cook had called with an update.

We don't have much to report. We're sending a helicopter and a small boat, and we have the radar data on the airplane's last known position.

Marsha was livid.

A small boat? Is that all you have? What about sonar? Get a big boat with sonar out there and find the airplane! Why was everything taking so long?

The cutter is on its way, ma'am. But sonar won't really help. The shoals out there are littered with shipwrecks. The sonar can't distin-guish between one hunk of metal and another. Besides, the Coast Guard wants to find your husband, not the airplane.

She slammed the phone down and felt tears coming. She rushed back to the bedroom and reached for a tissue on the side table.

It made no sense to Marsha. Just get the sonar out there to the place the radar said the plane was, find the plane and then factor in the tides or whatever and they would know where to search for Ron. The Coast Guard was supposed to know all about currents and things! Wasn't that their job?

Thank goodness Bob had come rushing over from next door. That was the advantage of rarely asking for help, she realized. Once you did, people snapped to attention.

Some people react to tragedy with denial, reassuring themselves that the bad news can't possibly be true because if it were, the world would collapse. Instead, wouldn't this be a good time to clean the grout in the kitchen backsplash? Others panic, screaming at the realization that the world has, in fact, collapsed and will never be the same.

Others delve into sadness, curling up and holding themselves tight as they wail. They indulge in pity, letting the dishes pile up in the sink as they give themselves permission to grieve, and then comfort themselves on the painful path back to daily life.

Marsha cried, of course, holding herself tight as she sat on the bed and rocked. But the overwhelming sadness alternated with another response, one to be expected from a strong, opinionated woman: Anger. She stomped into the bedroom, her eyebrows pinched together hard and making a line on her forehead. Ron was out there, she thought, and somebody needs to do something! Bob sat next to her on the bed as Marsha took deep breaths, sobs creeping in. Her anger and frustration steamed inside, waiting to blast out at the first opportunity.

Again the kitchen phone rang and Bob left the bedroom to answer it. She heard mumbling and then a shout.

Marsha! It's Andrew!

Andrew! She raced out of the bedroom to grab the phone. So he hadn't been on the plane!

Your father is missing, she said, the words tumbling out in a rush. I didn't know if you had come, I thought maybe you were with him.

No, I decided not to, Andrew mumbled in a standard teenager monotone. Mom, don't worry, he's been late before.

Andrew, you don't understand! Her voice went up a notch, lashing out at her son. He's really missing, they are looking for him and they don't know where the plane is.

119

He sounded a little more alert: Well, what are they doing? Who's over there?

The Coast Guard is out looking, she said. Bob from next door is here, and Uncle Eric and Aunt Trudy are driving down.

Andrew said something about coming out to the Cape.

You shouldn't drive out here tonight, Marsha said. It's late, the weather is terrible. It's pouring down rain. Wait and come in the morning.

Okay, Mom, call me if you hear anything. They hung up.

Relief flooded through Marsha—her son was safe and dry. Then guilt swept through her. How could she feel happy, even for a moment, while Ron was out there, lost? Relief, guilt, happiness, worry, anger, it was all so jumbled up that she didn't even know what she was feeling.

Marsha stood next to the wall phone and looked at Bob Corey. I should probably call Ron's parents, she said. It was a question.

No, don't, Corey said. Let them have one more good night's sleep. There's nothing they can do now anyway.

Marsha nodded. She looked at the phone and rubbed her forehead. Can't we call someone? Who can we call? Shouldn't we call the Coast Guard again?

Of course, Bob said. He walked over and picked up the phone.

As the Jayhawk slipped in and out of the cloud bottoms, Womack fought off vertigo. It had happened enough times in New England and in Alaska for him to recognize the signs—no horizon at night, eyes on the panel and then out the window to look for the target then back to the panel, head bobbing around. It was the perfect recipe for disorientation. Fortunately, he also knew how to fight that off. Ignore your ears and gut and just scan the panel—the artificial horizon, the intersecting Doppler bars that guided the hover position, the altimeter. It was getting tougher to fight. Even with Starrett in the right seat, working the radios and taking the stick from time to time, Womack knew they were on the edge.

But this was the reason he signed up for the Coast Guard. He had wanted to pluck people out of the water, to run missions that made a difference instead of some war game exercise for the Army. Nine years of that and he had switched to the Coast Guard aviation program and taught the Coasties to fly their new Jayhawks. Some of his Army friends had teased him, calling it the shallow-water Navy. But Womack knew that every day some Coastie was laying his or her life on the line. Maybe there weren't bullets flying, but if you drowned or crashed you were just as dead as if someone shot you.

With the night vision goggles, Womack and Starrett could see the scrubby tree line below as the Jayhawk popped in and out of fog banks. Over the shoreline and water the crew hadn't seen a thing. No debris, no oil slick. Now the ceiling was dropping and the blinding light from the night sun was just bouncing back off the fog.

This flat out isn't working, Womack said. I'm going up and see if we can pick up an ELT signal.

As Womack climbed, Starrett tuned one of the radios to 121.5. The ELT would have sent out a loud signal on that frequency on impact. But if the plane landed in the ocean that signal would have faded as the plane sank. ELTs weren't designed to work below about ten feet underwater.

Nothing on 121.5, no signal at all. Womack shot his second ILS approach into Provincetown to get below the clouds, breaking off from the approach path at 100 feet to fly along the coast. Womack had flown a lot of low-level missions in bad weather. Zipping along under a hard ceiling was no problem, but popping in and out of the ragged-bottom clouds was dangerous. Womack knew he could lose 50 feet in a moment's fight with disorientation. At 100 feet, that didn't leave much margin for error.

They had been up for an hour when they decided to call it quits.

We're not going to find this guy tonight, Starrett said.

Yeah, this is nasty, Womack agreed. We can recover to Otis, I'll call and tell them we're coming back in.

Hudnell got off one flare, popping the tube open and ramming the butt end into the cap to trigger the charge. It shot a few hundred feet into the air, lit, and floated down on its parachute, bathing the clouds, boat and waves in a wash of light for half a minute.

No sign of anything. No debris, no smell, no shiny fuel or oil floating on the water. The crew was finishing its search pattern, a tight series of parallel lines half a mile apart, when Chatham called. The 41-footer was underway from Cape Cod Canal to relieve them, it would be on site momentarily. The 36-footer was released.

The winds had calmed a little, but it was well after midnight and Hudnell's crew was exhausted. The waves had taken their toll and the adrenaline rush had worn off. Hudnell pointed the boat southeast in the dark rain and headed toward Provincetown harbor.

I don't know, the navigator said. It's weird that we haven't seen anything.

Hudnell agreed. The conditions were bad, but the crew should have drifted through some sort of debris field—wreckage, oil, fuel, something left from the crash. The helicopter hadn't found any clues either. There isn't anyone out here to save, Hudnell concluded. That plane had to be on land somewhere.

# Chapter 10

# No Joy

LATE FRIDAY NIGHT, pilots Scott Womack and Robin Starrett landed at Otis and recommended launching again at first light. Then they headed for the barracks to grab a room for the night. They were on duty for over 12 more hours, and would fly again in the morning.

Before bedding down, Womack called home to check in with his wife.

Oh, my cousin called, she said. Remember her from the wedding? She asked me if you knew anything about a friend of hers whose husband is missing out on the Cape. He was flying his small plane to Provincetown tonight and disappeared.

The coincidence was unsettling. Womack explained that he had been out looking for that plane. They hadn't found anything, he said. But the boats were staying out overnight, and he and Robin would launch in the helicopter again in the morning.

Womack said goodnight and hung up. It had been a long night. He was asleep almost as soon as he fell into the bed.

As Womack and Starrett rested, officials at Coast Guard District One got out the survival charts. The *Search and Rescue Manual* included several tables, one of which noted that life expectancy in calm, 55-degree water was two to eight hours. After that, the victim succumbed to hypothermia.

The manual included an admonition to regard the numbers as a guideline, since various factors can affect the times. Coast Guard personnel have performed many miraculous rescues of survivors who surpassed all survival expectations. That is why they search even in 34-degree water—so icy that it sends people into cold-water shock and they drown almost immediately.

On Friday night, the Coast Guard set the pilot's life expectancy in the water at 12 hours. Ultimately, the mission would stretch into 22 hours.

Hypothermia is the process by which the body's core loses heat and then stops working. It can happen in water as warm as 92 degrees Farenheit. The ocean tops out at 84 degrees, and so even at the beach in July you can feel hypothermia beginning after swimming just a bit too long. Your teeth begin to chatter. Children sometimes linger, pulling their arms close and crossing their legs to stay warmer while floating for just a few moments longer. Their instincts are good—swimming or other exercise increases heat loss and hastens hypothermia. The best survival technique is to huddle, floating in groups or alone, with arms and legs wrapped around the body's core.

That's because the core, at 99.5° Farenheit, works to keep the arms, legs and skin warm. The closer the limbs are to the core, the easier it is to warm them. Water is a better conductor than air, so it saps warmth away quickly, making the core push more heat out. The body becomes like a house in winter with open windows, the furnace desperately trying to heat up the whole outdoors. Insulation slows the heat loss, of course, which is why scuba divers wear wet suits. The neoprene traps a thin layer of water next to the skin, which the body core heats and uses as insulation.

People begin to feel cold when the body's core temperature drops from 99.5° F to 97° F. As it lowers to 95° F they begin to shiver uncontrollably. Teeth chattering, body shaking, it is the first serious sign that something dreadfully wrong is happening.

Severe hypothermia sets in around 93° F, as the body's core begins shutting down. People become clumsy, irrational and confused. They act drunk, slurring their speech. And they often begin to hallucinate, having heavenly visions, or more mundane ones of rescuers, of boats or (in the case of high-altitude mountain climbers) cozy tents.

Bodies of climbers are often found naked in the snow. In the euphoric latter stages of hypothermia they stripped away their clothing in a frenzy of feeling hot. At that point the hypothermic person may move around a lot, thrashing and panicking, which uses energy and sends the body to the next stage.

At around 91° F, muscle stiffness sets in as the blood starts to thicken. Then the body's core temperature drops below 90° F and the shivering stops. The person collapses into semi-consciousness—breathing but no longer aware of his or her surroundings.

Unconsciousness comes at about 86° F, but recovery is still possible if the victim's body is gently warmed and given moist, warm air to breathe.

When the body's core dips to around 84° F, pulse and breathing become very slow as the lungs and heart struggle to keep working. At around 82° F, the heart goes into cardiac arrest. By that point there are no vital signs and the person feels cold, stiff, and dead.

Coast Guard rescuers have saved people who passed that point, thumping away on chests to restart the heart, giving mouth-to-mouth resuscitation to spark the lungs. But those survivors were usually wearing life vests. A complication of hypothermia in water is that once a person becomes unconscious, he or she drowns. The lungs fill with water, and without a life vest to hold it afloat, the body sinks.

The sun rose just before 7:00 A.M. on Saturday morning but nobody saw it through the low clouds and thick rain. A few minutes later a Jayhawk lifted off from Otis and pointed its black nose toward Provincetown. Pilots Robin Starrett and Scottie Womack were once again in the cockpit. No night vision goggles this time, no flares or searchlights. Womack had recommended the dawn launch, knowing that daylight would bring better flight conditions. But inversely the late hour meant that survival time had decreased and the search area had grown. Floating targets swim or drift, and survivors of ground crashes start walking out, if they can.

The overcast had lifted slightly and the helicopter skimmed a few hundred feet off the ground, running under the cloud deck. The wind was still blowing, but for the moment had stopped gusting. In the back, the rescue swimmer and flight mechanic rotated their seats to face the side windows. Through the rain the crew could see almost a mile ahead and to the side. They scanned the low rolling waves for bits of debris, the flash of a life vest. No joy.

Below the helicopter the 110-foot cutter *Grand Isle* cruised the bay side of Provincetown in a tight pattern of parallel rectangles, making a five-mile run along Race Point Beach, turning south one mile, then heading back five miles and turning south again. After that it would turn toward the ocean side, sweeping another five-mile square area past the end of the runway. That was where the Grumman would have ditched if it had overshot the runway and flown past the airport.

Womack and Starrett were flying a 20-mile-diameter starburst pattern of overlapping triangles centered over the airport. On one of the last legs an excited crewmember announced over the helicopter's intercom system: debris in the water, debris in the water!

It was hard to tell what it was while hovering in the helicopter. Was it part of the plane? There were no apparent signs of life. Starrett radioed *Grand Isle* to tell the cutter they had something. The cutter sped to the debris field site, directed by vectors from the helicopter hovering overhead. False alarm. A child's flotation toy that had drifted miles out from the beach. The boat pulled it aboard and radioed in: No joy, it's not the airplane.

Low on fuel, the helicopter returned to Otis empty-handed.

In the gray light of morning, Troice Hudnell didn't have a clear idea of what time it was. It could have been six, could have been seven or eight. He and his crew had bagged only three or four hours' sleep in the station barracks before climbing back into the orange 36-foot boat and heading back out around 4:30 A.M. to relieve the 41-footer from Cape Cod Canal. Different time, same place, bouncing around off Race Point in the rain. His back was sore from leaning over the helm and he had a few extra bruises on his thick calves from the edges of the cabin door. As the morning wore on his search pattern grew and drifted south, to compensate for the prevailing winds that would be driving any debris.

He had a feeling they were not going to find this plane. No signs, no clues. Maybe it would turn out like that guy in the sailboat off Plymouth, the one who disappeared overnight. Hudnell had spent the night cruising the bay, searching for the missing boat, only to find it in the morning moored 150 yards from its home dock. He came alongside and sounded his air horn, waking the guy up. An argument with the wife, the man had explained. I didn't feel like going home so I slept out here.

Hudnell had let him have it, yelling about the wasted taxpayer money spent on the boats and helicopters scouring Cape Cod Bay in the dark, all night long. The guy was a Harvard professor, but super clueless. He could have at least called his wife.

The search patterns of parallel lines had grown from a tightly-focused area right off the end of the runway to the entire hook and miles out to sea around it. Hudnell wanted to find the pilot. He didn't mind spending a wet night and day in high seas, as long as he knew there was a life to save. But heading into 15 hours and no debris? If the plane had crashed into the water, surely something would have spilled out or broken off, Hudnell thought. Seat cushions, luggage, fiberglass trim.

In Boston, the District controller was working the phones hard on Saturday morning, briefing the various Coast Guard stations. First was the discussion about divers. Boston guessed that the wreckage site was not very far offshore: Were there rescue divers from Woods Hole available to work the area and find the plane, so they could pinpoint the drifting search area?

Woods Hole did not think that plan would work. The water was over 170 feet deep. Divers would be able to stay down there for mere minutes before heading back up to decompress. Sending divers down for a few minutes at a time would not be an efficient way to cover the bottom.

Then came the calls to and from the Coast Guard public affairs officer, who was faxing out press releases. Calls to and from the District Commander, the air station, the various marine stations, the Air Force Rescue Coordination Center in Langley, Virginia. The command center's notes, terse as they were, spilled over onto a fourth page as the search stretched into mid-morning on Saturday.

By the time Marsha woke up, Bob Corey had already made coffee. Eric and Trudy had arrived late the night before. Marsha had managed to sleep for a few hours with Trudy curled up tightly next to her. As she walked into the kitchen, her dark hair was wild around her face. Her eyes were puffy with dark circles showing through her deep tan.

She saw Bob and asked, What happened? Did anything happen last night?

No news, Corey said gently. He had already called the Coast Guard for an update, and explained what they had said. There had been a boat from Cape Cod Canal out there all night, cruising off the coast of Provincetown. The cutter arrived shortly after four this morning. They sent another helicopter out half an hour ago.

And they still haven't found anything? Marsha was shaking, her whole body shivering as if she were cold. She couldn't stop. She felt so helpless, stuck in the house waiting for the phone to ring, relying on other people to save Ron. Wasn't there something that she could do?

Right out of law school, Ron had worked for Mary Ann Krupsak, who was then the Lieutenant Governor of New York. That was years ago, but Ron had stayed in touch. Krupsak had connections, Marsha thought. Maybe she could light a fire under the Coast Guard. It was worth a try, and better than just sitting there, waiting. She picked up the phone and dialed. When she got through to Krupsak, Marsha launched right into the problem.

Mary Ann, it's Marsha Sinzheimer, Ron's wife. I'm out on the Cape and Ron's plane is missing. Please, can you do something? I'm not getting anywhere with the Coast Guard.

Krupsak was shocked and sympathetic; she had always been fond of Ron. She gave Marsha the number for an aide to a New York state senator or representative, someone who had contacts in the Navy. Marsha thanked her and hung up.

The aide sounded anxious to help. Don't worry, he said. We'll push for a Navy cutter from Virginia, a big boat with sonar.

Thank you, Marsha said. Navy ships, sonar, more helicopters, anything, she thought. Just get stuff out there and find him.

She hung up and headed back to the cocoon of her bedroom, huddling under the covers. It was still raining outside.

A few minutes later the phone rang and Corey answered. Then he came into the bedroom: It was the Coast Guard again, with a question for Marsha. One of Boston's public radio stations, WBUR, had called. They wanted to run a news story about the accident, and they were asking the Coast Guard to release Ron's name.

More reporters. Marsha hadn't talked to any of the ones who called. There was no way she was going to smear her emotions all over the nightly news. Some dogged journalists had already come up to the house that morning, and Eric had chased them off. In Albany, the night before, reporters had banged on the door at 2 Manning Boulevard, and Andrew had called her in a panic. Ignore them, she had said.

They ran stories on Friday night's news and in Saturday morning's paper anyway, of course. They quoted people who were not close friends, who did not realize that Marsha preferred media silence. And so the stories and articles were full of mistakes, Marsha noticed. Like the newspaper article that called Theo a Pomeranian.

Corey stood by the bedroom door, waiting for her to answer.

Ron's name? Marsha's anger and frustration boiled over, pouring out and splashing Corey.

He's shivering out there waiting to be rescued and the Coast Guard is worried about releasing his name to reporters? No, she barked. I just can't deal with that right now.

He dutifully reported back to the telephone.

By the front door a small pile of sneakers and loafers was growing as people arrived and followed Bob Corey's lead, removing their wet and sandy shoes to pad around the carpet in their socks. Eric began answering the telephone and jotting down names, phone numbers and messages in a spiral-bound notebook. Trudy sat with Marsha.

Nobody here to tease Trudy now, Marsha thought. Nobody to flick her with a rolled-up towel or jab at her with a raw hot dog as Ron had done at one party. Probably years of therapy, Marsha thought, for Trudy to get over the trauma of that hot dog. Trudy didn't get Ron's humor. She thought he was a little egotistical. But in his absence the big modern house was silent and plain, and Trudy cried.

Saturday before lunch, Andrew arrived with his girlfriend. Another friend had driven them. Andrew was tall, over six feet like his father. But his coloring, dark hair and olive skin, was all from his mother. He didn't say much as Marsha hugged him fiercely. With Andrew she felt like a family again. A family waiting, scared and wounded, but a family nonetheless.

For the rest of the day the teenagers bound together in a tight group, sitting on the couch and not talking much to the new arrivals beginning to crowd the house. Andrew slipped periodically into Marsha's bedroom to ask how she was doing. He hovered for a few minutes, asking if she was hungry. They talked about Ron, about what might have gone wrong with the plane to force him to make an emergency landing, and where he might be, what he might be doing. Marsha could see that Andrew was taking it hard, not accepting the fact yet that his dad might not come home.

Later on Saturday, Ron's parents arrived from Manhattan in a hired car because neither of them could drive. Marsha showed them to the living room, and mentally tallied the guest beds. Eric and Trudy, Andrew and his friends, now Ron's parents. She wondered if she had enough clean towels.

She made her mother-in-law comfortable on one of the couches and Sulamith broke down immediately.

How could you, Marsha? How could you not call me when it happened? Why did you wait until today?

Marsha was apologetic. I'm sorry, she said. Maybe I should have called.

Bob Corey, still recovering from open-heart surgery a few weeks earlier, stepped into the fray. Don't blame Marsha, he said. It was my fault, I told her not to call you. There was nothing you could have done.

Sulamith looked Corey in the eye, staring him down. I could have prayed, she said.

The Coast Guard can trace its origins back to the lower Cape's fine and drifting sand. Cape Cod's upper arm was formed from glacial outwash material, mostly rock and granite. But that ends at the Highlands, a few miles south of Provincetown. From that point north to the hook itself, it's all sand. Real sand, not the standard layer of small rocks that passes for "beach" across northern Massachusetts and Maine.

The sand spills onto Route 6 and the smaller side roads. In winters past the state had to dig the roads out from under tons of sand to keep them open. The fine sand drifts into Pilgrim Lake, which served as a storm harbor at Cape Cod's wrist until its sand threatened to spread into Provincetown's main harbor. Then residents closed off the entrance and turned it into a lake.

The spectacular dunes at Race Point and around Pilgrim Lake are sculpted by the constant wind into giant waves of sand. They are known as "parabolic" dunes. When the pilgrims arrived, these dunes were covered with a foot of soil with mature beech and oak trees. Those were later cut down to build houses, and the domesticated animals grazed the shrubbery. Residents have been fighting the shifting sand ever since, as it blows south and threatens to bury Provincetown. To hold it back, the National Park Service began planting beach grass in the 1800s and continued through the 1980s. That helped stabilize the giant dunes, and erosion is under control now. Signs still warn visitors to stay off the dunes lest they uproot the fragile beach grass. The sand still slips through, blowing across parking lots, through hotel rooms, and into faces. It slips and flows over the ground like water.

On the floor of Cape Cod Bay the sand drifts into treacherous bars and shoals. Until Cape Cod Canal was opened in 1914, every ship between Boston and New York had to sail around the north side of the hook. Thousands of them didn't make it, as the tides and winds pushed them aground on the sand bars a few hundred yards off the beach. The heavy surf would break the boats up, then drag them into deeper water where they still litter the bottom.

Wrecks began to pile up on the sandy shoals, poking up into the shallows and causing more wrecks. The waters to the east of the Cape began to be known as the Graveyard of the Atlantic. In 1785, volunteers in Boston Harbor took pity on the growing number of stranded sailors and started the world's first lifesaving service. It was called the Massachusetts Humane Society, and offered food and shelter to area shipwreck survivors.

Rescuers started whisking out to the imperiled boats themselves a few years later, when Congress funded lifesaving outposts along the Eastern shore. Cape Cod had nine stations, at Race Point, Highlands, Peaked Hill Bars, Pamet, Cahoon Hollow, Nauset, Orleans, Chatham and Monomoy Point. They initiated a romantic era of dangerous and daring lifesaving rescues. Patrols walked endless hours of beach each night and during storms, when most accidents tended to happen. They held wooden shingles in front of their faces to protect against the blowing sand. If a ship ran aground, patrollers would send up a flare and the shout the alarm, "Ship ashore!"

The old station at Race Point still stands on the beach. From there, lifesavers ran back and forth to the small surf boat at the water's edge, loading it with rescue equipment. Five oarsmen and the helmsman pushed the thousand-pound boat into the surf and rowed out to the wreck. There, they struggled to pull survivors out of the waves—the boat held five at a time—and bring them back to shore. Back and forth, fighting exhaustion, until no more survivors could be found.

When the water was too rough for the boats, which came to be known as "Race Point" or "Monomoy" types, lifesavers used the "breeches buoy." A small cannon, called a Lyle gun, shot a lightweight line to the damaged ship. The crew anchored the line to the mast while the lifesavers set a 12-foot wooden support on the beach for the other end. With a block and pulley they could pull back and forth a pair of canvas pants attached to a life ring. The pants went out to the boat, and in went a sailor who was pulled to shore on the line. He was often dunked several times into the cold water as the ship's mast rocked back and forth, slackening the line. A man in the breeches could slip into hypothermia and drown on the long, wet journey to shore.

In 1915 the lifesavers were folded into the newly-formed U.S. Coast Guard, some of whom informally adopted the lifesaver motto, "You have to go out, but you don't have to come back." The Coast Guard prides itself on the lifesaver tradition, and the Cape's stations still hold demonstrations of the old-style techniques. They shoot off the Lyle guns and tug the breeches buoy pulley for an offshore ship.

By the early 1900s Cape Cod Canal had opened. New steel ships motored through the canal and then the protected bay, with engines strong enough to keep them from blowing onto the shoals.

And yet, the Coast Guard stayed busy. On February 18, 1952, personnel from Station Chatham made international headlines by pulling off the Cape's most daring rescue. In a ferocious Nor'easter, Coxswain Bernie Webber and his crew saved 32 men from a sinking tanker. They did it in a wooden 36-foot boat, the same size Troice Hudnell worked in his search for Ron Sinzheimer.

The violent storm had broken two tankers in half. The *Fort Mercer* managed to make a distress call, and most of the Coast Guard headed for it. But Station Chatham's radar had picked up the two pieces of the sinking *Pendleton*, which had lost its radios and was unable to call for help. Two boats launched, but could not cross the Chatham Bar. The shallow shoal was treacherous in the 10-foot waves, which were reaching 60 feet out at sea.

In the 36-footer, Webber managed to cross the bar. But in the violence of the breakers the boat lost most of its rescue gear. More importantly, it lost its compass. With no navigational equipment, Webber opted to continue the mission. He steered via radio headings from personnel in Chatham who were watching the boat on radar, and finally reached the wrecked tanker.

It took 45 minutes to load the survivors. The crew timed each jump with the waves, maneuvering to keep the tiny boat from smashing into the side of the steel hull. Only three men went into the water. Two were saved, one was fatally thrown against the wreck.

On the return trip, the overloaded boat tipped in the heavy waves, several times nearly capsizing. The visibility was zero, in driving snow and ocean spray. Blindly following radio headings from Chatham, Webber successfully steered the boat around the shoals at Morris Island and back across the bar to a safe landing.

After 16 more years' work CG36500 was retired and restored. It now floats around the Cape as a museum piece. Most of the Coast Guard's rescue work has historically been done in smaller boats. But by 1998, the hardy little 36-footers had largely been replaced by steel-hulled 44-footers and the Jayhawk helicopters.

By lunchtime on Saturday, the Coast Guard had been searching the water for 17 hours with multiple trips by three boats and a helicopter. The strange lack of any evidence began to convince officials that the plane was not in the water. And then a phone call came from a local resident that seemed to confirm it.

The caller lived in Truro. He had read about that missing airplane in Saturday's paper, and thought he should call in with some information. He had heard a plane fly over his house in Friday night, heading south. It sounded like maybe the plane then turned back to the north.

The dispatcher at District One thanked him and passed the information to Woods Hole. With nothing showing up in the water it did make sense to turn the mission toward the interior. It would be tricky because the shoreline and dunes of the National Seashore between Provincetown and Truro were wild. No houses, no lights, nothing but beach grass, a few pine trees, scrubby scotch broom and the wild roses.

District One duly informed the Air Force Rescue Coordination Center that the mission was shifting to land. AFRCC knew that Park Service personnel had been walking the dunes at Race Point since daybreak, but there were not enough of them to cover the interior. The Rescue Center contacted their Civil Air Patrol volunteers. They would be able to send more foot patrols and maybe launch pilots to fly the ground search. They could listen for ELT signals and fly low and slow over the search area, scanning the ground for glints of metal.

Al Slaney lived in Whitman, Massachusetts, south of Boston. He was on call for the weekend, ready to coordinate any Civil Air Patrol missions that AFRCC asked for. His pager beeped just after noon. Slaney launched into the phone calls to CAP volunteers and caught a series of answering machines. There was a New England Regional drill for the CAP, in Rhode Island, and most of the volunteers had gone there. Finally, Darrell Lipman answered. He and his wife Shelley, both CAP volunteers, were in the middle of a squadron activity with a bunch of teenaged cadets. They couldn't launch until the parents came to pick them up.

Slaney told them to stay on standby.

I might be able to find someone else, he said. But it's getting down to the bottom of the list. Stay by the phone, I'm pretty sure I'll need you.

The CAP air crew reached Beverly airport, north of Boston, within the hour. But the weather was not promising. Dick Schafner had flown CAP missions for 20 years. He knew a sucker hole when he saw one, and Provincetown was sitting right in the middle of a sucker hole. The weather looked decent for the moment, with ceilings up around 400 feet, but the unstable air circling around it was a mess and completely unpredictable. It could close in at any moment, leaving the pilot stranded in hard IFR conditions with ceilings too low to land. None of the airports along the coast had high enough ceilings to be considered trustworthy alternate landing sites.

The Provincetown airport was open, but not the ILS approach that Sinzheimer had flown. The signal had been shut down until FAA personnel could make the standard check flight in clear weather. They would compare the electronic signals to the airplane's true position from the ground, making sure the signal put the plane on an accurate path.

Until then, and the weather showed no signs of breaking, pilots were stuck flying Provincetown's Non-Directional Beacon, or NDB, approach. It was the trickiest kind, relying on a wobbly beacon signal and a series of non-precision maneuvers that brought the plane down in a kind of stair-step descent instead of the slanting path of the ILS glide slope.

Schafner called to consult with Slaney, the mission coordinator. Slaney made the call. Don't go, he said. It's too risky. We're sending ground crews for a foot search.

Mike Lorenz lived in Dennis, just down Route 6 from Chatham. He reached the Provincetown Coast Guard station before any of the other CAP volunteers. With Slaney several hours away in Whitman, Lorenz took over coordination of the ground crews. The Coasties let him hook a radio up to one of their antennas, and he pulled up a chair in the communications room and began organizing a foot search by the Coast Guard, his volunteer teams and the AFRCC.

At 5:00 P.M., Darrell and Shelley Lipman arrived at Race Point after a three-hour drive from Stow, Massachusetts, 25 miles west of Boston. One 14-year-old cadet still in tow, they stopped and picked up a Park Service volunteer who gave them a drive-on pass for the beach.

Darrell had taken a four-wheel driving class when they lived in California, so he was the one who drove the Isuzu Rodeo out onto the beach. Before easing it out onto the sand he stopped and got out to bleed some air out of the tires. He reminded himself to drive slowly and not make any sudden turns. Then he passed out flashlights for Shelley, the cadet and the park ranger, who got out and walked ahead of the truck. They scanned the area lit by the car's headlights in the dark rain.

Shelley was thinking of the cadet walking next to her, thinking of how it might shake him up to see a body. She could handle it, had seen plenty when she worked as a paramedic, and as a firefighter. But she knew that seeing a gory crash site could provoke strange reactions from people, send them right into depression. She ran over her training in her mind as she snaked her light along the scrubby tree line: Unless there is a life to save, protect the accident scene. Keep the cadet away from the smoking hole in the ground, don't let him peer over just to see what the body looks like.

Overhead, the Jayhawk roared by, returning to base from its third and final trip of the mission. Solid IFR, Shelley thought as she looked up at the sky, wondering if Friday night had been similar. She had her instrument rating, but decided that she would not shoot an approach in this rain and cloud cover. The ceiling was too low, you would have to go around. The Rodeo crept along behind as the volunteers scanned the waves, the shoreline and the beach.

It went on like that for hours. Every few minutes someone radioed Mike Lorenz back at the Provincetown station with a briefing, or for a briefing. Found anything yet? Nothing here, how about you? Got an ELT signal or anything? Nope, nothing.

For Marsha, time was both compressing and stretching out, hours one on top of the other in an indistinguishable mish-mash of phone calls, casseroles and rain. People had begun arriving—other neighbors, friends from the Provincetown Tennis Club. They filled the living room. Some attempted jokes, thinking maybe of Ron, how he could always break the ice with humor. But Marsha didn't feel social. She wanted to climb into bed and never come out. She was hanging on to her anger, mad at the Coast Guard for not finding Ron. Furious with Ron, however irrationally, for not coming home. Irritated by the well-meaning friends in the living room.

I wish, she told Andrew, that they would all just go home.

Everywhere she looked in the house she saw Ron. They had been coming to Provincetown and Wellfleet since they started dating in 1977. When they decided to buy a vacation house they looked in Truro, halfway between the two towns they enjoyed, and had loved the house at first sight. It had been designed by architect Charlie Zehnder in a spare, modern style with fir paneling in the living room. The location was perfect, a heavily-wooded lot near the end of a secluded sandy road.

It had been a bit small, so after they bought it Ron and Marsha added a few bedrooms and the large tiled entryway. The main bathroom had just been finished a few days earlier. Marsha wondered if Ron would ever get to see it. She had kept the giant sunken tub which Ron loved, and replaced the sliding doors to the deck with glass block and a clear glass panel. From there, Marsha could look out toward the Sagamore Bridge. On clear days, she would have been able to watch Ron's plane cross Cape Cod Bay.

Instead, all she saw was the empty space he had left. She had married him on the spur of the moment in front of a justice of the peace in East Hampton 21 years ago, and stepped into a life full of variety and love. If he were here, Marsha thought, he would turn the roomful of moping people into a party and make her laugh.

Late Saturday afternoon the phone rang. Eric answered and called to Marsha to come talk. It was a friend who lived up toward Provincetown, on the Atlantic side of the Cape. The neighbor's voice sounded peppy, he had a little joke for her.

Hey Marsha, I don't know what's going on out here, all these helicopters overhead are really annoying. It's like Ron is buzzing the house or something. Are they flying over by your house?

She was shocked—he didn't know about the search? It was on the front page of the morning paper.

Um, it's the Coast Guard, she said. They're searching for Ron. His plane is missing.

Oh God, Marsha, I'm sorry. I didn't mean... his voice trailed off. Marsha could tell he was mortified. He made an excuse to go and hung up.

Marsha's brother-in-law, Eric Eslinger, had taken over the phones, talking with the Coast Guard and Park Service people. Marsha was thankful for it. Eslinger was the serious type, a geology professor with brown hair and a beard. He took careful notes every time someone called, and explained it all to her later.

What Eric explained to Marsha late Saturday night was that the Coast Guard had suspended the search for Ron.

Crews had been out all day, Eric said. The helicopters, boats and foot patrols flowed back and forth along the ever-lengthening lines of their search patterns, finding nothing. They had scanned the water on both sides of the hook and Provincetown Harbor. Search teams had walked the dunes of Race Point, peering under the trees and shrubs along the shoreline. The general feeling among the rescue teams, Eric concluded, was that the plane was either buried deeply in the under-brush, or if it had gone into the ocean it crashed at some distant location or sank before rescue crews arrived on the scene.

The explanations that Eric passed along made sense, the survival time and all, but to Marsha it still didn't feel right because she didn't have any proof one way or the other. She was torn by the uncertainty, by not knowing what decisions she should be making or what her future held. Was there a chance that her husband would come back, would be found shivering under some dune tree? Or was he gone, never to return?

Marsha slept roughly on Saturday night, tossing between hope and despair. Where was Ron? What was he doing? An answer, any answer, would be a relief.

On Sunday she woke up and decided to press for more information from people in a position to know. Could Ron still be alive? She called the Coast Guard men in Boston and Woods Hole whose names Eric had written down.

She asked the question right out, daring them to answer honestly: Is there any chance that my husband will be coming back?

They had all responded in the same way, with varying degrees of hedging: No, we don't think he is still alive. If we did, we would still be searching.

They explained, as Eric had, that the search and rescue mission had been converted to "recovery." That meant they thought Ron had not survived. Would she like to continue the effort? There was a man, Mike somebody, who she could hire for marine salvage. He had called the Coast Guard to leave his number for her.

She couldn't decide about the salvage. If Ron were dead, there wasn't much point in hauling up an airplane wreck—what would she do with that? But on the other hand, if the wreck held Ron's body... well, then she would have a definite answer, and could say goodbye.

It seemed to Marsha that the Coast Guard should look for the plane. The radar track showed where it had gone down, they had the cutter out there. Why didn't they just send divers down to get the wreck? She decided to push them to get the plane, to insist that they do something right after fumbling around on the rescue mission.

The promised cutter from Virginia, the one with sonar that the New York representative had talked about, never materialized. All those promises, that concern in the political aide's voice, it had all amounted to nothing. What difference did it make now, she asked herself.

The people in the house did not give up hope, Marsha noticed. She had decided to accept the worst and grieve, but perhaps hope was helping Andrew through the process more gradually. Eric was particularly dogged in his efforts to gather as much information as possible. On Sunday he had gone out to the airport, carrying a copy of the radar data track of the Grumman, and found Alan Davis and Pete Kacergis at the picnic bench outside the waiting room. They had explained the regulations about shooting approaches and talked about what the weather had been like that night.

Eric, the scientist, was frustrated by the lack of proof. He was unable to accept Ron's fate as fact without more information, without empirical evidence that the plane was not to be found.

I'm organizing a foot search, he announced Sunday afternoon. The Park Service only looked near the beach. I think we should cover the dunes more inland.

Andrew volunteered to go, as did some of the other neighbors who still lingered in the house on Sunday. As the men prepared to leave, Ron's father, Hans, called to Andrew from the couch.

Take two of Ron's cigars with you, he said. You can smoke one with your dad when you find him.

**Chapter 11**

# Swimming

GOT ONE FOR YOU, BOB.

The National Transportation Safety Board field investigator stuck his head into Bob Hancock's office on Monday morning.

The call came in this weekend, the investigator said. I figure it for a limited. Missing Grumman AA-5 in Massachusetts.

Hancock looked up from the large fake-wood desk, cluttered with paperwork. He grabbed a pencil and dug around for a blank sheet of paper.

Okay, whatcha got?

Friday night it was on the ILS into Provincetown and disappeared from radar. Coast Guard searched all weekend and didn't find anything. The Fizz-doh guys have the details, Otto is the one who called.

As the investigator disappeared down the hall, Hancock wrote it all down: Barry Otto, Boston FSDO, the Flight Standards District Office.

A "limited" meant that Hancock would add it to the dozens of current files on his desk, but would not rush out to the site. There wasn't anything to see, yet. No wreckage to tear apart and analyze. Hancock would call Otto in Boston and see if he had collected any eyewitness statements or logbooks. Hopefully the plane itself would turn up in a few days, Hancock thought.

Bob Hancock turned heads. A 56-year-old beefy man with a shaved head is high-profile enough to attract a few second glances. But it was the mustache that made people stare. Hancock's trademark facial hair was almost completely white, and long over his upper lip. It was thick with wax, the sides pulled straight out sideways and flattened, like a little propeller above his lip. The effect was that he seemed to be slightly smiling most of the time. Age had created a crinkle around his sky-blue eyes.

Six other field investigators worked in the nondescript square office building that housed the Parsippany, New Jersey office, headquarters of the New York region. After 16 years there, Hancock had seniority. His workplace was one of the six aviation-related NTSB regions scattered across the country. Anytime an airplane scraped, bumped, bent or bored in for whatever reason, the National Transportation Safety Board was the government agency charged with finding out how it happened. Other arms of the organization investigated major highway, railway, marine and pipeline accidents.

There are about 2,000 small aircraft accidents each year, and New York handled about 350 of those. The most common causes were not mechanical, but operational. Non-instrument-rated pilots flew into instrument conditions and got disoriented. Pilots turned too steeply on landing, stalling and spinning the plane into the ground. Sometimes the pilot lost control for no apparent reason. These causes all fell under "Pilot Error," a term popular among pilots. But one the NTSB did not itself use because it wasn't very specific. It meant that the plane was operating properly, but somehow the pilot had screwed up.

Bob Hancock reached across his desk for the phone and dialed Boston.

Marie was talking to her, Marsha realized. What had she said? Something about Andrew?

I'm so sorry I woke Andrew up early Saturday morning, Marie was saying.

I called the house to find out if it were really true, I had seen the news and just couldn't believe it. Andrew said yes and that he had been up most of the night. I felt so bad for waking him up.

It was Monday morning. Marie Newman, the bookkeeper for Ron's law firm, had driven from Albany on Sunday night, through the driving rain that still had not stopped. This morning she was in the kitchen, Marsha had come out of her bedroom to eat. More baked ziti. Everyone seemed to be bringing baked ziti.

Marsha's dark hair was wild around her face. She hadn't exactly been giving it loving attention over the past few days. Hair she could ignore, but her hunger and her tiredness were more insistent. She was sleeping better now, her sister Trudy still in the bed, but the bags under her eyes were pronounced.

As Marsha spooned out the pasta, Marie kept talking.

Someone actually asked me if Ron had disappeared! They made it sound very mysterious, as if Ron had taken a bag of money and flown south. I said, "Don't be ridiculous."

The house was still filled with neighbors from Truro. Friends who would normally be meeting Ron to play tennis now walked through the kitchen and said kind, mournful things about him. People from Albany were trickling in. Marie had brought along the two other lawyers who worked in Ron's office.

Ron had been missing now for three days and Marsha was beginning to accept the fact that he was not going to call her to pick him up, or walk through the door with some wild story. She was beginning to think less about him and more about his body. She wondered whether or not it would be found so that she could see him, find out what happened, and say goodbye.

The only person who seemed to hold bottomless hope that Ron would be found alive was Eric Eslinger. He kept organizing the foot searches of Race Point, taking crews of volunteers with him to walk the dunes. Marsha did not go. Although she wanted him found, she did not want to be the one to discover Ron's body. She made sure that when Andrew went, someone was devoted to keeping a close eye on him, in case he might stumble upon the wreckage himself and break down.

She thought of her own father, dead at age 49, when Marsha was 11. She could not escape the coincidence that Ron had turned 49 in June. Things would not be as difficult for Andrew, she hoped. He was older, at 18, and they were better off financially than Marsha's family had been. She hadn't seen a speck of spending money until she graduated high school, earned her beautician's license and went to work.

She thought of Andrew. He was not a talker like his mother. He had always been quiet, a characteristic complicated lately by an adolescent's tendency to speak in one-word sentences. When they talked, it was about Ron. The two people who knew him best, sharing stories.

Mom, he had said one night. I just keep wishing I had been there. I could have helped. I'm a real strong swimmer.

Marsha held him and didn't say what she really thought, which was that she would have lost both of them, and that would have killed her.

She looked around the bedroom, at the towels hung over the naked windows. Ron had been bringing the window shades in the plane. Everything in the house screamed out for him. She could feel his absence hurt, physically hurt, deep in her gut. It would have been less painful if on Friday night someone had walked up to her and hacked her arm off.

Ron was not around to simply *be*. Suddenly he was just a memory, a handful of photographs in the album. He was reduced to being a construct of people's reminiscences. He was not here to contradict them by being the whole person, the unpredictable mix of impulses and insights—thoughtful and devilish, generous and infuriating. You didn't know him, she wanted to shout at the crowd in the house. You only knew a part of him, each of you, and now he is frozen as just that part. He was more than that, he was everything to me, my best friend for over twenty years and I don't know how to live without him.

Each day that followed—Sunday had melted into Monday which turned into Tuesday—was nothing but another formless morning to wake up and realize again that Ron was not coming home. People with long faces drifted in and out of the living room. Eric took some of the men out to walk the dunes. Newspaper reporters rang the house— How did Marsha feel now that the search was called off? No comment. The Coast Guard called, Eric talked to them. Events ran together, without much to distinguish one from the other.

Until Wednesday, five days after Ron disappeared. Eric answered the phone.

Oh really? He looked up as Marsha came out of the bedroom.

Are you sure? Eric scribbled on his notepad. Okay, yes, someone will be down there right away. He hung up.

Animal Control, he said. They found Theo yesterday afternoon washed up on the beach near Sandwich. It's him, they checked his tags. If you want, Eric continued, Trudy and I can stop by there on our way back to Albany.

Marsha roused herself: No, I want to see the puppy. I'll go.

Oh Marsha, do you think that's a good idea? Voices raised in the living room: She shouldn't have to do that! Let someone else go. Eric, you go!

The arguments swirled around her, pushing her back. The crowd had thinned a bit over the past few days but there were still plenty of people who wanted to protect her.

I'm going, Marsha insisted. I need to know. What were they trying to protect her from? Ron was dead, and that horror she had already embraced. How much worse could it be to see the dog? She needed tangible proof that the whole awful thing had really happened. A concrete image to latch onto each morning as she woke up and blearily sorted through the hazy nightmare.

It was decided that a neighbor would drive Marsha. Eric and Trudy would go along, then leave from Sandwich for New York.

In the car, Marsha also began to think about returning to Albany. There was the law firm to think about. Marie Newman and the two lawyers were leaving tomorrow morning. Ron's estate loomed—the will, the law firm, the trusts and investments. A new and dreadful life filled with paperwork. She did not talk much during the 10-minute drive.

At the animal control center, the dog looked terrible. Marsha had known he would not be pretty, but it was still a stark contrast to the last time she had seen him, brown and fluffy, his silken fur puffed out around his body.

Now he was frozen stiff from the storage cooler and stuck in a plastic garbage bag, his fur matted and sandy. Theodore T. Bear had been the proud offspring of champion Chows. Ron had brought him home just a few months ago, and since then Theo had been his constant companion.

Marsha stared at the dog's hind legs, protruding from the bag, as the animal control person talked. No external signs of injury, the control officer was saying.

No sign of injury? Did the dog drown? And if the dog drowned . . . suddenly it was as Marsha had imagined it: Ron having some sort of mechanical trouble or something. Gliding the plane down on the waves, sliding the canopy open and jumping out. Swimming.

Outside, as she waved goodbye to Eric and Trudy, Marsha's mind raced. Swimming, she thought. Ron had always said that if he ever had to ditch over water, he would just glide the plane down, get out and wait to be rescued.

Marsha asked her neighbor to drive the half hour to the Coast Guard Group at Woods Hole. She wanted to talk to Captain Webster in person.

Barry Otto at the Boston FAA office had said something interesting over the phone. One of the guys from the FSDO in Bedford, Massachusetts knew this plane. He had never met the pilot, but had ramp-checked the Grumman a month earlier, when he walked past it tied down on the ramp at Provincetown. He had chosen it at random for a thorough visual inspection, and found a few problems. He was faxing over a copy of the Aircraft Condition Notice.

Good, thought Hancock. Some hard facts on the accident. He was curious to see what the problems had been, if they were something he should look into further.

When people asked Bob Hancock how he could possibly bear what he did for a living, how he could stand the grisly visions he had seen, he explained about the safety recommendations. Digging through the details and finding something wrong with an airplane system or flight procedure, then submitting it to the FAA to be corrected, that's what an NTSB job was about. That was stuff that would save lives. Hancock submitted more recommendations than any of the other investigators in the region.

Like the error he found on an aviation chart—a heliport's elevation was off by 40 feet. That had been corrected. Or the shoulder harnesses on Piper Malibus, which Hancock had discovered broke on significant impact. Piper put out a repair notice and kit, and also modified their assembly line to correct the problem.

A few years earlier a pilot had survived a crash, but died of hypothermia when search crews took too long to find him. His ELT had been turned off and did not send a signal on impact. Hancock had himself gone to the aircraft charter company, who had gone along with his recommendation to add an ELT check to their preflight checklist.

Hancock was particularly proud of teasing apart the cause of the fire in the rear of a Cessna Citation. He had reproduced the accident scenario and discovered that the fuel and hydraulic lines were too close to the electricals, which arced a spark and caused the fire. The Board faulted both Cessna, for not setting the lines further apart, and the FAA, for failing to catch it while overseeing the production facility.

Changes like that justified the late hours, the travel, the slogging through muddy crash sites to find that one important detail, the life-threatening problem that could be fixed.

Not every accident resulted in a recommendation, of course, even with Bob Hancock bulldoggedly digging around. Fortunately the job itself was inherently interesting because no two accidents were ever the same. Hancock also liked the independence. The field offices were left to run things their own way, without Washington breathing down their necks. The desk jockeys in Washington thought of the field investigators as cowboys.

The New Jersey office investigators worked in two teams of four, on rotation for three weeks at a time. When an accident came in, the investigator in the number one position took it, then number two moved up. If there were more than four accidents during the three weeks, the second team stepped in. Each person ended up handling just over 40 limited and about 8 field investigations per year.

At any given moment, Hancock was working 15–20 other accidents in varying stages of the process: rounding up paperwork, performing a field exam, filing the report and any recommendations, then waiting for the Board's final conclusion. He worked closely with the Federal Aviation Administration.

FAA officials act as the police for aviation, and are accordingly feared and loathed by pilots, mechanics and airlines. These police have an infamous conflict of interest. The Administration is charged by the government with both supporting and regulating aviation. Pilots have an old joke about the conflict, "Hi, I'm from the FAA and I'm here to help you." Yeah, right. Help me lose my license, you mean.

Imagine the highway patrol being directed to both support and regulate interstate traffic. Hurried drivers would push for higher speed limits, a change that would support traffic by moving more trucks and cars through the system. But faster traffic would create some nasty accidents, which would cry out for lower speed limit regulation. What's a confused officer to do after pulling someone over—make the driver happy or save his life?

NTSB investigators joke that their budget would not run the FAA for more than eight hours. It is true that the FAA is better funded and has more personnel in the Flight Standards Department Offices around the country. FAA officials usually reach an accident site first and start rounding up witness statements and certification paperwork. In some accidents, mostly non-fatals, they are the only ones who show up.

Investigations are always overseen by an NTSB desk, but sometimes the FAA rep is the one actually poking at the wreck.

The NTSB's tiny budget forces it to prioritize. At the top of the list are accidents in the types of planes in which lots of innocent fare-paying passengers ride. They are the rarest, but they grab headlines. Preventing future accidents there could save thousands of lives, and so those investigations get the most resources. Next come air charter operations, smaller planes but also carrying passengers. Hancock worked both of those, but more often he got the commonest type of aircraft accident—a lone pilot, maybe with family or friends riding along, crashing a small, general-aviation airplane. Finding a safety recommendation there—the seat belt in the Piper, for example—could still save lives, just not as many.

When calls came in to the NTSB, the investigator on phone duty made the decision. Would an accident be a "limited," a desk job? Or would it be a field investigation? It depended on whether or not it was fatal, what type of plane, and what the preliminary data was.

In each case, an NTSB investigator filed a "factual report." That summarized just the facts, no conclusions. A supervisor reviewed before sending along to the Board members in Washington. The Board read it and decided on the probable cause of the accident, then released the final report. The Board also forwarded any attached safety recommendations to the FAA.

The FAA might or might not slap the hands of the aircraft charter company or manufacturer involved. The frustrating thing about those recommendations was just that, they were merely recommendations. The NTSB had no power to enforce them.

On Monday morning, Hancock had a dozen other investigations to puzzle over. Like that helicopter that crashed in Pennsylvania last month—it was beginning to look as if the maintenance shop had not kept track of who worked on it and when. That might explain why the number-five cylinder had not been tightened down after repair. Was there a recommendation in there somewhere? Hancock opened the file and started flipping through the helicopter maintenance reports.

At Group Woods Hole on Wednesday, after leaving the Animal Control Center in Sandwich, Marsha seethed as Captain Webster tried to explain how his mission had run. He pulled out his charts and diagrams to illustrate how hard crews had tried to locate the target. William "Russ" Webster was a handsome man, she thought, in a West Point kind of way. Chiseled, erect, controlled, with carefully groomed silver hair. He had good manners. He asked if she wanted a sandwich when he noticed her shaking. But he was very formal and, Marsha thought, cold. Icy.

He showed Marsha a printout that plotted the search pattern in bright green, red and blue overlaid on a map of the hook. The parallel lines represented boats, he explained as he pointed out the large ocean-based grids. The large triangles had been the helicopter. The vivid colors surrounded the Cape's tip, obliterated it on the map. See, he said. We searched both land and sea thoroughly.

Next he pulled out copies of pages from the Coast Guard Manual that explained about hypothermia and survival ratings. In water that cold, survival rates are six, maybe eight hours, he said. We went beyond our required time, he explained. We searched for 22 hours, for most of Saturday.

Marsha lost it: Saturday! What use was searching on Saturday! What about Friday night?

She couldn't help herself; her anger, propelled by grief, overwhelmed her as she practically screamed at the man. He was so pompous and pleased with his charts and graphs. By Saturday, she said, Ron had been beyond saving! Wasn't the most important part of a rescue to get there quickly? As her voice got louder, Webster turned away, showing the charts to the neighbor who had driven Marsha to the station. He probably thought she was hysterical. Well, okay, maybe she was! And why not? None of the graphs and reports that Webster waved around impressed Marsha. None of them explained why it took two hours—two long, cold, rainy hours!—for the Coast Guard to reach the crash site.

Marsha spent a bad night alone in the bed and woke up Thursday morning ready to leave the Cape. They would never find Ron's body, she decided. The tides and the graveyard of shipwrecks had gotten hold of him. Or the tangled scrub of dune vegetation. It was fortunate in a way, she told herself. No grisly scene at the coroner's office. No more photographs in the newspapers. No horrible vision stuck in her head. Ron just went off one day and never came back. It was a good argument, but it annoyed Marsha that she would never know for sure what happened. She still wanted answers, for herself and for Andrew.

Her brother drove her back. They made it into Albany just in time for the afternoon meeting at the law firm. The lawyers were to discuss the liquidation of the firm, tearing apart what Ron had spent years nurturing and growing into success. Her husband was truly gone, Marsha realized. If the law firm was dissolving then Ron wasn't coming back.

The two lawyers and secretaries who had worked with Ron were there in the conference room with the tall gilt-framed mirrors. Marsha looked around the room and saw Ron's restoration work in the carefully-chosen paint, the period chairs on which everyone sat. The familiar faces of people who had worked so hard alongside her husband. Now it was over, for all of them. She waited to discuss the dismantling of her husband's dream.

One of the lawyers was talking about the clients, about drafting some sort of form for them to sign when they received their files. Suddenly, Marie stuck her head through the doorway. She motioned to Marsha, her face stricken, her words rushed.

It's Eric; you have to speak to him.

Marsha knew it had to be something out on the Cape. Eric would never have interrupted the meeting otherwise. Had they found Ron? A witness? A piece of the wreck? Her stomach tumbled as her thoughts ran through the possible options, jittering between expectations of good news and bad. Was the nightmare getting better or worse? Heaven or hell?

The conference room door clicked behind her as she picked up the receiver and asked in a shaky voice, What is it? She waited, her insides churning. How much more of this could she take?

Eric's voice was calm: Marsha, they found Ron's body today on Cahoon Hollow Beach.

So it was not as simple as good versus bad, Marsha realized. This news was both. Her legs collapsed.

Somehow, probably by her brother's help, she got home and heard the details. Ron's body floating in the shallow water at the beach, spotted by a beachcomber who called the Fire Department. They found his wallet, got Eric's number from the Coast Guard.

She wanted to go out to the Cape, to see her husband's body and know that it was all true. But nobody offered to drive her, and when she asked, Marsha was exhausted enough to listen to the arguments. No reason to go all the way out there for a terrible sight. The doctor would do a positive identification.

The medical examiner could not identify him after so long in the water. He asked for dental records. Ron's dentist, a family friend and also a pilot, was horrified by the grisly request. But he dutifully sent the film by courier out to Pocasset, and the identification was made: It was Ron.

It would be days before they fixed the cause of death: hypothermia and drowning, according to the autopsy. But as soon as she got the phone call, Marsha already knew. Swimming, she thought. He was swimming out there while the damned Coast Guard sat around, oblivious.

Why else would he and Theo have washed up on opposite sides of Cape Cod's slender arm, miles from each other? With the winds out of the north that night, the waves would have been pushing into the bay. The tides would have worked for a few days, zig-zagging anything floating or on the bottom, until it worked its way to the bay shore. That's where the dog was found.

To make it to the ocean side, someone would have had to swim against the waves to reach the Atlantic current. It swept south along the ocean side of the Cape, pushing down past Cahoon Hollow Beach, where Ron's body was found.

**Chapter 12** ———————

# The Paper Trail

MARSHA DECIDED to have a Jewish service. Ron had always been enthusiastic about the bits of the faith that she brought to the family—the Hanukah prayer, Andrew's Bar Mitzvah. Not that they had gone overboard. For Ron's memorial service she chose a reformed rabbi, and a funeral parlor instead of a synagogue. She did not have much time after Ron's body was found on Thursday.

In a traditional Jewish funeral, the body is buried within 24 hours. It is not embalmed. All bodies are wrapped in simple white shrouds, symbolizing that everyone in the cemetery is equal. Burial is in a wooden box with no nails or other metal parts. Ron's case, however, presented a bit of a problem. The 24-hour limit had passed, and the body was too decomposed to ship to Albany without embalming.

Marsha decided on cremation, and the rabbi agreed. But it could not be scheduled until Monday because of the autopsy. The service on Sunday would be a memorial, a service without the body.

Planning the service gave Marsha something to do, and it was something for Ron. It brought him back to her, in a way. Each choice she made, including planning the gathering back at the house afterwards, made her feel as if she and Ron were together again. She was doing what she had always done: arranging the houses, the trips and parties for Ron.

151

The service began shortly before noon on October 18, a sunny Sunday that was brisk but not cold enough yet for overcoats. Marsha arrived early and was sitting in the front row with her brother and sister, half-paying attention. Something happened in the back, some noise or other, and she turned to look. The place was packed.

The large room at Levine Memorial Chapel seated 240. All the chairs were filled and people spilled out into the aisles, through the door. She saw friends, colleagues, many people she didn't even know.

A notice had run in the Albany paper. That had attracted some of the colleagues whom Marsha had not met. The notice asked people to donate to a cause Ron had been championing, "Save the Pine Bush." It was an area west of Albany made up of stabilized sand dunes—much like Cape Cod—which had been protected from development. Ron had fought to save the land because in the dunes grew a flower, a particular lupine, which was the sole food for the larvae of the endangered Karner blue butterfly.

Marsha could see Ron's cousin Hugo, who had flown in from the Netherlands. Ron's middle name was Hugo. Both cousins had been named after their paternal grandfather, a famous labor attorney who escaped the holocaust and resettled in Holland. An institute at the University of Amsterdam had been named for him and his pioneering method of combining the study of sociology with labor law.

Those who could not fly in had called—old high school friends, distant relatives. Everyone at the service was somber, very serious looking. They were not chatting like everyone at the house had been, Marsha noted. They had accepted the finality of the situation.

The rabbi began to speak, and Marsha turned back to the front. She tried hard to pay attention as he spoke about Ron. Mary Ann Krupsak, the former New York Lieutenant Governor, spoke. So did Ron's aunt, the one who had been in a concentration camp during the war, and had taken her first airplane ride with Ron out to the Cape years ago. One of Ron's friends, and then a colleague took the podium. They each spoke with feeling. The kind words were all blurry to Marsha, everything running together.

The service lasted for about an hour, and she hardly remembered a word.

Honestly, although it sometimes got gruesome, Hancock liked being in the field a heck of a lot better than shuffling paperwork. He had been out on hundreds of investigations, from Virginia to Maine, Kentucky to New Jersey. They were each different, each interesting.

Things moved quickly on a launch. The pager would go off at 2:00 A.M., or just when you sat down to dinner or got into the shower. Whichever investigator had phone duty would hand out the details, then pass along the phone number of the local police. Call them, secure the crash site, hop in the car or get a flight out there.

A site could be anywhere. Hancock had recently worked one in the East River in New York City. Or the wreck might lie on the side of a mountain in Tennessee, accessible by a two-hour hike through dense woods. Many were off the end of a runway, a scorched hole poked into a soybean or corn field.

The first thing you noticed on the walk out there, hauling the heavy tool kits and biohazard bags, was the stench. The unnatural odor suddenly sharp in the woods—the stink of dripping gasoline, burning seat cushions, sometimes cooked flesh. Jet crashes smelled like the kerosene fuel they burned. Propeller airplanes reeked of low-lead gasoline. The smell meant the site was getting close.

Then things began to look surreal. Strange fruit swinging from the nearby trees—a seat back, a shoe or a large curl of white metal. Trenches carved into the muddy ground. Thousands of bits of metal, fiberglass, Plexiglas and fabric making a glittering pathway, leading to the plane.

Often it did not look much like a plane. It may have left most of itself behind on the trail that ended at the engine. Or it may have hidden. Sometimes the whole damned thing dove right into the ground, tunneling and compressing until the back end of the engine was six feet under and the investigator had to dig it out.

You had to be prepared for anything: to tear the engine down and run a thumb-compression check while standing ankle-deep in a muddy field, in the rain; to cut the crunched metal airframe apart in order to reach the instrument panel; to saw an engine from its thick metal mounts.

The bodies, or what was left of them, were tough to take at first. Almost nobody walked away when a small plane hit the ground, and cockpits were often covered with sticky blood. Hands and feet, or worse, were sometimes scattered along the debris path.

The police or coroner handled the larger parts, or at least covered them up. But there was always plenty left. Enough to attract the flies.

153

Investigators wore rubber gloves to handle the gored instruments and tried not to think too much about someone's beloved being smeared all over the airplane. After a while most investigators learned to accept it as part of the job, and to think of the blood as just a bunch of red stuff that got in the way of the examination.

The debris field held the most useful evidence of the investigation. Anyone standing at a site could see where the plane tunneled through trees, touched the ground and slid. An experienced investigator could tell by the bits whether the plane had been level, upside down or in a turn. Key marks on the propeller could indicate whether or not it had been turning at impact, powered by a running engine.

But those were conclusions, requiring an investigator to make assumptions about what might or might not have been happening just before impact. That was outside the scope of the NTSB. An investigator was to gather facts about the accident. Period. Not to conclude that the engine was running as the plane bored in, but to state that "witnesses claimed to hear engine noise" and "propeller tips were curled backwards." NTSB reports are filled with facts and no conjecture, to the extreme point of reporting that fuel tanks contained, not blue low-lead aviation fuel but "a blue liquid similar to aviation grade gasoline."

Without a wreck, without a site, Hancock had to get his facts on the Grumman somewhere else. It would be a story told not through the airplane, but through paperwork. In the weeks following the accident, Hancock spent a lot of time on the telephone, backtracking along the plane's paper trail. He began by rounding up the data—Air Traffic Control kept voice and radar tapes for 15 days, then recycled them to make new recordings. After that, the Grumman's flight plan would disappear.

Fortunately for Hancock, pilots and their airplanes trail a wide wake of documentation. Boston Center sent him a copy of the airplane's radar track over Cape Cod Bay. Flight Service sent a weather report for conditions at the time of the accident, and also a transcript of the pilot's conversation with the weather briefer early Friday afternoon, long before the flight took off. Cape Approach and the rest of the radar facilities that had worked the Grumman—Providence, Bradley and Albany departure—sent statements from the controllers who talked to the pilot. Albany tower and ground control sent theirs also, although they were very brief and straightforward. The dialog consisted of: You can take off now. Okay, thanks, bye. Hancock added them to the file, anyway. Another data point for the report.

Hancock called Signature Aviation and requested a copy of the fuel bill. Fuel starvation is a leading cause of small airplane accidents, and it was a useful fact to know that the Grumman took off with full tanks holding 38 gallons. That was enough to fly for over four hours.

The FAA people in Boston dug through their files for copies of the pilot's medical records, his certification information and the airplane's registration data.

Hancock read it all, combing for clues. Pushing paper. Too bad the NTSB could not afford to recover water crashes. Hancock knew that the paperwork might be all he would ever have on this accident, particularly because the plane had gone into the water. Currents and tides spirited away airplanes with alarming speed. It happened off the coast of Cape May, New Jersey. The pilot radioed his position to Air Traffic Control, and several eyewitnesses saw the Cessna 195 dive in. They triangulated its location for the Coast Guard, who arrived within 30 minutes with side-scan sonar. Despite an extensive search the wreckage was never found. Another New Jersey crash involved a Cessna 182 that ditched just offshore in 40 feet of water. Radar data pinpointed the crash site, but FBI divers never located it.

By now, Cape Cod currents had had their way with the Grumman for two weeks. Hancock knew that sand and shifting tides had shoved it around and probably broken it up. The pilot's body had washed up on the Atlantic side, on the other side of the Cape from where the dog's body had been found on the bay side. Who knew where the plane itself was headed?

At the end of Ron Sinzheimer's memorial service, the rabbi gave a reading. It was not what the mourners expected, was not from scripture or some famous poet. It was from Eric Eslinger, written a day earlier when he still thought he might have the emotional wherewithal to speak during the service.

It was supposed to be Ron talking to Marsha, explaining what happened in the airplane. It was unorthodox, smart-alecky and funny. Just like Ron:

So here I was, still on the approach, but I couldn't see *anything* outside—rain was coming down and now Theo was trying to crawl into my lap! I couldn't tell my descent rate. I started looking for the runway but I must have been too far out.

Marsha, wait a minute! Come back! Are you listening to this? All of a sudden, I could see what I thought was water, but that didn't make sense—I should have been seeing the runway! I pulled up a bit but I still couldn't see anything. All of a sudden we went down fast—I don't know what happened. I had no control and we hit hard—look at my head here—this is where I hit the window! I must have been knocked out. The next thing I know my legs are in cold water and Theo is standing on me and licking me in the face. My head was throbbing and my left leg was numb. I tried to look out but couldn't see anything but rain!

I wrapped Theo's leash around my wrist and shoved Theo out and then I went out. We sat on the plane for a few minutes and then left it as it sank. Theo kept trying to climb onto my head. We started to swim, but I was doing all the swimming and Theo was climbing onto me. Marsha, I kid you not!!

I kept hearing a buzzing sound but couldn't figure out what it was. We swam for a while but I couldn't tell which direction to swim. The waves were pouring over us. I was getting tired and then a warm tingling feeling came over me—I decided to drift and wait for help. I laid back and Theo climbed onto my chest. I was thinking of the new tile in our bathroom and how glad you would be to have me see it. I put my arm back and was about to slip under when the buzzing got louder and something grabbed my arm and wouldn't let go. Then, a light hit my eyes but blinded me so I still couldn't see anything.

It was amazing! All of a sudden I was lifted up, Theo still on my chest, and was laid out on a cushion and blankets were on me and I went out. Later, I wakened—I heard a buzzing and a gentle rumbling and the light was soft and I was warm and comfortable and I looked up and into the eyes of this gorgeous woman with full lips and large dark eyes just a few inches from my face and she smiled and said:

"It's about time, Ron. You're OK—I'll take care of you now."

I looked at her and tried to imagine what was happening. Then, slowly, I realized that she was absolutely one of the sexiest women I had ever seen—*I kid you not!* Brunette, short curly hair, long, long legs and cleavage from heaven! And, would you believe—you'll never believe this, Marsha: she was puffing on a cigar and drinking straight out of a Stoli's bottle. I still don't believe it!

She smiled at me, reached over and placed her cigar between my lips and said:

"Wait 'til you see my Harley!"

Marsha, come back! I can tell, you don't believe me! Marsha—there's more! What? We're late for the Spectrum? Are we meeting Trudy? She'll believe me! OK, OK, I'll tell you the rest later, but just listen to this: She was sooo nice to me. She wouldn't tell me why she was out in a low, fast boat in a rainstorm, but it must have been something illegal, because she wouldn't take me to shore. She took me with her—all the way to the Bahamas!! Then arranged a flight home for me and Theo.

I told her all about you. She can't wait to meet you. We're meeting her for a drink next weekend in P-Town. She wants me to represent her if she ever gets caught.

How long did you wait at the Cape? Did anybody find my plane? We'll have to order a new faucet for the bathroom. Where's my keys? Marsha—I'm sorry I didn't call ahead—do you forgive me? I wanted to surprise you! You weren't worried, were you? Wait'll I tell the office! Where's Andrew? He'll never believe this! Andrew!!! Andrew?

As the rabbi read, Marsha could hear the mourners struggling to suppress their laughter. Until the end and that part about Andrew. Marsha thought of Andrew, who in a few weeks would turn 19. He had been a late bloomer, had goofed around far too much at Boston University. He had not yet proven himself to his father, hadn't stood in front of him as a man. Marsha knew that she was a survivor, that she would somehow find a way out of this. But she worried about Andrew.

Bob Hancock sat at his wide desk and shuffled through the stack of papers that documented the Grumman's last flight. He started with the radio transcripts from ATC. The stuff from Albany, Providence and

Bradley was pretty straightforward. The pilot crossed through at such-and-such a time, made his turns, climbs and descents. He had been low-maintenance. No issues.

Cape Approach did have that one thing, when the pilot asked about alternates on the Cape. Was the pilot a little nervous about his chances of getting in? Or was it the opposite—he was relaxed enough to think ahead and use some leisure time during the cruise to plan alternatives to the landing? Whichever it was, Hancock had no idea. He decided to mention it in the report. And also to mention that the pilot never radioed in with any trouble. He would let the Board draw their own conclusions when they read the facts.

The radar data held the most compelling information. Hancock studied the report from Boston Center, examining the path the airplane took through the sky. When a plane follows an ILS approach, it flies a path that looks like a child's slide. The side-to-side track is called the localizer, the descent path is called the glide slope. In the cockpit, the pilot keeps the instrument needles centered to stay on both paths at the same time.

The Grumman crossed Phony, the final approach fix 6.6 miles from the runway, at 1,800 feet instead of the 2,000 listed on the approach plate instructions. It then began a standard 500 feet-per-minute descent, which was about when Cape Approach lost it on radar. The descent continued, just as it should have, but because the plane started out 200 feet low, it stayed about 200 feet below the glide slope. By itself, that's not a problem when there is nothing but flat ocean underneath. There wouldn't be anything to hit on the descent, and the plane would just reach the decision height a few seconds early and level off.

Then, about four miles from the runway, something happened. The Grumman suddenly steepened its descent, heading down at twice the rate as before—1000 feet per minute. It dropped from 900 feet to 700, then 500 and 400. Within 12 seconds it dove from 400 feet to 100, a rate of 1,500 feet per minute. Maybe the airplane stopped developing power, Hancock thought. Did the engine stop? Did a cylinder fail, reducing power? Did one of the fuel tanks run dry? Did the pilot panic and lose control of the plane?

Probably not the panic. Hancock noticed that during the descent, the airplane stayed on the localizer path. Although the plane was diving, there was almost no side-to-side deviation as the plane stayed on track, was not meandering around in confused circles. It looked as if things were at least partly under control.

Until that last drop. At 400 feet, the plane was two degrees left of the localizer. Not more than a few hundred feet, close enough that it was still on the path. But it was the furthest it had deviated on the approach. The drift to the left continued over the next 12 seconds. The distance increased to 2.59 degrees as the plane dropped to 100 feet on the next radar hit. The plane was trending toward disorder, away from the localizer on a too-steep descent.

Then, whatever happened stopped. The pilot corrected the flight path. By the last radar hit, the plane had leveled off at 100 feet and had moved back to the right, toward the center of the localizer path.

What happened? Fuel problem? Engine failure? Hancock would never know unless he could look at the wreck, test the cylinders, check the fuel lines and tanks. He studied the radar data again to see what facts would be useful to include in the report.

The plane leveled off, but 100 feet was too low. The pilot was supposed to descend below the decision height of 208 feet only if the runway environment—lights or threshold, for example—were in sight and the plane were committed to landing. When it descended to 100 feet, the Grumman was still about three miles from the airport.

Could the pilot have glimpsed the runway lights?

Hancock put the radar chart down and picked up the weather data printout for Provincetown. The weather that Friday night was all over the place. The ceilings were up, down, and back up again from a few hundred to a few thousand feet. Visibilities ranged from a few miles to almost nothing. The winds twisted all around the compass within a few hours, ending up out of the north by evening as the front camped on the coastline, swirling rain and winds over the shore.

Hancock had pegged the accident at 7:44 P.M. EDT, one minute after the last radar hit on the airplane. Pinpointing Provincetown weather at that exact time was a problem because of the automated weather system. It reported at 14 minutes and 54 minutes after the hour. At 7:14, visibility was two miles with a broken layer of clouds at 1,300 feet. In that weather, the pilot could have come out of the clouds and seen the runway lights, descending to the airport.

But by 7:54 the clouds had closed into a solid layer at 200 feet, right at the decision height. Visibilities dropped to three-quarters of a mile, the minimum on the approach plate. Hancock wondered if perhaps these low conditions had closed in earlier, say by 7:37 as the Grumman was cleared for the approach?

He picked up the phone, dialed Cape Air's main operations center at Hyannis and asked for Pete Kacergis.

He'll be landing here in a few minutes, the desk clerk said. Want me to have him call you?

Yes, Hancock did. He left his number, hung up and opened a new file on his desktop computer: Summary of Telephone Interview. Pete Kacergis, Cape Air.

A minute later, the phone rang. Kacergis was between flights, he had about ten minutes to talk during the turnaround.

Hancock asked Kacergis about the runway lights. Did he remember whether or not they were on?

Yes, Kacergis said. I keyed the mike myself when Cape Approach told me someone was inbound. I taxied to the runup area, shut down the engines and waited.

How about the weather? Hancock didn't tell Kacergis about the two miles versus three-quarters. Just asked him what he remembered.

I remember it was pretty bad out there, Kacergis said. I could see a glow from the lights in town, about three miles to the south. But I couldn't see the lighthouse from the end of the runway. Never saw or heard the airplane either.

Hancock looked at his map. How far away is that lighthouse, about a mile?

Yeah, a mile, Kacergis said. I remember the ceiling about a hundred feet. It was that low when I took off after the accident.

Thanks, Hancock said. Kacergis had to go, had to run the next load of passengers out to Boston. He hung up.

Okay, Kacergis had seen the glow of lights from the city. On the map that was two or three miles away. But he had not seen the lighthouse, a mile away. A glow of lights did not count as good, sharp visibility, Hancock decided, and went with the lower weather. He marked it on the report: 200 feet and three-quarters of a mile at the time of accident.

The FAA had copies of all the medical records, pilot's licensing records. Pretty dry stuff. Pilot was 6′2″ at 175 lbs, brown hair, brown eyes. No meds, no heart trouble. He was a fit 49-year-old who earned his glider license in October 1978, pilot's license in August 1980, and instrument rating in November 1985.

It was all up-to-date. Sinzheimer had a valid medical, had passed his most recent one in May with no notations or restrictions, did not even have to wear glasses. His license was current.

Hancock fingered the files, and noticed something interesting. On his medical form Sinzheimer had listed a total of 1,400 hours, but none in the past six months. He hadn't flown in the six months before May? At all? What about afterwards? Had this flight out to Provincetown been his first in 11 months? There was no way to tell. Nobody tracks those hours except the pilots themselves, in their logbooks, which are often carried along in the airplanes. Hancock wanted to know how much flight time Sinzheimer had in that Grumman, and how much time in last 30 and 90 days. Was the guy current or was he rusty?

What did not show up in Hancock's paperwork was that Sinzheimer had sold his Mooney to a friend in the fall of 1994 and quit flying for three summers. By May, he had been out of the cockpit a lot longer than just the six months the FAA medical form asked about.

Hancock knew that many pilots earn a license but then life gets in the way. No time to fly, until suddenly there is a trip to take. The pilot dusts off those flight skills, makes the trip, lands, and feels confident again. Then a long dry spell, a month or two, and another trip. This can go on for years of smooth, uneventful flights.

But one day, the flight gets complicated. Pilots who are proficient can handle higher workloads, but the rusty pilot reacts slowly as events pile up: Bad weather worsens, a controller changes the routing, crabby passengers ask questions and complain about the bumpy ride. Maybe the airplane is a rental, with some new equipment to get used to. It takes forever to tune out the distractions and focus on what the instruments say. The pilot starts second-guessing, fights to remember key details as time and air run out.

To keep pilots current, the FAA mandates minimum flight requirements—six instrument approaches in the past six months, for example. Many pilots struggle to keep up with just these basics. They fall out of currency and have to fly check rides with instructors to become legal pilots again.

That had been a factor on the other accident on Cape Cod that Hancock had worked. A month earlier another Grumman had stalled and crashed while going around from an aborted landing in Chatham on a windy day. It was a limited—no injuries—so the NTSB did not launch. Instead the FAA rep interviewed the pilot, who had gotten his license just a month earlier. He had logged 75 total hours and only 12 of those in the Grumman. Hancock included those little details in the report, and the Board ended up citing the pilot's lack of experience in their probable cause.

Would it be a factor for this Grumman? Hancock did not have a pilot to interview. He could only hope to recover the logbook, somehow.

Sinzheimer's little Grumman generated a lot of paperwork. Built in 1976, at a time when small aircraft manufacturing was in its heyday, the Grumman Traveler was a sturdy, basic airplane.

It was a lucky little plane. Although it was a good trainer, with its fixed landing gear, fixed-pitch propeller, and small engine, this one had not done flight school time. That could wear a plane out, being jerked around by inexperienced students who stressed the engine by throttling back and forth on endless touch-and-goes. It spent its first two years at a leasing company, which probably rented it out to certified pilots, not students. After 1979 the Grumman belonged to private owners.

The plane spent six years in Georgia, a year in Arkansas, then was sold to a doctor in Louisiana in 1986. He flew it for four years, upgraded the navigational radios, and added an exhaust gas temperature kit (for engine monitoring) in 1988.

From there it made a brief hop back to Georgia, and then up to Maine where Richard Agostin bought it. Agostin was a crusty old-timer who had been flying since the 1940s—helicopters, planes, seaplanes. He had an IFR rating but did not fly the Grumman in the clouds much. Too many mountains near the tiny town of Oquossoc. Besides, by then the plane had a few squawks which Agostin did not bother fixing. That problem with the ADF radio dial, it tended to slip as you were trying to select a frequency. He did not have the IFR-required system check done at the annual (the pitot-static system which drives most of the key gauges). Flying VFR, out where you could see the ground and horizon, you did not need IFR-quality instrumentation. While Agostin owned it, the Grumman was legal, but not for instrument flying.

Agostin usually took the plane to Pete Conner in Plymouth, Massachusetts for maintenance. Then he could visit his girlfriend who lived nearby. In 1992, Conner installed a modification to the nose of the plane, splitting the cowling that covered the lower part of the engine. With the mod, you could get at the engine to work on the alternator, say, without having to take the propeller off to remove the cowling. That saved Agostin a little money on Conner's labor costs.

Agostin flew the Grumman around Maine for eight years. And then its engine manufacturer, Textron Lycoming, came out with a regulation to inspect the crankshaft on the Grumman's engine. That required a major overhaul at high expense. The insurance was due at the same time. Rather than go broke, Agostin decided to sell. He had been hanging around Plymouth for years, so he already knew Steve Vosburgh, the broker at Plymouth Aircraft Sales.

Vosburgh bought the plane right away. Just after Agostin sold, Lycoming lifted the engine-inspection requirement. But it turned out to be just as well that Agostin sold when he did, because six months later he had a heart attack and successful five-way bypass surgery. No flying for a while.

So the Grumman came to Plymouth. Because manufacturing of new planes had tapered off since the early 1980s, well-kept used ones appreciated in value. The Grumman sold for $14,000 in 1980. Steve Vosburgh bought it for $20,000 in 1989, updated it to be instrument-current, and sold it to Sinzheimer a few weeks later for $25,000.

When Sinzheimer bought it, the Grumman was 22 years old and had flown for 2,365 hours, about a hundred hours a year—low time for a plane that age. The engine had been overhauled a few years earlier. It had only flown 445 hours since then and could go another 1,555 before it would have to be overhauled again.

To stay airworthy, every year N7100L had its requisite annual inspection, sort of like an automobile inspection on steroids. An FAA-certified mechanic spent about a week examining the entire airplane—removing panels to test control cables and fuel tanks, replacing spark plugs and other worn engine parts, retiming the engine and testing its compression, testing the control cables. Licensed mechanics signed the aircraft logbooks for every major repair or change that was made.

If Hancock could recover the logbooks, which the family told him were kept in the airplane, he would have an intimate history of the airplane's mechanical systems and airframe. Until then, all he had was the Condition Notice from the Bedford FAA.

When the fax came, Hancock had a look at the items listed on the Grumman's ramp check by the FAA official: "Left aileron has hole in trailing edge. Landing light not secured. Floating in bottom of engine cowl. Hole in right elevator tip."

Holes in two of the control surfaces, and a loose landing light. Well, how big were the holes? Had the plane been fixed before the accident? The FAA guy thought the problems were important enough to mark the plane as unairworthy, requiring a special permit if it were to be flown before repairs were made. Hancock also received a copy of the registered, certified letter that the FSDO had sent the pilot and to the Provincetown airport manager. Sinzheimer's copy had been returned. Nobody signed to receive it.

Pilots know that holes in airplanes don't necessarily make them fall out of the sky. Hundreds of bombers and fighters have landed at their bases full of bullet holes, with shot-up tails and wingtips. The holes made this plane imperfect, certainly, but would they have made it crash? Once again, Hancock needed the wreckage to know.

# Chapter 13

# Fishing for Clues

ON MONDAY, OCTOBER 26, Bob Hancock arrived at the office to a voicemail message from the Coast Guard at Woods Hole. It was both good news and bad: A fishing vessel, the *Chico & Jess*, had snagged his missing airplane in its fishing net. It had pulled the whole thing almost all the way out of the water. But then the net tore and the plane dropped back down the 180 feet to the bottom.

So, Hancock thought. The pilot ditched after all. He went in the water.

The Coast Guard figured Hancock would want to know where the wreck was, but Captain Vicente wasn't telling. He wanted a reward, some insurance money to repair the holes in his net. The Coast Guard had threatened him, telling him he was blocking an active investigation. Vicente stood firm, the officer from Woods Hole explained. Would Hancock please call him?

Hancock called the fisherman. Yes, he understood about the damage. No, he didn't know if there was any insurance money to be had. The pilot's brother-in-law was handling all that. Hancock passed along Eric Eslinger's phone number.

Vicente was never heard from again, but a few hours later Hancock got another message from the Coast Guard at Woods Hole, this one markedly calmer. Another fishing vessel, the *Joan & Tom*, had caught something in its nets. The boat was bringing the pieces to the Coast Guard station at Provincetown. Hancock didn't know what they were, but "pieces" didn't sound like the whole airplane. He was not sure if it would be enough wreckage to be able to examine and determine anything useful.

A few hours later, Hancock got a call from an official at the Massachusetts Aeronautics Commission. He had met the boat at the wharf. The crew had given him the top of the engine cowling, the passenger-side control yoke and the airplane tow bar (used to hook to the nose so a pilot could hand-tow and park the airplane). It did not sound like enough for Hancock to launch. But he asked, just in case. Was there something unusual that he should examine?

Not really, said the official. Well, the metal tubing of the control yoke was bent up at a 90-degree angle.

Something must have hit it on impact, something in the passenger seat. The seat itself? It could have broken off of its two sheet-metal flanges and jammed forward. Luggage? The dog? The bent yoke raised more questions, but there was not enough evidence to answer them. Hancock decided not to go to Provincetown.

One new fact he had was that Sinzheimer had "ditched," making an unplanned landing in water. It is, surprisingly, a highly survivable event when the pilot has advance warning and prepares for it. According to a study of NTSB records by the journal *Aviation Safety*, the ditching survival rate is 90 percent.

That is because the pilot sets the plane down on a relatively flat surface. Even with waves, an ocean is smoother than a mountainside, for example, or clumps of pointed treetops. Or roads and fields edged with power lines and fences. Instructors tell their students that should they be forced to choose between rough terrain and water, take the water.

There are three phases to ditching: the initial phase, the egress phase, and the survival phase. The initial phase involves recognizing the emergency and planning the landing. The key is to land parallel to the waves, flaring the plane into position just at the top of a swell. A wide trough between waves is also good. Radioing for help is an added bonus because rescue crews will launch immediately.

In a retractable-gear airplane, pilots leave the landing gear stowed so that the plane's slick belly can skim along the waves. Fixed-gear aircraft are trickier. If a wheel, or a wing, catches a wave, the plane can cartwheel or nose over. A banged-up airplane tosses its passengers around. Disoriented and injured, they struggle to find the exit.

The most important part of the egress phase is to get out of the plane, and get out quickly. Airplanes do not usually float. Even if one lands intact, it will sink within minutes. Planes are usually well underwater before the passengers get out.

In a best-case scenario, the plane lands upright and remains floating long enough for the passengers to fling open the door and jump out. They swim away from the wreck to avoid being sucked into the vacuum created when the hulk sinks.

Then comes the survival phase. The ditching survival rate found by *Aviation Safety* was 90 percent. But the successful egress rate was 95 percent. That means 5 percent of the people survived the crash only to drown later.

In planning a flight over water, most pilots forget the survival phase. They focus on the ditching itself. After all, that is a pilot's job: Keep flying the plane all the way down, keep thinking, do not give up. Few think about what comes next—life vests or rafts.

Even if they do weigh the risks and benefits of carrying survival gear, the gear rarely wins. Rafts are expensive and heavy. The vests are a hassle, taking up room in an already cramped cockpit. Besides, pilots claim, who would have time to don a life vest in a true emergency? They would be too busy doing their primary job: ditching and egressing. Let the search and rescue teams worry about survival. The problem with this attitude is that it does not factor in the delays that can happen in any rescue launch.

Sinzheimer's plane remained in the 180-foot depths, but Hancock was optimistic about recovering it. Don't worry, the Coast Guard had said. It's in a prime fishing area. One of the fleet will snag it and bring it in.

The whiting that fall had been plentiful for the lucky fisherman who held permits. The Marine Fisheries Division had given out 17 to the Provincetown fishing vessels. The Division was testing a new style of net, an experimental net, and the permit-holders were required to use it. If it worked then everyone who wanted to fish for whiting would have to switch over when the restriction was lifted.

The old nets had dragged the bottom, scraping up the flat flounder and lobster on the sea bed. The holes in the mesh had been small—whiting are about a foot long—and so the net also hauled in squid. Flounder and squid were by-catch which the fisherman threw overboard. Usually the fish were already dead, or died shortly thereafter. A few flounder and squid were not worth the trouble to keep when compared to the tons of whiting a boat could haul in. But the combined New England fleet had been pulling in enough by-catch to make a dent in the population off Cape Cod. Thus the restriction.

The mesh of the new net was a bit larger, with two- to three-inch holes in the nylon filament. Orange ball-shaped floats held up the top of the net and kept it from collapsing on itself. The bottom was edged with a small chain to weight it and keep it steady and straight as the net was pulled through the water. The idea was for it to hover a foot or so off the sandy bottom, above the flounder, and for the mesh to be large enough for squid to escape.

As a fishing boat motored along at about three knots, it paid the net out and let it billow and settle behind. Then the boat dragged the net along for short hauls, maybe ten minutes if the sonar painted the shadow of a big school. The net cut a swath 60 feet high and 80 feet wide. It strained the ocean for everything that lay underwater behind the boat. Ten minutes of trolling in a big school could fill the net, and fisherman were careful not to overdo it. Crushed fish were less valuable at market.

The Marine Fisheries experiment was working. Permit-holders were hauling in whiting and almost nothing else. Fisherman were using the new net, which cost in the neighborhood of $6,000. But the nets earned their keep. A day's haul could earn a fisherman between $2,000 and $10,000.

Which explains why Captain Rodriguez of the *Carla Bee* was not happy when his fishing ended at about 9:00 on the morning of Sunday, November 1, 1998. His whiting net had caught an airplane.

After three weeks of chasing paperwork, Bob Hancock had a wreck. He had no idea what condition it would be in, but the message from NTSB headquarters on Sunday said that Woods Hole believed the fishing vessel had netted the entire plane. Hancock told his wife that he'd be driving up to Provincetown in the afternoon. He spent the morning on the phone, making the usual arrangements for a launch.

First, secure the wreckage. The Coast Guard planned to get it to MacMillan Wharf, the commercial pier in Provincetown Harbor. The harbormaster had garnered a flatbed to tow it wherever Hancock wanted.

That sounded fine, Hancock said. Go ahead and take it out to the airport.

He gave his pager number to the Coast Guard at Woods Hole and hung up after assuring them he would notify the pilot's family.

Now that the Grumman merited a field investigation, Hancock rounded up the official NTSB "parties." He called a couple of guys from the FAA who had been following the case and had already been briefed about the wreck recovery. Hancock also called the official from the Massachusetts Aeronautics Commission who had organized the flight check of Provincetown's ILS in the days after the accident, and had also examined the few parts the *Joan & Tom* had recovered a week earlier.

Normally Hancock would also contact someone from the airframe manufacturer, but the Grumman was an orphan. Its parent, Grumman-American, abandoned the light-airplane business in 1979, and later split into two companies. Gulfstream-American, now simply Gulfstream, built business jets. Northrop Grumman was a defense supplier, making aircraft and surveillance equipment for the military. Nobody from either company cared much why a little legacy airplane had crashed in Provincetown.

The engine manufacturer, however, was a different story. Hancock paged Textron Lycoming in Williamsport, Pennsylvania and got Gregg Erickson. Erickson was one of the company's accident investigators who visited crash sites involving their company's engines—and about 75 percent of them did. Most of the rest belonged to the other major manufacturer, Continental Engines. Erickson worked up to a hundred each year. He was covering the Massachusetts area at the time, and would launch immediately, he told Hancock. He'd catch a flight from his home near Chicago to Boston, then drive out to Provincetown and meet Hancock at the airport Monday morning.

By late afternoon Hancock had notified the parties, eaten lunch, and packed his work clothes—jeans, boots, the navy blue t-shirt with "NTSB" emblazoned on the front and back in bright yellow. He grabbed his blue NTSB hat, in case he would be standing out in the sun.

He called his contact at the pilot's family. The plane was out of the water and in a hangar at Provincetown, he explained to Eric Eslinger. I'm leaving now to go examine it, I'll be back in my office middle of the week. Give me a call then and I should have more information.

Hancock preferred to drive. It was easier to just jump in the Ford Explorer and haul all of his equipment to the site. When he took a commercial flight he first had to spend half an hour or so sorting through his bins full of supplies. The problem was he never knew what he would need until he reached the site. The basics were always the same. The various tool kits full of testing and demolition equipment—wrenches, screwdrivers, hacksaws, pliers, wire cutters, bolt cutters, hammers. Ink pens and notepaper. Half a dozen leather work gloves, half a dozen rubber biohazard gloves. Hand cleaner. But did he need the biohazard bags and full body suits? Goggles? What about the waders—the tall ones or the shorter boot-style? First-aid kits?

At some sites it was impossible to stay clean, to avoid the "HR," or human remains, that covered the crash site. The waders and biohazard suits were a necessity then because the stuff got everywhere. It wasn't like you could just wander over to a sink and wash it off. If it sounded like a wreck would be pretty clean, it might be better to chuck the suits and instead take a bunch of extra work gloves and goggles in case the other guys didn't have any. Was the wreck in a hangar or out in someone's field? Might want some extra hand cleaner.

In his years at the NTSB he had been buying his own tools, building a kit and stocking supplies. He had enough now to fill half a dozen giant Rubbermaid containers that he kept stored in the back of the Explorer. He preferred to just hop in the car, take everything and be prepared.

Along the drive he could think about staging the teardown, and about what section of the plane he wanted to start with. On this accident the best data Hancock had so far was the radar printout. The plane was on the approach, then quickened the descent and leveled off. Engine failure and a restart? Hancock was curious to see what details the engine would reveal. Better get Erickson from Lycoming on that right away, examining the insides of the cylinders for cracks, testing the pistons for compression, checking the fuel filters to see if there was anything that could have blocked fuel flow.

Hancock worried about the condition of the wreckage. It had been on the ocean floor for three weeks, corroding in the salt water. It had been picked up twice and dropped by fishing nets. Who knew how many times it had been snagged and dragged, losing stray bits along the way?

If the plane broke up a lot when it hit the water, there might not be much of it left. Parts would have drifted with the tides and currents. The tow bar, top cowling and passenger control yoke had already been recovered by the *Joan & Tom,* proving that some of the plane had separated from the main fuselage. Hancock wondered if there would even be wings and a tail with the piece he would see tomorrow. They would offer clues about the intensity and direction of impact. Would there be a propeller, with its clues about the engine power? What about the engine itself? That Hancock could open up and test for a multitude of possible problems. He doubted that the fuel lines would still be intact.

Hancock was curious about the details mentioned on the Aircraft Condition Notice that was handed out during the ramp check in Provincetown. Were the holes in the aileron and elevator big enough to compromise the airframe structure? Had they grown bigger since the ramp check? Could the airflow have pushed into them, widening a hole as the plane flew, working the fiberglass or metal loose until the wingtip or end of the tail fell off and the plane dove into the water? And what about the loose landing light, how would that have affected the bottom half of the engine cowling? He wondered if the wings and cowling had been dredged up with the wreckage.

Hancock thought about the transcript of the pilot's conversation with the Cape controller. He had asked about alternate airports, then decided to try Provincetown. How comfortable was he in instrument conditions? And with the Provincetown airport? Perhaps they would find the pilot's logbooks in the airplane.

Pilots log their own hours, on the honor system, but there's not much point in lying. After a few minutes in the cockpit an instructor or check pilot can usually tell if a pilot has exaggerated. At any rate, the total number of hours wasn't as important to Hancock as time logged in the past few months. Like any complicated skill, flying—particularly instrument flying—comes most easily to those who do it often, who spend enough hours in the cockpit to be comfortable and relaxed. Had this pilot been knocking off some rust, reacting slowly at the controls after too much time on the ground?

Hancock had some hunches, some ideas of what to look for. But he knew that the best way to approach an investigation was to clear his mind and let the data from the wreck point him in its own direction. As he drove, he didn't turn on the radio. He just thought about the plane as he headed north on Interstate 95.

The Mayflower Pilgrims set sail for Virginia, not Plymouth Rock. They had intended to join the Jamestown colony, which had landed 13 years earlier and was in need of reserves. But the *Mayflower* was blown off course. On November 19, 1620, it anchored off the shore of what would later become Provincetown. The Pilgrims didn't see the Cape's potential as a summer resort. They hated it, and only stayed a month.

Bad weather prevented the ship from heading south for Virginia. Instead, the *Mayflower* stayed near the Cape and anchored offshore. The captain landed the group of 100 Pilgrims and pressed them to find a suitable wintering-over site so that he could return to England.

The Pilgrims could not find a decent camp site. The area looked promising at first. The hooked harbor where the *Mayflower* lay anchored was large and calm, and there were enough fully-grown trees to provide building timber. But the problem was that there did not seem to be a source for fresh water. Nevertheless, the settlers explored the area, desperate for food. They were not farmers, and had few survival skills and no knowledge of the area. The *Mayflower* captain refused to share the ship's food, hoarding it for his sailors on the two-month return voyage. The Pilgrims were facing a New England winter with no stores and no crops.

In their explorations they quickly tangled with the Wampanoag people, mainland natives who fished from the Cape. By that point the Wampanoag had survived sporadic Viking, Italian and British explorations in the area. Their number, however, had been severely weakened by a recent plague of smallpox, which had nearly wiped out the nearby native Patuxet people.

The Pilgrims discovered and pilfered a cache of corn, which turned out to be a native offering stored on sacred burial ground. The area, near Truro, is still called Corn Hill. Whether the natives were angry about the stolen corn or just fed up with European infiltration is unclear, but when the two groups ran across each other on a beach still known as First Encounter, shots were fired and arrows flew. The skirmish was the last straw for the hungry and frustrated Pilgrims, who by then had discovered a more hospitable harbor nearby on the mainland. They decided to relocate.

Because the settlers always intended to join the Jamestown colony, they had been given no guidelines from King James for establishing and governing a new one. The group returned to the ship and there, in

Provincetown Harbor, the men quickly drew up the Mayflower Compact. It was a radical document of self-governance—the first such document in the New World.

In the Compact, the Pilgrims agreed to run the new colony themselves, creating whatever laws would be necessary. They then bade good riddance to Cape Cod. The *Mayflower* took them to Plymouth and put the group ashore before returning to England. The following spring, after winter had killed off half their number, the Pilgrims met their savior in Squanto, a surviving Patuxet who spoke English and taught them to grow native crops.

Although the Pilgrims abandoned the Cape, it jutted into a rich fishing ground that was well known to both natives and Europeans. Fishing would shape Provincetown's future for the next four hundred years.

Throughout the 1600s and 1700s, Scandinavian and English sailors criss-crossed the area frequently. There was enough traffic to attract pirates and "wreckers" who raided the ships that broke apart on the Cape's treacherous shoals. Soon Portuguese sailors, hardy souls with a long history of venturing to distant fishing grounds, began to work the nearby Stellwagen, Georges and Grand Banks. They set up summer camps on the Cape where they could mend nets and salt the cod for the return voyage to Portugal. Before long, some of those fishermen began to winter over in the Province Lands. By the early 1800s, Provincetown was an established fishing village full of year-round residents. They hauled in most of the world's codfish, to be salted and shipped across the planet.

Cod and salt-making were the main industries for Provincetown. Until the mid-1800s, that is, when whaling hit. The village's natural harbor—the largest in New England—shot the town into the white-hot center of the era's biggest commercial enterprise. Before it was eclipsed by Nantucket, Provincetown ruled the whaling industry, home to 52 wharves and 5,000 residents. Ship captains and owners spent their fortunes locally, building spectacular houses and a railroad line.

Whaling declined in the 1900s, and then a massive storm wrecked Provincetown's salt works and warehouses. The town's glory days at sea were behind it, but its tourist season was just beginning. For years, rich Boston and New York vacationers had been riding the railroad to the picturesque town at the tip of the Cape. The fishing community was soon outstripped by the arts. Provincetown became known as flourishing arts colony, where internationally-known painters, playwrights and writers lived and worked.

In the late 20th century, the little town with cheap real estate became a hippie mecca, then a stylish summer address for the gay community. It has grown into a town full of jolting visuals. Salty Portuguese fishermen walk the wharf next to pairs of buff men holding hands. Studded leather accessories fill shop windows. A ten-foot tide leaves shallowly-anchored boats beached along the coastline. Because of the way the hook curls, Provincetown's sun sets over the ocean—a sight normally associated with the West coast.

Today, Provincetown real estate is far from cheap. Whale-watching has replaced whale-hunting. But some things have remained the same. MacMillan Wharf is still home to a hard-working fishing fleet that hauls out each morning.

The fishing boat that caught an airplane made the Sunday evening news and the front page of Monday morning's *Cape Cod Times*. Visitors whipped out their cameras. Even jaded locals were impressed.

The picturesque *Carla Bee* was a dark blue boat with white trim at the gunnels and along the waterline. Its paint was charmingly chipped, with a little authentic rust accenting the back end. Just perfect for photographs. It was one of those old-style trawlers that so prettily dotted the New England coast from Gloucester, Massachusetts to Point Judith, Rhode Island. A working boat, obvious from the wooden crates and buckets on deck. But it was not one of those floating fish-processing-plants with a metal hull and giant arms sticking out all over the mast. This was a wooden boat, 50-odd feet long. "Eastern-rig," the fishermen answered when tourists asked, "What kind of boat is that?" It was so labeled because the net hung from the mast over the side, instead of off the back end as on more modern boats.

Captain Rodriguez had learned his trade as a boy in Portugal, and then immigrated to New England's southern fishing coast. He owned the trim little boat, working it with a small crew of one or two family members, or sometimes other fishermen. He spoke little English; there wasn't much need in the area's vibrant and thick Portuguese community.

That it was an airplane he could clearly see. But Rodriguez had not read the papers or watched the news about Sinzheimer's accident. He didn't know if the plane had been there for a week or a year. He didn't know if anyone was looking for it. But there it was, in his net. Might as well call the harbormaster and find out if anybody wanted it hauled in.

The harbormaster called the Coast Guard, the Coast Guard called Bob Hancock. The *Carla Bee* motored into the harbor at about 11:00 A.M., its green polypropylene net full of airplane dangling off the left side of the boat. Captain Rodriguez and his crewmember were both deeply tanned by working long days under the glaring ocean sun. They shouted in Portuguese to dock workers as the boat motored toward the pier. A crane and flatbed truck, called for by the harbormaster, stood waiting at the end of the pier, next to the tractor-trailers lined up at the fish packing plant.

The fishing vessel docked at the end. The crumpled white, orange and brown plane hung between the wharf and the boat. Half a dozen shouting men reached out with hands and straps, to secure the wreck to the crane. They cut away with serrated knives at the net. Once the plane was free, the crane winched it up onto the flatbed. The crane motor chugged, and everyone watched as the plane landed with a gentle crunch on the truck.

Captain Rodriguez looked at his ruined net, dangling from the mast. A new one was too dear, this one would have to be mended. Days of work, days of no whiting. He sighed and circled the *Carla Bee* back toward the side of the wharf, to its mooring spot.

The flatbed made a slow three-point turn at the fat end of the wide pier and drove to the entrance. It drove past the parking attendant, past the ice-cream and t-shirt shops. It did not make the tight left turn onto Commercial Street, the narrow one-way lane crowded with bicycles and foot traffic. Instead it headed straight, and then turned onto Bradford, the wider road that ran the length of Provincetown. The driver shifted into higher gear and headed out of town on the mile-long drive to the airport.

# Chapter 14

# The Wreck's Story

THE CRUMPLED SHEET METAL that was once the Grumman sat in the sole hangar at Provincetown airport on Monday, November 2. Much of it was missing and would never be recovered. The vertical part of the tail and most of its left horizontal surface were gone. Both wingtips and most of the right wing were missing. The entire bubble-shaped canopy and windscreen had disappeared, as had the bottom half of the engine cowling. The pilot's seat was never found.

The missing pieces could have been on the ocean floor right next to where the wreck was recovered, sliding just under the whiting net. Or they could have been carried miles away by currents. Nobody would ever know.

What was left did not look much like an airplane. The orange and brown striped fuselage was tilted forward, resting on its nose and the main landing gear. Its stubby half-wings stuck out from the sides. Both ailerons, the flap-like control surfaces running along the back edge of each wing, were broken off. What was left of the tail was separated from the fuselage, connected only by the slender control cables. The nosewheel was bent backward.

The engine was still attached to the fuselage. The whole thing was the size of a canoe, crumpled and creased as if some giant making origami had pinched at it and broken off a few extra bits. On the side the entire registration number was clearly visible, "N7100L."

Bob Hancock looked at the chunk that was left of the Grumman and saw an intact airplane.

Sure, it was missing some of the softer peripherals like fiberglass and plastic. But Hancock was delighted to see that the core was there. He had a complete instrument panel with gauges. The engine and propeller were attached. Most major flying surfaces were there and still connected to their control cables. It hadn't crumpled into tiny, fragile bits like many wrecks do. The fishermen's nets hadn't sliced it up or dropped the engine. Hancock had something to work with.

Hey, Bob, whatcha got here? Gregg Erickson was a stout, grey-haired man dressed in a mechanic's jumpsuit and baseball cap. He walked through the small side door into the hangar, carrying a metal toolbox. The two had worked accidents before, and ran into each other in person and on the phone regularly in the small aviation world.

Gregg, good morning! Bob smiled and then turned back to his wreck. We have ourselves a pretty complete airplane here.

They talked for a few minutes, Hancock briefing Erickson on the details of the accident. The two men were both pilots who had logged thousands of flight hours—Hancock as an instructor in California, eventually teaching in Douglas DC-3s, the glamorous "Gooney Bird" tail-dragger that pioneered commercial air travel after World War II. Erickson had more than 2,500 hours just in Grummans. His personal airplane was a Grumman Tiger, with a similar airframe to this Traveler and a larger engine. The men looked with practiced eyes at the pieces that had broken off this plane. They studied the wrinkling of the metal skin, the crushing and folding of the airframe.

Erickson did not seem surprised by the missing canopy. He had seen plenty of Grummans balled up, and almost every time the canopy had been ripped off by the impact. He had seen seats shear off like this one had, the worn pins that held the seat to its metal flange snapping as the weight of the strapped-in pilot pulled the seat forward.

The crushed airframe did not necessarily indicate a slam of an impact. Aluminum sheet metal is fragile; a person can bend it with bare hands. Almost everything around the cockpit was crumpled, but the core of the plane had been preserved, and so had the engine. The plane had suffered a "moderate" impact. In a full-speed nose-down crash, both the cockpit and engine would have been severely smashed up.

Hancock scribbled notes about the condition of the wreckage: missing canopy, bent and broken tail, missing wingtips, lower left engine mount bent in, wing skins torn and rotated around the spars.

Well, let's get started on the engine, said Hancock. The FAA guys will be here in a little while; they're coming in on Cape Air.

He hitched up his belt and slid on a new pair of suede work gloves with blue trim. Hancock and Erickson stepped up to the wreck and lifted, grunting. Hancock's thick bull neck bulging with the effort. He slid a cinderblock underneath the nose with his foot and they lowered the front end.

The propeller caught their eye first. It was odd, with the ends bent forward instead of the usual twisting or backward bend associated with a crash. To Erickson, it looked like what propellers do when a pilot doesn't put down the landing gear. The plane floats down onto the runway at a slow speed and shallow angle. The propeller tips are rotating faster than the airplane is moving forward, and physics dictates that they bend outward, biting into the ground.

Hancock was not so sure, remembering that the plane had been muscled around a bit before arriving at the hangar. Maybe the propeller hadn't been turning on impact, and the tips were bent later, as the wreck was handled. It would have taken a powerful force to curl the tips of a five-inch-wide aluminum propeller blade, but it was possible. Or maybe the plane had crashed in some weird trajectory, flipping and twisting so that the propeller hit the water from behind. Impossible to know which scenario was the truth.

The propeller alone did not offer much of a clue about whether or not the engine was running on impact. Hancock made some notes and took a few pictures. Then he moved to the engine.

With the propeller tips bent forward, it was easy to turn it, which "rotated" the engine (moving all four pistons up and down in the cylinders) for a compression check. Erickson had already removed the valve covers from each cylinder. As he turned the prop blades, that turned the camshaft and Hancock could see the tips of the valves moving in the heads, one on top of each cylinder. The valves are connected to the rocker arms, which are connected to the push rods, which are connected to the valve train, which is connected to the camshaft. The fact that the valves moved when the camshaft turned meant that those internal workings of the engine were rotating properly.

I've got valve train continuity, Hancock announced, and scribbled on his clipboard. It was one fact arguing that the engine had been running at impact.

Using a wrench he unscrewed the spark plugs one by one, numbering each with a Sharpie marker. He carried them out of the hangar and held them up in the sunshine, staring with his bright blue eyes. The tiny electrodes were corroded from the salt water. No telling if they had been in good enough shape to spark.

Hancock walked back to the engine block and stuck his thumb over each of the spark plug holes as Erickson pulled the prop through again. As each cylinder slid down into firing position it sucked at his thumb and made a quick gasp. As it slid back up into the exhaust position, it pushed out a puff of air.

Looks good, said Hancock, writing on his clipboard.

Compression, an operating valve train. The facts were beginning to tell a story, agreeing with each other on the subject of the engine. But that alone did not solve the mystery, did not explain why the airplane had made that sudden dip to 100 feet.

Next came the engine peripherals: the vacuum pump, carburetor and magnetos, which fired the spark plugs. For a few minutes Hancock got excited about the engine-driven fuel pump. He got out the camera and took some photographs because the pump had separated, falling into two pieces. If that happened in flight, the engine would stop receiving fuel. Could this be the cause of the accident?

But as he and Erickson talked about it, they realized that the screws holding the part together were made of magnesium, a metal that dissolves in salt water. The screws had disintegrated after the accident. A false lead.

The fuel lines had blue fuel in them, the filters were clear. The magnetos were too corroded to test, but there was enough data on the engine and fuel lines for the Hancock's Board to draw conclusions about the condition of the engine and the fuel system.

By early morning, one of the Cape Air flights touching down across from the hangar had brought in the FAA and Massachusetts Aeronautics Commission officials from Boston. They were anxious to look at the problems mentioned on the Condition Notice.

Well, the bottom half of the engine cowling wasn't recovered, Hancock said as he ushered them around the plane. So we can't check the landing light but we ought to be able to find those holes. We've only got one side of the tail though, which elevator was it? Right side? Yeah, we've got that.

Hancock walked around the wreck, poking at the pieces lying on the hangar floor, looking for the broken-off aileron first.

The aileron was about four feet long and less than a foot wide. Hancock picked it up and ran his hand along the smooth aluminum skin. Ah, here it was, a quarter-inch hole plugged with something. Bondo? Epoxy? Some kind of filler. He handed it to the FAA guy who had originally slapped the notice on the plane: Is this it?

Yeah, it was. It had been plugged with something, but that was the hole all right.

A tiny hole, really. And it was on the trailing edge, not the all-important leading edge that attacked the air and created lift. Hangar rash, probably, from bumping into another plane as it was parked by a tow tug. Not an issue.

How about the elevator? That hole was larger. A couple of inches wide and over an inch high, in the fiberglass tip of the horizontal tail section.

Gregg Erickson came over to have a look. If it had been his plane, he said, he would have fixed that right away. Would not have risked having a hole that large right in the airflow, especially on fiberglass. It could have gotten worked open, become a larger hole and then a gash and finally two pieces, one falling off into space.

But the hole, large as it was, had not caused any further airframe damage. It probably had created a little drag, slowing the airplane down by maybe a mile an hour. But it hadn't opened further. The FAA official said the hole was in the same condition as when he saw it a month earlier.

Hancock made more notes, deciding to include the fact that the holes were still there. More data for the report, for the Board to sift through.

A pile of debris was collecting under the airplane as the team tossed gaskets, bolts and used parts on the floor. Airplane mechanics normally kept tidy track of each washer and nut, ready to pop them back in exact order. Lycoming's trainees for investigative work often found themselves standing next to a wrecked engine, bolt in hand, looking for a clean shelf to put it on. They had to be reminded to just toss it on the floor—nobody was putting these planes back together again. The wrecks were usually released to the insurance companies, then sold for scrap metal.

Hancock reached into the cockpit and wiggled the yoke. One of the FAA guys hung onto the cables in the back and confirmed that the proper ones tugged as Hancok moved. Right turn on the yoke, right aileron up, left aileron down. Pull back, tail elevator goes up.

Okay, we've got control cable continuity, said Hancock. He made some more notes.

After a lunch break, sandwiches at a little place on the outskirts of Provincetown, Hancock poked around in the cockpit and found an important piece of data—the pilot's logbook. It was still wet, stained and falling apart, but as he laid it out on the concrete floor Hancock found that he could peel the pages apart with the tip of his knife. The ink hadn't run, and he could read the last entries. A lot of back and forth between the Cape and Albany. A flight to Syracuse and Buffalo. He pried open an earlier page. He could read the pilot's name.

Hey, this guy used to be a Mooney driver, he announced as he turned the pages. A Mooney? To a Grumman? Usually pilots go the other way around, stepping out of the smaller planes and transitioning up to the faster, more complex platforms. Kind of odd to see someone head in the other direction.

Hancock started doing the math, adding up Sinzheimer's flight hours, and his time over the past 30 and 90 days. Was he current? Or was he logging snippets of flight time here and there, still shaking off the rust from three years of not flying?

The logbook totaled 1,371 hours, an impressive amount compared to the mere 40 required to earn a pilot's license. Hancock added up the recent numbers, doing the math on Sinzheimer's last 30 and 90 days of flying.

In the past three months he had flown 36 hours in the Grumman. If a local news reporter had asked Hancock whether or not that was a lot of flight time, he would have hedged, saying it was all relative. His job was to record the numbers, just the facts, and not to draw conclusions about them. But an average general aviation pilot would answer that yes, it certainly was a lot. And it was 36 hours in the Grumman, all focused on the same airplane instead of hopping from cockpit to cockpit and having to learn new procedures.

The time averaged out to 12 hours a month, but Sinzheimer had logged 17 in the past month. That meant he had increased his flight time through September, averaging an hour in the air every other day. More than four hours of flying every weekend.

The FAA required pilots to have three night takeoffs and landings within the past 90 days to legally carry passengers after sunset. That takes about half an hour. Sinzheimer had logged nine hours of night flying within the last 90 days.

He had six hours of actual instrument time over the past 90 days. The FAA required that instrument-rated pilots log six instrument hours every six months. Sinzheimer was averaging twice that. Plus, in May he had passed his biannual medical exam and an Instrument Proficiency Check (a flight test with an instructor). In April he had passed a Flight Review—a basic flight check that was good for two years.

Hancock did not know that Sinzheimer had taken a three-year break from flying, but that wouldn't have mattered to him. In the past four months, Sinzheimer had flown to Provincetown almost every weekend. He had shot many approaches there. He had flown regularly and recently at night and in instrument conditions. With 36 hours in that plane, he was well past the five or ten hours of transitional training that insurance companies often demand from pilots when moving to a new airplane. In short, Ron Sinzheimer was about as proficient as a pilot with a day job could be.

There were no new clues from the logbook, nothing to point the investigation in a different direction. From all appearances the pilot was up to date. Hancock wrote down the totals for the flight hours, slapped the damp logbook closed and moved back to the plane. Time to check the cockpit.

The pilot's side yoke was still in place. The power controls—throttle and mixture—were full forward at their maximum settings, which Hancock often saw in accidents. It was impossible to know if they had been set that way or had been pushed in after impact by the pilot's hands or some cockpit clutter.

Hancock noted the settings of the various instruments, including the altimeter window, which was set to 30.04. The actual setting for Provincetown at the time of the accident was 30.06, a minor difference of 20 feet. The error was in the pilot's favor: The plane was 20 feet higher than he would have thought it was.

Hancock knew that most of the other instruments were unreliable. As a plane smashed into something the needles tended to go haywire, and were not trustworthy as indicators of what the plane had been doing just prior to the crash. Still, it couldn't hurt to document it. Hancock made some notes, and then he noticed something strange.

Hey guys, we've got something here, he said.

Hancock had noticed the radios that were linked to the navigational instruments. The first one was set to frequency 114.05 on a course of 72 degrees. The second to 115.6 on a course of 91 degrees. The ADF radio was set to 390.

Those were the three navigational radios that tuned in the beacons for the plane to follow. In flight, the pilot tuned a radio to a beacon, set the instrument on a particular heading, then used those settings to intercept a highway in the sky to fly to the destination. With the radios on the wrong settings, a pilot would just wander around blindly. None of Sinzheimer's frequencies matched those for the landing procedure at Provincetown.

What the hell were 114.05 and 115.6? As Hancock flipped through the local aviation charts and plates, he found part of the answer. The frequency for the beacon at Providence, Rhode Island was 115.6. The Grumman would have been navigating from that beacon on a heading of 93 degrees. The needle on the plane's VOR instrument was set to a heading of 91 degrees, a negligible error at that distance. So that radio checked out.

But what about 114.05?

Instead, the primary radio should have been set for the landing approach frequency at Provincetown: 111.1. Or, if Sinzheimer had decided to go around, he would have dialed in the frequency for Hyannis, 108.95. Neither was even close to 114.05.

The closest navigational beacon to Provincetown was called Marconi. It was named for the nearby site from which Italian radio inventor Guglielmo Marconi sent the first transatlantic radio message from President Teddy Roosevelt to King Edward VII of England in 1903. That beacon was near Truro, and although it wasn't used as part of the Provincetown approach procedure, it was the closest beacon to the airport. Pilots could use Marconi to cross-check their position. Its frequency was 114.7.

The beacon at Martha's Vineyard was strong enough for pilots to receive at Provincetown. Like Marconi, its signal could be used for a position check. Its frequency was 114.50.

Marconi and the Vineyard were close to the plane's radio setting of 114.05, but why would the pilot be using those distant beacons instead of the ILS?

Radio knobs are round and rotate stiffly. It was highly unlikely that at impact something caught on them and turned the dials. The whole thing was weird enough for Hancock to bag the radios. He worked them out of the panel and wrapped them in a clear plastic garbage bag. They would be packed and mailed off to Narco, the manufacturer, for the insides to be checked. It was possible that the impact had broken the knobs somehow, so that the actual frequencies tuned in by the unit did not match what was on the face.

Hancock glanced at his stainless steel Mickey Mouse watch. Almost 5:00 P.M. One more thing to check before packing up and heading out for dinner.

Hancock didn't have to unscrew the small panel at the tail, where the Emergency Locator Transmitter was mounted. The tail was crunched up and torn enough that he could just reach through a hole and pull it out. The accident had not triggered an ELT signal. At the very least, it would have confirmed that the plane crashed. If a signal had sounded long enough before the plane sank, it would have pinpointed the accident site.

He pulled out the orange rectangular ELT unit and looked down into the recessed top.

Oh, this is interesting, he said.

The switch was in the "off" position.

On Tuesday afternoon, just as Hancock walked back into his office, the phone rang. Eric Eslinger calling: What did you find in the investigation? Do you know what happened to Ron?

Hancock wanted to explain, to offer some solace to the family, but he had to be careful how he presented the facts. He wasn't supposed to be drawing conclusions at all. What if the family decided to sue and pointed to something he said, some opinion he had offered? He would lose his job. But it was difficult when explaining aerodynamics to non-pilots. They couldn't interpret the telling details in the same way a pilot could. They sometimes needed a little hand-holding.

The facts were not clear, Hancock began, as he sat down at his desk. We found his logbook and keys in the airplane, but not the aircraft maintenance records. The exam didn't turn up any obvious mechanical problems. The cockpit was pretty much intact, not crushed.

The nose gear was bent backward. There was a slight crushing to the inboard portion of the wing. The propeller was damaged.

Eslinger interrupted. Damaged propeller? Did that mean anything, did it offer any clues about the impact?

It could, Hancock answered. Some kinds of scratches can mean that the propeller was probably turning on impact, so the engine would have been running.

The navigation radios, he continued. They weren't set for the Provincetown airport. We'll send them out for analysis, but regardless of the result the radar track shows he did fly the localizer for the approach. Somehow even with the radios set wrong, he was on the approach path.

Eslinger spoke again: What about vertigo, does it look like maybe he got disoriented in the clouds?

Hancock chose his words carefully: I don't see any evidence of that from the radar data. It shows the plane on a steady path during the approach. With vertigo you see more turns, climbs and descents.

Eslinger didn't ask any more questions, thank goodness. Didn't ask what caused the steep descent. Didn't ask if Hancock thought the pilot survived the crash. He hung up, leaving Hancock to his paperwork. So many forms to fill out.

The frustrating thing was that the facts just were not pointing in a clear direction. The pilot was very experienced, but had apparently used the wrong radio settings. It looked as if the engine was working, yet there was that steep descent on the radar report. The weather was perfect for inducing vertigo, yet the radar track did not show a single turn or climb—the meandering hallmarks of vertigo-stricken piloting. And what about the dog, which his wife had said always rode along loose, with no type of restraints? Had he created a problem?

In 14 years of field work, Hancock had avoided the burnout that claimed a lot of other investigators. He had learned to accept that on some cases he wouldn't turn up all of the evidence. He might have a hunch what happened, but NTSB reports weren't about hunches. They were thick with facts, built on concrete details that added up to a probable cause. An investigator could go crazy trying to figure out what happened in a cockpit. But without a data recorder there was no way to know for sure. No facts to turn to, no safety recommendation to make, no future lives to save.

To keep himself sane, Hancock knew it was better in the long run not to focus on the frustrations of an unsolvable case. All of the data here pointed in the same direction: a competent pilot flying a working airplane. He would write his detailed report, and the Board would likely conclude that the pilot had done something mysteriously and fatally wrong. What, nobody knew.

# Chapter 15

# Going Down

IN BOB HANCOCK'S OFFICE, taped to the wall above his computer, is the principle of Occam's Razor. It is a theory that underlies all scientific modeling. It reads, "One should always choose the simplest explanation of a phenomenon, the one that requires the fewest leaps of logic." What it means is that although life is unpredictable, and for any given set of data there are an infinite number of possible causes, the simplest explanation is the best.

In other words, Sinzheimer's engine could have failed, then re-started. He could have had a sudden, overwhelming death wish. The plane could have been forced off-course by aliens. But none of those are very likely. The facts point to a more probable scenario.

As Sinzheimer flew over Providence, Rhode Island, there were just clouds, no rain yet. The controller authorized him to begin a descent, and as he pushed the nose down he tuned in the Provincetown automated weather broadcast. He would have been hand-flying, holding the yoke with his left hand, turning the tiny black radio knob with his right. Over his headset came the computer-generated voice.

Provincetown had a low ceiling, hovering right at the decision height of 200 feet above the ground. The visibility, which determines whether or not a pilot can legally land, was also at the minimum of three-quarters of a mile. Conditions were so low that many pilots would have abandoned the idea of landing there altogether.

But Sinzheimer felt confident, remembering all the times he had gotten in to Provincetown in marginal weather. Mostly that had been in the Mooney, but at least once was in the Grumman, a few weeks earlier.

He then switched the radio frequency to hear the Hyannis weather, which was much better. But it likely never occurred to Sinzheimer to divert to Hyannis. When he asked controller David Loring for "an alternate," he seems to have meant an alternate in case he had to go around at Provincetown. Hyannis *after* Provincetown, not *instead* of Provincetown.

To divert would upset plans. He would be late for dinner, would have to rent a car or call Marsha to pick him up. Pilots divert if they have to, but it is so much easier to press on, to stick with the original plan instead of filing for some new routing, puzzling it out on the charts, yakking with the controller. Too much hassle.

And so, Sinzheimer started his descent into Provincetown. He crossed low over the navigational fix at Phony—1,800 feet instead of 2,000. The cockpit was dark, lit by the dim glow of the panel lights. Outside the cockpit window, the left wingtip light flashed red, surrounded by a hazy halo. Sinzheimer started a normal descent, just below the approach's glide slope path.

Then the descent steepened at around 1,000 feet and increased until the plane leveled off at 100 feet. According to pilot Pete Kacergis, who took off shortly after the accident, the cloud layer began at 1,200 feet above the ground and reached down to 100. The air was smooth, with only occasional turbulence in the clouds.

Perhaps as the Grumman bumped through the cloud layer and Sinzheimer searched for the airport, he struggled with one of flying's illusions. It happens in the clouds, the feeling that the plane pitches nose up. He may have reacted to correct the perceived error by pushing the yoke aggressively, lowering the nose and steepening his descent.

It is possible he did that. But Sinzheimer had enough experience to recognize and correct for that illusion. It is more likely that he was determined to get down.

Had he done this before, with Bill Newman? It looked like he was "dipping," or flying below the glide slope in an attempt to break out of the cloud cover as soon as possible. Maybe he saw the runway lights at

200 feet, and descended the extra 100 allowed by the regulations. That is doubtful; he was still several miles from the runway on a night with less than a mile visibility.

At any rate, he was in control of the plane at that point. He descended toward the cloud bottoms while holding the localizer path. The plane pointed straight toward the runway heading.

Did something then distract him, pulling his attention away from holding a steady descent? Something large was in the front seat at impact, something big enough to hit the passenger-side yoke, bend the metal arm straight up and break it off. Theo may have panicked and struggled forward, clawing his way into the front seat while Ron lost track of his descent speed and drifted to the left.

Then he recovered. He leveled off at 100 feet above the ocean.

Although Sinzheimer was below the decision height (illegal unless the runway is in sight), flying that low would not itself have caused the crash. When Lindbergh crossed the Atlantic he often dipped as low as five or ten feet off the water, just to watch the waves and keep himself from getting bored.

Flying that low over the water, at night, is hard work. The gauges would have competed for Sinzheimer's attention, each blaring its own crucial information. The plane slogged along close to the water at low power. Sinzheimer strained his eyes ahead to spot the runway lights. Below, he would only have seen darkness. In that configuration, the slightest distraction can throw the whole thing askew.

It could have been the dog again. More likely it was the radios.

Sinzheimer loved electronic gizmos and flew with a Global Positioning System unit, a small handheld radio that tracked his course and altitude. It was much more sophisticated than the navigational radios installed in the Grumman. It was not recovered with the wreckage, but there was a GPS-type power cord snaking around the cockpit and plugged into the cigarette lighter. That's where Grumman pilots plug in their units.

With the GPS pointing to Provincetown, and the plane clear of the clouds, Sinzheimer started scanning below for runway lights. He was holding the plane on a fixed heading using the Directional Gyro. In a few seconds he would either see the runway and make a visual landing, or he would go missed, flying the new heading for the go-around procedure.

In go-arounds, the pilot's workload skyrockets because several procedures must be performed almost simultaneously. Did Sinzheimer anticipate this by setting up the navigational radios in advance? Maybe he was thinking of the Mooney, of how it forced him to set up in advance for go-arounds because it was such a fast airplane and could quickly speed ahead of his checklist duties.

If so, he would have been busily turning the radio dials from the Provincetown landing settings to the go-around settings. He would have been focusing more on the radio dial windows, trying to get the frequencies right, and less on the Attitude Indicator and other gauges that monitored the airplane's position. A moment's distraction as he leaned forward, reaching to turn the dials. Just enough for the airplane to drop a hundred feet.

That would explain why the primary radio frequency was not found set for Provincetown, Hyannis or anything nearby. Sinzheimer may have been in the process of changing the setting when the plane hit.

It took seconds, and he probably never saw it coming. He never noticed the waves rushing up, never had a second to think about climbing or adding power. Or perhaps at the last minute he did yank back on the yoke, hoping the plane would respond like the powerful Mooney. But the Grumman didn't. It kept sinking for one precious second.

The plane probably hit on the left wingtip or landing gear wheel at about 75 miles an hour, nosing down as the water grabbed and bent the nosewheel back. Then it cartwheeled, flipping over as the contents of the cockpit tossed violently around—the bathroom faucet and window blinds ramming into the seats, sides and ceiling. Something smashed into the panel, bending the yoke and breaking it off. Maybe some baggage, or the dog. Theo had no signs of external injury, but he could have had serious internal damage. There had been no autopsy to determine his condition.

The plane hit the water upside down, so that the canopy and tail bore the brunt of the impact, bending the tail down and yanking the canopy off. Sinzheimer's seatbelt held.

The Grumman tumbled, and the top of the plane seems to have crashed into the waves backwards, enough of an impact to rip the canopy loose and bend the propeller tips forward. The canopy jammed into the windscreen and broke that loose also.

The plane may have continued rotating, righting itself before it sank in the dark water. Or it may have stayed upside down as Sinzheimer struggled to orient himself.

Some pilots who have been in accidents talk about how quickly the whole thing happens. One minute you're flying, the next you're upside down, strapped into a smashed airplane. Others say it all happens in slow motion, and you keep processing information while you're going down, "I'm crashing, how do I minimize the damage?"

It was probably instinctive for Sinzheimer to release the seatbelt and kick free of the plane—easy with the entire canopy broken off. He may have been surprised to find that he was not hurt, just a few bruises. The strong honeycomb construction of the cockpit had held together well. Sinzheimer floated through the water to the dark surface, pleased to be alive.

And then, his real problems began.

As Cape Approach, Boston Center and the Coast Guard worked through their bureaucratic dance, Sinzheimer floated offshore. He probably cursed himself for not packing a life vest. It's one of those things that just takes up space. It's a bother, a hassle, until you need it, of course. Without it, he was forced to either tread water or swim.

Sinzheimer was a healthy man, a strong swimmer with (as indicated by the autopsy) minor injuries. The mile or two toward shore surely felt like something he could make, particularly for an aggressive person like himself. Sinzheimer was someone who never gave up, who had supreme confidence in his abilities.

Did he know which direction to try? Perhaps. He knew that the wind was out of the northeast. Wind drives the waves. If he swam into the waves, or kept them to his left, he would be heading toward Race Point beach. It was a small spit of land; missing it meant heading out into the wide Atlantic. Perhaps Sinzheimer listened for the surf of the breaking waves to tell him where the shore was.

He started out strong, confidently stroking into the dark waves. He may have worried about mundane things—would the airplane insurance cover the accident? Would Marsha be eating dinner without him by now? Should he cancel tomorrow's tennis game? He expected either to make the shore or be rescued. He knew that Air Traffic Control would be concerned when he didn't cancel his flight plan, and they would launch the Coast Guard.

Then the icy water began its work. Sinzheimer was dressed in a short-sleeved shirt and cotton pants. He had low body fat, little insulation. The extra exertion of a difficult swim through rough water hastened the onset of hypothermia. Within minutes, he would have started shaking. Maybe he didn't even notice it as he kept swimming, focusing on finding the beach. Next, his muscles would have started to stiffen, and swimming would have become difficult.

At that point, it was a quick transition from heroic self-preservation to shock. People who have experienced shock after terrifying events describe the feeling of detachment, as if the events weren't happening to them, but instead to that disconnected body floating around out there. Although Sinzheimer would have struggled in the water, he would not have felt involved. How interesting, he probably thought, that my body can't manage to swim right now.

Eric Eslinger's memorial wasn't far off the mark. Hallucinations would have followed, and perhaps Ron was delighted to see a speed-boat heading his way. A beautiful woman. A fine cigar. Warm blankets. How divine to fold himself into her arms.

In water that cold it all would have happened quickly, with no time for panic. It could have taken as little as an hour from the crash until the moment in which Sinzheimer relaxed into the sea.

The Grumman disappeared at 7:45 P.M. The first Coast Guard boat arrived just before 10:00 P.M. The Coast Guard and Air Traffic Control personnel who looked at the mission timeline afterwards were appalled that it took two hours to get equipment to a site so close to the stations.

In search and rescue missions, the first few moments are critical. It is imperative to hit the site while the target area is still small, and while survivors are at their strongest. When the alarm sounds, Coast Guard pilots run to their aircraft to shave seconds off the response time. When the rescue crews at Station Provincetown can't find a nearby car to make the drive, they run the entire quarter-mile pier in their bulky survival suits, arriving at the boats out of breath. Every moment counts.

In this case, over an hour had passed by the time the crews started running. What caused such a delay?

One problem was that there was never a sign of distress. There was no radio call from the pilot saying that the airplane was in trouble. Nobody heard an ELT signal to indicate the plane had crashed.

Controller David Loring began to worry at 7:46. He sensibly spent four minutes, then the supervisor spent another nine, checking the ramp at Provincetown and nearby airports to see if the pilot had landed and forgotten to radio in. All of Loring's previous "vanishing" airplanes—and it seemed like 99 percent of the other controllers'—had ended up either at other airports or in the air on the go-around. There was no reason for him to believe this one would be any different.

But it was. When that became obvious, Cape Approach followed FAA procedure and called Boston Center at 7:59 P.M.

"I was always under the impression that when we called Boston Center they put on their Superman cape and sprang into action," said Loring. "The plane was cleared for the approach at 7:37 and Boston Center didn't call the Coast Guard until 8:35? Oh my, that is sad."

Another complication was that nobody communicated a sense of urgency to the Coast Guard. Cape TRACON neglected to mention that someone called the airport looking for the pilot, declaring him late. When Boston Center called the Coast Guard half an hour later, they used the phrase "*possible* downed aircraft." If Cape had mentioned Marsha's phone call, or if Boston hadn't used the word "possible," District Controller Pat Cook would have launched the Jayhawk and asked questions later.

"If we thought he was in water when we first talked to Cape Approach at 8:45, the rough position they gave us was enough to launch," Cook said later. "Normally we're getting some type of ELT signal. You watch for it to try to settle somewhere. Then you call Boston Center and ask them if they have anything. But we didn't have that. I was going on the information from them which wasn't everything I was looking for."

It took 20 minutes for a frustrated Cook to confirm the distress call and decide that he did, in fact, have a mission. Once that happened, he initiated the Search and Rescue crews within two minutes, well within the five-minute goal of the Coast Guard's mission statement.

The complexity of three government bodies working together—Cape Approach, Boston Center and the Coast Guard—caused its share of bureaucratic delays. Then the weather weighed in, further slowing mission briefings and launches. That couldn't be helped.

By far the biggest lag for the search and rescue response was caused by the lack of an ELT signal.

The Emergency Locator Transmitter in the Grumman was, as in most airplanes, bolted in the tail, as far away from the usual point of impact as possible. The pilot can access it by unscrewing a dozen or so screws and lifting away a sheet-metal panel, but rarely does. He or she would have to unbolt the unit to be able to see the face plate, or head, where the switch is. The switch has three positions: "On," which sends a continual signal (used for testing or when a downed pilot wants to manually trigger the unit), "Off," and "Armed." They are supposed to be set to the "Armed" position so that the emergency signal activates on impact. Testing and setting the ELT is not usually part of the pilot's checklist. The mechanic normally sets it to "Armed" at the required yearly battery check, and then nobody touches it until the following year.

Sinzheimer's ELT was found in the "Off" position. Is it possible that the unit was originally "Armed," but somehow malfunctioned and did not signal on impact? Then during recovery the switch was flipped to "Off"?

Occam's Razor says that it's possible, but not probable. In 16 years of NTSB investigations, Bob Hancock had never seen an ELT not signal when it was in the "armed" position on impact. It does occasionally happen. There are cases of antennas being ripped off, or antenna cables being severed at impact. But they are rare.

The likelihood of both an antenna malfunction and the switch being flipped to "Off" is even slimmer. The tail was mangled at impact, the aluminum skin brushing near the ELT unit. But the switch itself is in the recessed top. It faces the front of the plane and is protected on all sides by walls that are higher than the tip of the switch. The nearest thing to that switch is a panel about six inches forward. The Grumman was minimally compressed along the longitudinal axis, so that panel remained in position. Nothing came near the switch.

Bob Hancock noted that the ELT unit's battery expiration date was August 2000. This meant mechanic Pete Conner had replaced the two-year battery at the July 1998 annual. Did he check the switch?

Two and a half years later, Conner could not remember whether or not he had checked the ELT at all at the Grumman's annual. He refused to consult a copy of the checklist which mechanics are required by the FAA to use for airplane annual inspections. When asked how he normally checked ELTs, Conner was silent for several seconds. Then he said, "on the annual you have to check the ELT battery date, not the switch."

It was possible, Conner explained, that he or one of his mechanics unscrewed the rear access panel, unclipped the ELT unit, looked at the battery date label, replaced the expired battery—disconnecting and reconnecting the wires to the head, where the switch is—but never bothered to check the switch's final position. That switch, Conner claimed, is an owner responsibility, not a mechanic's.

He went on to explain in detail about the "slam test" in which a mechanic holds the ELT unit in one hand and slams it into the palm of the other, approximating a five-G longitudinal impact, which should trigger the signal. The FAA had recently mandated yearly slam tests for all ELTs. Conner explained that although he was likewise not required to slam his customers' ELTs (that being another owner responsibility), he usually did it anyway while he was performing the required battery check.

The manufacturer's inspection checklist (from Gulfstream) is used throughout the industry for Grumman maintenance. Under "fuselage and empennage group" for the Grumman AA-5's annual inspection, the second item is "inspect ELT for security, operation and battery expiration date." To "inspect ELT for operation," a mechanic must move the switch to the right, to "On," and then listen for a signal. The switch must be turned back off, to the center position, to stop the signal. For flight, it is supposed to be moved to the left, into the "Armed" position.

FAA officials at several Flight Standards District Offices disagreed with Conner's reading of the regulation. The rule itself is indeed found under the Part 91, the "General Operating and Flight Rules" section for pilots in the Federal Aviation Regulations. But, officials pointed out, so are the rules regarding the annual inspection itself. Owners do have final responsibility for making sure the work is *done*, but legally they must hire an FAA-qualified mechanic to *do* it and sign the aircraft maintenance logbook.

Although he believed he was not required to check the switch, Conner admitted that he regularly did anyway. When asked how he checked ELTs prior to the slam requirement, Conner answered, "Our procedure was to look at the unit, make sure it was in the armed position, but we didn't pull it out for the slam test."

He remembered examining other ELT switches, "We often see that they're off, not armed. Maybe we've done it ourselves, turned the switch the wrong way. I put one in once and turned it to 'on' instead of 'armed.' The airport manager called and said he heard it on the frequency."

Like many pilots, Conner does not take ELTs too seriously. "They're the stupidest things to put in an airplane. Worst thing Congress ever mandated. It just costs people money to maintain them, and they never seem to work." Although the Narco-manufactured ELT in the Grumman, Conner pointed out, is "a great unit, one of the few that still work."

Few pilots think much about their ELTs, which are usually installed in nearly impossible-to-reach places, as far back as possible to avoid being crunched by impact. Pilots rarely bother to unscrew the access panels to test them, and so the units can go from year to year—from annual to annual—without ever being touched. The pilot relies on the mechanic to do it, and many, like Conner, either do not accept the responsibility or they forget. Anecdotes abound of pilots who do bother to check, and find their ELTs with the switches set to "Off."

In Sinzheimer's case, a functioning ELT would have sent up a brief alarm, a sound picked up by ATC and Flight Service Stations monitoring aviation's emergency frequency. Combined with the plane's disappearance from radar and the pilot's failure to cancel his flight plan, it would have been enough to launch Coast Guard crews immediately. They could have been on the scene within one hour instead of two.

As Hancock sat in front of his computer, typing up the final report eight months after the accident, he thought about a lot of things. He thought about those radios, and why the pilot might have been fiddling with them. He thought about the weather, and the stress of flying an approach to minimums. He thought about that dog, loose in the plane and maybe scared enough to cozy up to Master.

But he could not write any of that down in the report. He knew what had happened—the plane had gone into the water. But he would never know why.

It was damned frustrating. He was a detective who had a pack of facts but still could not solve the case. All he could do was type up the key details in his report, hope that the Board could make sense out of it, and move on to the next accident.

It took four more months for the Board to review and finalize the report. The summary was released on October 15, 1999. In the formal document, the board listed the key findings from Hancock's investigation, and drew conclusions as to probable cause:

The pilot initiated an ILS approach in IMC conditions, at night, from over water. After tracking on the localizer and glide slope for part of the approach, the airplane entered a descent and leveled off at 100 feet for about 12 seconds prior to disappearing from radar. No evidence of a mechanical failure or malfunction was found with the airplane. Both wings had sustained moderate impact damage. The outboard portion of the left wing was not recovered. The pilot had told approach control that if he missed, he would request the approach to a nearby airport. The navigation radio frequencies did not match the instrument approach flown, the missed approach, or the planned subsequent approach.

The National Transportation Safety Board determines the probable cause(s) of this accident as follows.

The failure of the pilot to follow the published instrument approach procedure, which resulted in inadvertent collision with water. Factors in the accident were the dark night and low ceiling.

The stilted bureaucratic language did not reveal anything new, it merely summarized what everyone following the accident already knew: Something happened which caused Sinzheimer to dip, then the "inadvertent collision with water." But what? Whatever it was, the Board concluded, it was the pilot's fault that he didn't recover.

It was, in other words, Pilot Error.

Since the NTSB did not delve into the real cause, readers had to draw their own conclusions. Many pilots read Hancock's report after it was posted on the NTSB web site. Even more read the summary published a year and a half later in *Aviation Safety*, the newsletter of small airplane accidents. Editor and pilot Ken Ibold took issue with the NTSB, pointing out that, "there are too many unanswered questions to firmly conclude that this was simply a case of a poorly flown ILS." He warned his pilot readers to respect the complexity that goes into making an airplane flight:

Mysteries such as these feed that little voice that questions a pilot's preparation. Poorly flown approach, maybe. But the fact that it could have been something much more mysterious demands pilots pay attention to the potential troubles that surround them.

A few cautious pilots put down that article, thought for a minute and created their own safety recommendations. Maybe a pilot who flew regularly across Cape Cod Bay began carrying life vests, even though they were not required. Perhaps another pilot bought a seat-belt harness for the family dog.

But others, old-timers who have made enough successful landings to feel invincible, used the phrase to dismiss the accident as no threat. A mechanical problem could happen to anyone, they think, but Pilot Error is for bozos. It won't happen to me because I'm smarter than that. I have more experience, better judgment and sharper skills. Pilot Error is what happens to the other guy, the stupid one.

The truth is that pilots like to deny the possibility of Pilot Error because it's flat-out scary. There is no surefire way to protect against it, against the possibility that in a moment of crisis, when lights are flashing or warning horns blaring, you may forget the key piece of information that could save your life. It will be one of the thousands of interlocking bits of data you memorized for an exam years ago and haven't used since. You are expected to recall it instantly and apply it as skillfully as the professional test pilot who flew your airplane model when it was first manufactured. If you don't, you're a loser.

Pilot Error also encompasses those moments when the airplane turns on you and bites, hard, for something that you have always got-ten away with before. Every pilot has pushed the envelope a bit—land-ing in too-strong crosswinds, burning too far into the fuel reserves, steepening the sharp turn to final approach. You picked up a little ice on the wings once. Nerve-racking, but you descended carefully and the warmer air melted it away. Ice, now that wasn't so bad, was it? You can punch through that again, can't you? Yes, until the day that it builds up so quickly that the airfoil that is the wing stops flying and you crash. Terrible judgment: Pilot Error.

When your plane crumples up and the NTSB comes to look at it, they will dismiss you with that phrase as just another chump. A pilot who couldn't hack it. Your flying buddies will nod their heads regretfully.

And until the day it happens, those who are left are the best. They are the ones who make successful steep turns to final approach, who get the plane down just before the microburst hits the airport, who punch through a cloud or two before earning instrument ratings. All pilots take calculated risks. Usually, they get away with them.

# Epilogue

Bereaved spouses are often angry at their loved ones for dying—the ultimate act of abandonment. Marsha was no exception. As she read the NTSB report she blamed Ron for making a bad decision. The weather had been terrible. That air traffic controller had suggested diverting to Hyannis and Ron had refused. What had he been thinking? He should have just gone to Hyannis, damn him.

She knew that he was a good pilot. She decided that he must have hit an air pocket or bad turbulence as he was coming in for the landing. Perhaps that slammed him into the water. Or maybe he suddenly realized he was not going to reach the airport and made an emergency landing. There was no question in Marsha's mind that Ron survived the landing.

Unlike most aviation widows, she never filed a single lawsuit. Not that there weren't suggestions. She was, after all, surrounded by lawyers and the phrase "wrongful death" was mentioned. But what reason was there to sue without the accident being someone else's fault? In a lawsuit, Marsha figured, the lawyers would just make a bunch of noise and bill their fees until someone decided to settle. Frankly she didn't need the money, or the hassle, and it would not bring Ron back.

One July day the summer after Ron's accident, Marsha got a call at the house in Albany. It was her sister, Trudy.

Marsha, have you seen the news?

No, I've been out all day. What is it?

Trudy didn't say. She just told Marsha to turn on the television.

John F. Kennedy Jr. had crashed into the Atlantic Ocean, and Marsha watched, transfixed, for the next several days. It seemed as if the previous summer was coming back to haunt her. CNN reporters were tossing around the same vocabulary, "radar track," "instrument conditions," "vertigo." As the drama progressed, "search and rescue" turned into "recovery."

The Coast Guard crew was familiar too. Captain Russ Webster was running the operation out of Group Woods Hole. Some of the talking heads for the NTSB were the same men who had given news briefs about Ron's accident.

Over the days that followed, friends began calling, offering sympathy. Surely it was like a slap in the face, they said, for Marsha to watch the energy spent on Kennedy. Wasn't she furious that the Coast Guard would use sonar for him and not for Ron? She must resent all the fuss.

Strangely, she didn't. Like millions of other Americans, Marsha had always been fond of "John-John." She followed the news coverage with the hope that he would be found alive. She didn't begrudge his family any of the resources they received. But as the story unfolded, she began to see some unsettling dissimilarities between this rescue effort and Ron's.

For various reasons, the Coast Guard and NTSB continued calling the Kennedy mission "Search and Rescue" for days—much longer than Ron's had been. Some of those reasons were emotional. It was obvious that long after all hope for survival had passed, still nobody wanted to break the news to the American public. But there was also a logistical reason.

Technically, a search and rescue mission is one in which there is still a chance that someone is alive out there in the water. Once that window passes, once the hypothermia tables have been exhausted, it becomes a "Recovery" mission. That means there are no longer any survivors, only bodies or wreckage to salvage. After that point, the Coast Guard withdraws. Their job is to save lives, not recover wrecks.

Unless, that is, a request is made by some other organization, like the NTSB, for example, or the president of the United States. And that is exactly what happened in Kennedy's case.

Marsha watched Captain Webster give one press briefing after another on television. He became a media darling with his silver hair and white suit. She watched him be congratulated on his masterful execution of the search effort—locating the airplane wreckage with sonar. A shoe had washed ashore on the Vineyard and the Coast Guard tracked it backwards, factoring in buoyancy, gravity, tides and currents, to pinpoint the wreckage. She particularly noticed that as they talked about recovery, the Coast Guard was still running the mission.

She began to seethe. What Webster was doing for Kennedy was what she had asked him to do for Ron when she visited Woods Hole after viewing Theo's body. She had begged for sonar, screamed at him about tides and currents. And he had done nothing. He had told her that the Coast Guard didn't do recovery missions, but she was welcome to pay for it herself.

As the Kennedy story unfolded, Marsha did not realize that Webster wasn't working under his own initiative to sink $250,000 of Coast Guard resources into the search. The orders had come from President Clinton, who did not want private salvage hunters hauling up grisly souvenirs.

All Marsha knew was that clearly Webster could have done the same for Ron.

At first, she complained to friends and family, but not to the news media. When reporters called, begging for her perspective on comparing the two accidents, Marsha said "no comment" and hung up, just as she had done during the search for Ron.

But then, she was stung by a quote in the *Cape Cod Times*. On July 28, a story described Captain Webster as being at dinner with family and friends the evening before Kennedy's accident. He was quoted as saying, "I was commenting on how I survived my first year without a major incident."

He was talking about massive launches on the scale of the TWA 800 disaster, or the grounding of the Queen Elizabeth 2. He did not realize how callous his comment might sound to the families in New England who had lost loved ones under his watch.

Marsha struck back. She wrote an editorial for the *Cape Cod Times*.

Her story criticized Webster for the unthinking comment. What hurt Marsha the most was that Ron had been forgotten, swept under the carpet in the aftermath of a more glamorous mission. It had been nearly a year. Although the wound was still fresh for her, she feared that Ron's death had been merely a blip for the rest of the world. A tiny mission for the NTSB and Coast Guard, completely insignificant.

Ron, Marsha decided, deserved more respect than that. She concluded her editorial by writing:

"I would like to think that each of our lives is significant. When a public servant from an agency such as the Coast Guard is allowed to be a representative spokesperson, he should do so with more sensitivity than Webster displayed. I doubt if someone in his responsible position could have had a lapse of memory.

"On the other hand, it is even a worse scenario if people other than celebrities are so easily forgotten."

The following summer, Marsha made herself return to Cape Cod. She headed for the house as usual, curious to see whether or not she could handle it. Would it dredge up painful memories? Or would she be able to play tennis and see friends as before?

Of course it was not the same. The house was emptier and quieter, even with her family, Andrew and other houseguests coming and going. As the summer wore on, some of her Cape friends turned out to have been Ron's friends. They were not as interested in seeing Marsha alone. She questioned whether the house had been Ron's dream, whether or not she should sell it and start a new life of her own, maybe on another coast.

On October 9, 1999, the first anniversary of Ron's accident, Marsha climbed the Pilgrim Monument. From the 252-foot-high observation deck of the granite tower she could see the airport and gaze out over the bay where Ron had been flying the night of the accident. It had been years since she had been in a plane and she wanted that perspective. At the top of the monument she could look out over the water and see what Ron had seen the night he died.

Being in the tower, looking down at the ocean, made her feel closer to Ron. She could conjure him up again and miss him, curse him, thank him and explain things to him. A one-sided conversation was better than nothing at all.

As she stared out over the water, Marsha thought about the past year. She thought about the legal details through which she had wrangled in executing Ron's estate. The property, the trusts, the law firm— she had learned about the things that Ron had always handled, the legal and financial details that she never expected to be able to comprehend. She had published that story in the paper. Ron would have loved that, she thought, giggling. He had been such a bookworm but could hardly get her to read—a thick book just made her nod off. And here she was, a published author!

She had survived her year from hell, Marsha thought. No, she had done better than that, she had risen to the challenge. Ron had always taken such good care of her that Marsha had forgotten how strong she could be. She turned to walk the 116 steps back down to the ground.

If I survived this past year, she thought to herself, I can do anything.

# Index

visibility, 58–59
VOR beacons, 32–33, 73–74
Vosburgh, Steve, 99–101, 163

Wampanoags, 172
WBUR, 128
Weather Channel, 81
weather forecasts, 8–10, 80–82
Webber, Bernie, 132–133
Webster, William "Russ," 146–147,
    202–204

whaling, 173
whiting fishing program, 167–168
Wiltshire, Tom, 25, 96–97
Womack, Scott, 40–41, 111–112,
    114–115, 120–121, 123–124,
    125–126
Woodstock, 12
wreck. *see* Grumman N7100L (Ron's
    plane)

# About the Author

Phaedra Hise earned her pilot's license when she was 21. She has flown many types of planes, has piloted her Beech Bonanza across the country in trans-continental air races, and regularly flies up and down the East coast, from Boston to Key West. She understands how airplane systems operate, having worked closely with mechanics in repairing and maintaining her own airplane.

As a staff writer and professional freelancer, Hise has written about flying and other technical subjects for general-interest publications like *Inc.*, *Salon*, *Sports for Women*, *Forbes*, *The Boston Herald*, *Health*, and *Glamour*. Her previous books focused on business and technology: *301 Great Ideas for Managing Technology* (Inc. Business Resources, 1998) and *Growing Your Business Online: Small Business Strategies for Working the World Wide Web* (Henry Holt & Co., 1996). Her most recent book is *Entrepreneur America* (HarperBusiness, 2001), with coauthor Rob Ryan, founder of Ascend Communications. She has lectured at national conferences, appeared at seminars, on radio talk shows and television.

Hise and her husband, also a pilot, have owned six different airplanes and fly regularly with their five-year-old daughter. Hise lives and works in Richmond, Virginia.